To Walk Together Again

Richard M. Gula, S.S.

To Walk Together Again

The Sacrament of Reconciliation

Paulist Press • New York/Ramsey

Acknowledgments

Excerpts from *Theological Dynamics* by Seward Hiltner, copyright © 1972 by Abingdon Press, are used by permission. Excerpts from Louis Monden, *Sin, Liberty and Law,* copyright © 1965 by Sheed and Ward, Inc. are reprinted with the permission of Andrews and McMeel, Inc. All rights reserved. Excerpts from *Medieval Handbooks of Penance* (New York: Octagon Books, Inc., 1965) by John T. McNeil and Helena M. Gamer are used by permission of Columbia University Press. Excerpts from Bernard Häring, *Free and Faithful in Christ,* Vol. 1: *General Moral Theology,* copyright © 1978 by the Crossroad Publishing Company, are used by permission. Peter Fransen's "A Parable" from *The New Life of Grace* (New York: Desclee Company, 1969) is reprinted by the permission of Desclee De Brouwer of Paris, France. A story of hospitality told by Philip Hallie in "From Cruelty to Goodness," *Hastings Center Report* 11 (June 1981): 27–28 is reprinted by the permission of the Institute of Society, Ethics and the Life Sciences, Hastings-on-Hudson, N.Y. 10706. Excerpts of Frederick McManus taken from the *Rite of Penance: Commentaries,* Vol. 1: *Understanding the Rite,* co-authored with Ralph Keifer (Washington: The Liturgical Conference, 1975) used with permission of The Liturgical Conference. Excerpts from Eugene Walsh, *The Theology of Celebration* (Old Hickory, TN: Pastoral Arts Associates, 1977) are used by the permission of the Pastoral Arts Associates of Old Hickory, TN 37138. Excerpts from Robert Bolt, *A Man for All Seasons* (New York: Random House, 1962) are used with permission of Random House Publishers, Inc. Paul Tillich's statement on grace from his sermon "You Are Accepted" in *The Shaking of the Foundations* (New York: Charles Scribner's Sons, 1948) is reprinted by permission of Charles Scribner's Sons. Copyright 1948 Charles Scribner's Sons; copyright renewed 1976 Hannah Tillich.

IMPRIMATUR
+Most Rev. John R. Quinn
Archbishop of San Francisco

August 5, 1983

The *Imprimatur* is an official declaration that a book or pamphlet is free of doctrinal or moral error. No implication is contained therein that anyone who granted the *Imprimatur* agrees with the contents, opinions or statements expressed.

Library of Congress Catalog Card Number: 83-82021

ISBN: 0-8091-2603-6

Published by Paulist Press,
545 Island Road, Ramsey, N.J. 07446

Printed and bound in the
United States of America

Contents

Foreword

This is a hospitable book.

For people who sometimes have not felt "at home" in the Sacrament of Reconciliation because of bad experience in the past or no experience in the present, this book itself models the hospitality and welcome which Richard Gula recommends to all who celebrate this sacrament and "walk together again."

The reader is "welcomed in," welcomed to a dialogue, not a monologue, with the author. The method of reflection which structures each chapter invites the reader to recall and reflect upon his or her own experience. That experience is sacred ground where readers have experienced God's absence or presence. To integrate and reverence that experience is a mark of hospitality. Readers are invited to be at home with their lives and history. The method also attempts to put the author's reflections in dialogue with their own experience and their own real questions which have been discovered and named. Within Fr. Gula's own reflections, he often invites us to stop and think to be sure we are in dialogue. The final movements in the method invite us to name where we have been affirmed and also challenged so that we can return home a richer person who can now decide and act more responsibly. I felt respected as a person.

The book also welcomes a wide range of characters—from Big Nurse of *One Flew Over the Cuckoo's Nest* to Moby Dick, from Godfather Michael Corleone to St. Thomas More, from Willy

1

Loman to Thomas à Becket to Linus of "Peanuts" fame. The Gospel is inhospitable to none of these human stories, because wherever a story raises ultimate questions about sin and grace, the story of Jesus can offer good news and meaning and reconciliation. Wherever these stories connect can wake us up to see our story in the Jesus story. "Aha! That's what has been happening to me!" Sometimes we need those other characters to help us translate good news and allow Jesus to be at home in our journey.

In these pages we also "walk together again" with both our personal past and our history of reconciliation as a Church. It is hospitable to ask us where we are coming from. We need to be at home with our funny experiences of examining our conscience and confessing and perhaps also our tragic times of alienation even in a sacrament aimed at reconciliation. Then we can move on. We also need to know the history of this sacrament in the wider Church, not primarily to return to forms of the past but to be liberated for the future because we know our past is one of constant change. Knowing the past is a welcome doormat to the future.

Finally, a whole galaxy of theological disciplines are welcomed in this book: biblical theology, systematic theology of grace, sacramental theology, moral theology and ethics, liturgical celebration. If I might be permitted a personal note: this book also represents the journey of conversion in Richard Gula himself. Ten years ago I can remember him protesting the bankruptcy of studying liturgy. Now we find him integrating liturgy and ethics, liturgy and other theological interests. Bernard Lonergan suggests that all theology (biblical, systematic, moral, liturgical) should be reflection on conversion: God turning toward us in grace and our turning to God in faith. Conversion is the turf where all these disciplines meet. Appropriately, Richard Gula welcomes in all these disciplines to tap their wealth of insight into conversion and reconciliation. In so doing, he gives witness to conversion and broader understanding in his own life and is a sign of hope for the rest of us fragile mortals straining for conversion.

James B. Dunning
North American Forum on the Catechumenate

Introduction

A "quiet revolution" has been going on in the Catholic Church with regard to confessional practice. People have simply stopped going in the great numbers that were characteristic of the Church of the 1950's and 1960's. No warning was given. The lines simply vanished. This once regular sacramental practice has fallen on hard times almost everywhere. As one professor in a leading Catholic school of theology said to me when I mentioned I was writing this book, "You had better hurry up with it before it is completely useless. Most people I know have simply given up on that sacrament." Yes, the sacrament which the Baltimore Catechism listed as one of the "sacraments of the dead" seems to be dying. Is there time to resuscitate it?

Reasons for the quiet revolution are surely many. Some see no reason for the Church to be involved if sin happens within a family or between friends. "Why should I confess to a priest? I can take care of seeking forgiveness by myself with the one I offended. Why do I need the middleman?" This is a commonly expressed attitude. Less dependence on clerical leadership in other areas of Church life has had its effect on attitudes toward sacraments too, especially the Sacrament of Reconciliation. Those who got fed up with routine confessions of the same old sins, and routine recitations of the same old prayers for a penance, have found the atmosphere of renewal in the Church an occasion for giving up this sacrament entirely. Other Catholics (and there are many like this, unfortunately) are still stung from a

3

bad experience in the sacrament at one occasion in the past, and will not tolerate the possibility of encountering another gruff, tactless, insensitive priest again.

Another reason frequently given is the loss of a sense of sin: "We are all human. We all have our faults. I haven't done anything really vicious anyway. I have stopped going to confession because I simply have nothing to say. What is sin, anyway?" Such an attitude is quite common. It reflects a great deal of confusion about sin and personal responsibility. It also reflects the effects of the groundswell of a popular "no fault" theology which has made confession a meaningless ritual, since it has done away with moral guilt and an awareness of sin. While we no longer see mortal sin lurking around every corner, we have gone too far in not even noticing nor admitting guilt of morally wrong conduct that is offensive to God and harmful to our neighbor. Those who have come to see sin only in terms of large social realities, such as racial exploitation, sexual discrimination, national colonialism, or world peace, have found the private rite quite beside the point.

Many other Catholics recognize that God forgives sins even apart from the Sacrament of Reconciliation. Penance is not the only Sacrament of Reconciliation. Baptism and Eucharist are too. With more people receiving Eucharist these days, many are asking: "Why do we need a separate Sacrament of Reconciliation? What does this sacrament do for me that Eucharist can't? Isn't Eucharist enough? Why should I have to go to confession if I can be forgiven elsewhere?"

Other reasons for the decline can also be given. Perhaps you have a few of your own not identified here. Whatever the reason though, few will deny that this sacrament no longer occupies the place in the lives of Catholics it once did. It has simply become a marginal practice in the lives of many. For still others it has gone, or is now going, the way of Wednesday night novenas and Sunday afternoon Benediction. Like the once regular novenas and Benediction, the regular practice of the Sacrament of Reconciliation is quickly becoming part of Catholic memorabilia.

Will the implementation of the new Rite turn this situation around? Not in itself. No amount of changing the ritual can altogether solve the problem. The roots of the problem lie deeper than rites. The quiet revolution is part of a larger problem of faith, God, Church, personal conversion, and more. If the renewal of the rite can result in the interior renewal it hopes for, then we may find an increase in the number of persons who find in this sacrament a renewed significance of its place in the life of the Church, and in one's personal spiritual growth.

My experience of this sacrament as both priest and penitent, as well as my experience in adult and clergy education programs on this sacrament, has convinced me of the great need for good catechesis on Reconciliation. Priests are no less in need of this catechesis than are other adults. This fact comes home to me time and again when I celebrate Reconciliation, or conduct education programs on this sacrament. How often I have heard from interested, though often frustrated, adult Catholics questions like these: "Father, do the priests know about this new Rite of Penance? I have been in this parish for fifteen years and we do not have anything like what you are explaining. What Church do you belong to? I never heard, nor have I experienced, anything like what you are talking about. Are you sure you are representing the Roman Catholic Church?"

I assure them that I am, and that what I am talking about is reflected in the new Rite of Penance first promulgated by the Congregation for Divine Worship on December 2, 1973. This was later made available in English in the United States in Advent 1975. This new Rite was to be implemented in all parishes in this country by the First Sunday of Lent, 1977. The Rite of Penance was the last of the sacramental rituals to be reformed in response to the mandate of Vatican II that all liturgical books be revised.

The first clue that new thinking and new attitudes toward Reconciliation are afoot in this revised Rite can be found in the official change of the name for designating the ritual forms of this sacrament. Each of the three rites begins, "Rite of Reconciliation of . . . ." Why "Reconciliation" and not "confession" or "penance"? What's in a name?

This sacrament has been and is called by various names—penance, confession, and Reconciliation being the most common. Penance is the most ancient designation. It suggests the

5

change of heart which the Gospel designates by *metanoia,* or conversion. When used to mean conversion of heart, Penance is a proper designation for this sacrament. However, when "penance" is taken to mean only the acts of satisfaction the penitent does to make up for sin, then this designation is improper as a name for the whole sacrament. In this narrow sense, penance becomes a way of identifying the whole ritual by only one of its parts, namely, a part which the penitent does.

"Confession" is perhaps the most popular way of designating this sacrament. It is also a name which designates the whole by one of its parts. Again, it emphasizes a part which only the penitent does. This way of naming the sacrament came into vogue when the sacrament took on its private form, and attention shifted from doing acts of penance to making a right confession. Then the juridical meaning of confession as recognition of guilt and self-accusation before a judge quickly overwhelmed and replaced the biblical sense of confession as an expression of praise to God and an affirmation of faith. In our time, the juridical meaning has dominated our use so that the fullest sense of confession has been nearly forgotten. Given the attitudes expressed in the new Rite, "confession" is the least favorable name for this sacrament.

The preferred designation of this sacrament is "Reconciliation." It designates the whole of the sacrament of which confession and penance are only parts. The roots of this name lie in the Old Testament idea of atonement and in St. Paul's sense of healing the alienation between God and us (see Eph 2; 2 Cor 5). "Reconciliation" is the most theologically correct way of naming this sacrament, since it describes God's initiative through Christ and in the Spirit to restore harmony, or friendship, between God and us, and among ourselves. The first part of the new formula of absolution expresses in a concise fashion the whole mystery of reconciliation:

> God, the Father of mercies,
> through the death and resurrection of his Son
> has reconciled the world to himself
> and sent the Holy Spirit among us
> for the forgiveness of sins . . .

"Reconciliation," as the proper name for this sacrament, also has the advantage of expressing better than "penance" or "confession" can that the initiative comes from God, not from us. Only God's love can restore the broken relationships that need healing because of sin. God's action in Christ effects reconciliation. We need to appropriate this healing action which is already available by responding through faith and cooperating with the saving action going on in the community. The Church possesses a ministry of reconciliation as the continuing expression of Christ among us in a visible way. The Sacrament of Reconciliation is one way that the Church concretely proclaims this message of pardon and peace. The name "reconciliation," then, captures better than any other both the action of God's initiative in saving love, and our response of conversion in cooperating with this loving action present in the believing community through the Spirit. This sense of reconciliation, and not confession or penance, guides the reflections of this book.

This book's title, *To Walk Together Again,* reflects one of my favorite images of reconciliation. This image came to me one evening as I was walking back to my room after dinner. I live in a seminary community. A common practice after dinner here is to walk around the circle of our front lawn before returning to our rooms. Most often we walk together in small groups. Rarely does anyone walk alone. But one Monday evening I saw one of our deacons walking alone. This was especially unusual since his group most always walked together. I later learned that there was some sharp conflict in this class over plans for ordination. This particular deacon had alienated himself from his class by his conduct and remarks at a class meeting. But by Thursday I saw him walking together again with his classmates. He had been reconciled with his class at another meeting and was again incorporated completely into the life and hopes of his class. On this night the image of reconciliation as "walking together again" sat up in my mind.

This image sums up nicely the dimensions of sin, conversion, and reconciliation. Sin is to walk according to one's own vision and in one's own way apart from the covenantal community of God's people. Conversion is the turning around to come home again and walk in the way of the vision and life of God's covenantal people. Reconciliation is the growing unity with God and among ourselves that comes about when divisive selfishness is replaced by the vision of God's Kingdom and the commitment to a God-centered oneness. "To walk together again" is a powerful image of what we are about in the process of reconciliation in life and in its celebration in sacrament. Because God loves us, we are able to overcome the selfish divisiveness of our sin and restore the harmony of our covenantal relationship with God and with one another. The unity or harmony of walking together becomes a living witness of our commitment to conversion and reconciliation.

This book does not intend to be an apology for the Sacrament of Reconciliation. Nor does it intend to provide sure-fire ways of bringing Catholics back to this sacrament again. My purpose is a modest one. I want to respond to a clear need within the Catholic community for an adult resource on Reconciliation. One question has guided the writing of this book, and I hope this question will also guide its use. What do believing adult Catholics need to know about the Sacrament of Reconciliation in order to make this sacrament an integral part of their lives of faith and spiritual growth? I have tried to answer this question by providing a critical theological and historical framework for understanding this sacrament, as well as by offering suggestions for the pastoral implementation of the new Rite of Penance.

At the beginning of the ritual for the Rite of Penance is the *praenotanda,* or Introduction. This is a set of theological notes which provides us an understanding of this sacrament as well as some pastoral guidelines for celebrating it. This book will rely on the theological understanding and the pastoral guidelines of this Introduction, but it will not be a detailed commentary on each paragraph. A fine commentary has already been provided by the Liturgical Conference in its *The Rite of Penance: Commentaries,* Vol. 1: *Understanding the Document,* by Ralph Kiefer and Frederick R. McManus.[1]

This book has seven chapters. Each one can serve as the focus for a single session of a series of adult discussions on Reconciliation. The first chapter sketches characteristics of a style of life committed to reconciliation. The purpose of this chapter is to establish an attitude toward reconciliation. Unless we have a grasp on what it means to live a life committed to reconciliation—unless we take a stand on this at the beginning—then we have no need to go farther in the book, nor do we need to give serious consideration to the Sacrament of Reconciliation as an integral part of one's Christian life. Chapter Two explores the mystery of God and grace. Whether we experience God and how we experience God have a great deal to do with the quality of our sacramental celebrations and our moral lives. Next is a consideration of the fundamentals of a sacramental theology which support and give life to the new Rite of Penance. Chapters Four and Five consider sin and conscience respectively. These will be efforts to clarify significant aspects of the moral life which are so crucial to Reconciliation. Chapter Six traces the lifeline of the development of this sacrament through the ages. This chapter hopes to give us a sense of where we have been so that we can appreciate where we are going. The last chapter gives a brief commentary, with pastoral suggestions for priest and penitent, on celebrating the new Rites of Reconciliation. The Appendix provides an example of each form in which Reconciliation can be celebrated. The examples try to provide a pastoral/liturgical illustration of the theology of Reconciliation expressed in the Introduction to the Rite and in the seven chapters of this book.

Please note: This book is for adults only! It is not for children. If it were ever made into a movie, I would want it to be rated PG since it is not something to which children ought to be exposed without parental guidance because of the difficulty of its concepts. I will leave to someone else the task of providing a comparable book suitable for children. I am primarily interested in adults—priests, sisters, catechists, parents, seminarians, catechumens and sponsors, as well as any other adult who wants to talk with other adults about Reconciliation.

In order to facilitate this conversation among adults, I have set up each chapter according to the method of religious education proposed by Thomas H. Groome in his highly acclaimed, *Christian Religious Education: Sharing Our Story and Vision.*[2] This book is one of the most comprehensive developments of religious education to appear in some time. Groome's method should be very helpful to catechesis on Reconciliation. There are five pedagogical movements in his approach. Each movement has a particular focus of attention. I can only summarize them here, but you might want to check the original source.[3]

FIRST MOVEMENT: PRESENT ACTION

In this movement, the primary question is "What are you presently doing regarding the issue at hand?" Each participant makes a personal statement of his or her feelings, ways of acting, or valuing the issue at hand. The important task is to make a personal statement of one's own activity. This is not the time to give a report of what someone else is saying about the issue.

SECOND MOVEMENT: CRITICAL REFLECTION

In this movement, the primary question is "Why are you doing that?" This movement explores the assumptions (theological, catechetical, psychological, ethical, etc.) that lie behind what you are doing, as well as the consequences of what you are doing. Each participant explores one's own story and vision by reflecting on reasons for doing what one does as well as envisioning desired or likely consequences of this way of acting. This reflection does not stop with surface observations of the obvious. This is not to be an examination of what you think you should be doing or why you think you should be doing that. Rather, it is after the assumptions and the visions which our actual practice reveals. We draw out the meanings revealed by what we are doing now, not by what we should be doing. This point is too easy to miss. We want to sneak in our "should's" too early, and consequently miss the call to conversion in our actual practice and vision. Critical reflection also looks to the future and imagines likely consequences of our way of acting.

THIRD MOVEMENT: THE CHRISTIAN STORY AND VISION

This movement explores the faith Tradition of the Christian community on the issue at hand as well as the lived responses and promises which the Tradition invites.

10

FOURTH MOVEMENT: APPROPRIATING THE CHRISTIAN STORY

In this movement, the primary question is "How does the Gospel and the Christian Tradition, along with insights from our culture, affirm or challenge what you are doing and why you are doing it?" This step invites each participant to appropriate the faith Tradition of the Christian community into one's own life of faith. The goal of this movement is not only to affirm each participant in one's faith experiences, but also to challenge and invite each to rediscover the Tradition of faith as one's own. Also, the dialogue that goes on between our experience and the Tradition can also expand and challenge the Tradition.

FIFTH MOVEMENT: CHOOSING A FAITH RESPONSE

In this last movement, the primary question is "What adjustments do you want to make in your future practice?" The reflection of the previous movements leads into decisions, possible changes, a new agenda. This is the opportunity to choose a personal faith response to the Tradition of faith newly discovered and in the process of being reappropriated.

Each chapter in this book will begin with a few questions to focus the first two movements of this method in order to engage those who will use this book in a dialogue fashion. The main text of the chapter will follow and serve to meet the needs of the third movement. Following the main text of each chapter will be a few more questions to focus the last two movements of this method. At the end of each chapter, I will provide a few suggested readings for those who wish to explore in more detail the tradition of faith on the issues of each chapter.

In order that the chapters may read smoothly and easily, I have tried to keep the acknowledgement of sources and extended quotations to a minimum. What cannot be acknowledged in the notes and references is my extensive indebtedness to the participants in my many adult education sessions who asked honest, searching questions, and who shared openly their experiences and frustrations with the catechesis and celebration of this sacrament. I am especially indebted to the many people who have given me the privilege of celebrating this sacrament with them. They know who they are. This book is dedicated to them.

Like all theology, and like efforts at reconciliation, this book is the result of the help and encouragement of many people with different gifts and perspectives. I want to thank those good people. During the months spent in writing this book, I have been encouraged and greatly helped by discussion about its contents with many colleagues and friends who took time to read all or significant parts of it along the way. I wish to give special recognition and thanks to my Sulpician colleagues: Frs. Gerald Coleman, Phil Keane, Frank Norris, Roger Statnick, and Larry Terrien. I am also grateful to Fr. James B. Dunning for his encouragement and Foreword to this book. Fr. Steve Rowan has helped me make this book readable. Everyone can be grateful to him for that. Mrs. Marguerite Fletcher has contributed a very practical catechetical expression on reconciliation with her script which she has allowed me to include in the Appendix. Sr. Barbara Hazzard and Mrs. Marilyn Neri have helped keep me alert to the intended audience for this book. To all of these people, "Thanks."

1

Reconciliation:
A Style of Life

FIRST MOVEMENT: PRESENT ACTION

What does reconciliation mean in your life? How do you serve as an agent of reconciliation? What does the process of reconciliation look like for you?

SECOND MOVEMENT: CRITICAL REFLECTION

What memories of being reconciled in life and in sacrament do you have? What has shaped your present attitude toward reconciliation? What hopes do you have for being an agent of reconciliation?

THIRD MOVEMENT: THE CHRISTIAN STORY AND VISION

Liturgy and life are not the same. We should not expect our sacramental celebrations to substitute for genuine human experience, and vice versa. Life is where our experiences happen.

Sacramental celebrations are our way of dealing with human experiences in faith. In our discussion of sacramental theology and principles of celebration in the chapters to come, we will see that, in a certain sense, sacraments do not give us something we do not already have. Rather, sacraments are our way of deepening an experience already going on in our lives by lighting up the religious dimensions that are already there. For example, in life we take the risk to trust in the goodness within ourselves and within another who wants to walk together again in pardon and in peace. Our trust is the energy that enables us to say, "I'm sorry for what has broken our relationship." In the Sacrament of Reconciliation we touch the source of that energy by proclaiming God's love and acceptance of us. Consider another example. In life we pay attention to each other. We try to keep open channels of communication by our efforts to listen more intently, to understand more clearly. We give time and space for others to grow into their best selves and for all of us to grow into communion with each other. In the Sacrament of Eucharist, we celebrate the sacred space that has been created in our lives by God's loving action accepting us in Christ and through the Spirit. Because we know we have been accepted and can feel at home with ourselves and with God, we have room to accept one another. In the Eucharist we celebrate that communion we share as well as the hope we have that there might be more.

While we cannot substitute a liturgical experience for a life experience, or collapse one into the other, we should not isolate one from the other. This means that only when reconciliation becomes a reality in our lives will the Sacrament of Reconciliation make sense. In fact, without a life of reconciliation, the liturgical celebration of Reconciliation is an empty charade. Or, at best, it is putting the cart before the horse. For a Church like ours that is rich in ritual, we are always in danger of ritualizing without adequate preparation. The Rite of Christian Initiation of Adults (RCIA) tries to safeguard against this danger with regard to the Sacraments of Initiation. When it comes to the Sacrament of Reconciliation, however, a narrow legalism seems to have turned what ought to be a celebration of forgiveness into a kind of clinical clerical legal pardon.

The decline of participation in this sacrament can be attributed in part to our gradually separating this sacrament from the life of reconciliation that must be lived before as well as after the ritual moment of Reconciliation. The new Rite of Penance tries to put the sacramental moment back into its proper context. This means that the effective celebration of the sacrament depends on a heightened awareness of the need for reconciliation, and of participation in it throughout the whole of one's life. For this reason, then, the Rite of Penance will be most effectively celebrated when this sentence from its Introduction comes true:

> Faithful Christians, as they experience and proclaim the mercy of God in their lives, celebrate with the priest the liturgy by which the Church continually renews itself (Par. 11).

The effective celebration of Reconciliation, then, demands more than knowing the proper way to celebrate the Rite according to the ritual. Effective celebration of this sacrament also calls for living a life of reconciliation so that we have good life experiences to deepen through the sacramental celebration. The purpose of this first chapter is to take a stand on reconciliation in life. Unless we are willing to commit ourselves to living a life of reconciliation and being agents of reconciliation, there is no sense in celebrating the Rite of Reconciliation.

The fundamental truth underlying this whole book is this: *God reconciles, and we proclaim it!* The gift of reconciliation calls us to an active ministry of being agents of reconciliation. St. Paul spells out the consequences of this unearned gift in his most pointed statement on reconciliation:

> All this has been done by God, who has reconciled us to himself through Christ and has given us the ministry of reconciliation. I mean that God, in Christ, was reconciling the world to himself, not counting men's transgressions against them, and that he has entrusted the message of reconciliation to us. This makes us ambassadors of Christ, God as it were appealing through us. We implore you, in Christ's name: be reconciled to God (2 Cor 5:18–20).

The ministry of reconciliation is the responsibility of the whole Christian community. Certain characteristics of a style of life facilitate this ministry of reconciliation. We need to embody these characteristics and live them if we are to celebrate Reconciliation effectively. This chapter explores in a brief way some of these characteristics in an effort to sketch what some might want to call a "spirituality of reconciliation."

Reconciliation must never become an isolated religious phenomenon, or sacramental practice, apart from the daily life of each of us. Just as sin involves multiple relationships, so does reconciliation. A proper approach to the Sacrament of Reconciliation must keep the multiple relationships and the interconnection of the relationships of our lives in proper perspective. We must not so stress our relationship with God that we forget our relationship with one another. And we must not so stress our relationship with one another that we have no need to look to God for forgiveness. Reconciliation involves both God and neighbors. Anyone committed to living a life of reconciliation must attend to the dynamics of love in relationship with God, others, self, and the world.

Before proceeding, take a moment to make your own sketch of a way of life committed to reconciliation. What qualities of character would you expect to find in a person living a life of reconciliation? When you have answered this question, check your list against mine.

HOPE

A reconciling style of life is marked by hope. Hope is that fundamental disposition which makes reconciliation possible. Hope is rooted in the confidence that life is more reliable than unreliable, that upholding all things and all events is a fundamental graciousness. Moreover, hope trusts that the future is open, that new possibilities for life exist, that we are not fated by blind necessity, that we can change, and that tomorrow can be different from today. Hope is a confidence in the power of good to break into each particular place. It is confidence in life and in the possibility that those things which are destructive of human well-being and fellowship can be restrained so that the possibilities for new achievements of well-being can be realized.

16

The disposition of hope is rooted in the fundamental biblical truth that all possibilities for life and its future are under the care and goodness of God. Reconciliation is a possibility for us because it begins with, and remains rooted in, God's love for us. The good news of Christian faith is that God's love is constant and undefeatable. This is most clearly evident in Jesus' being raised from the dead. The resurrection of Jesus (the best of all possible futures) is our ultimate warrant for hope. We cannot engage in reconciliation, or experience it, if we do not believe in God's love for us as a constant, undefeatable love—that is to say, unless we believe in "amazing grace." To accept God's unconditional love for us is fundamental to the process of reconciliation in life and in sacrament.

This is one of my favorite stories of accepting God's love. The old man in this story is well on his way to becoming an instrument of pardon and peace.

> One evening as the priest walked along the country road he came across an old man also out enjoying the twilight air. They walked and talked together until a sudden rain made them take shelter. When their conversation moved into silence, the old Irishman took his little prayerbook and began praying half aloud. The priest watched him a long while, then in a quiet whisper said, "You must be very close to God!" The old man smiled very deeply and answered, "Yes! He is very fond of me!"[1]

Yes, the Father is very fond of us! More importantly, each of us needs to be able to say with the old man, "He is very fond of me!" This is the beginning of being able to live a life of reconciliation. This is accepting the gift of grace, God's gratuitous love for us. This is the basic fact of life. We must never be willing to negotiate or compromise it. This is the foundation upon which we build a life of reconciliation. God loves us, all of us without reservation. God never stops loving us. God loves us when we are in sin just as much as when we are out of sin. We cannot win God's love. We cannot lose God's love. But we are free to receive God's love or not. Even so, we could not even use this freedom unless God continued to love us. God is forever loving. All we need to do now is to hope in this love, and to live out of this hope and in this love.

The Scriptures never tire of repeating the word of God's love for us. Our God is a God of covenantal love. Our God is forever faithful. Our God will not go back on this word, "I love you." We find this word frequently repeated by the prophets; Jesus lived by the truth of this word; and St. Paul spoke about its truth out of the depth of his experience. Listen to God say, "I love you":

> Do not be afraid. . . . I have called you by name—you are mine. . . . You are precious to me. . . . I love you. . . . Do not be afraid—I am with you (Is 43:1–5).

> Even if a mother should forget her child, I will never forget you. . . . I have written your name on the palms of my hands (Is 49:15–16).

> How can I give you up? How can I abandon you? . . . My heart will not let me do it! My love for you is too strong. . . . I, the Holy One, am with you (Hos 11:8–9).

> I love you just as the Father loves me; remain in my love (Jn 15:9).

> For I am certain that nothing can separate us from his love: neither death nor life, neither angels nor other heavenly rulers or powers, neither the present nor the future, neither the world above nor the world below—there is nothing in all creation that will ever be able to separate us from the love of God which is ours through Christ Jesus our Lord (Rom 8:38–39).

Our efforts at reconciliation are to respond to this love being offered us all the time. Then we are to live this love in deed: in the way we welcome each other, communicate to each other, pay attention to each other, hold each other, and, in short, bring life to each other. All of this makes our hope a very active virtue and not some passive waiting for some future apocalyptic victory.

Because our disposition of hope is rooted in the undefeatable love of God, we do not give in to despair. Hope enables us to lean on the future trustingly with the expectation that something good will happen. Our hope points to the love of God which is the basis for renewal of life, for reconciliation between enemies, for the fulfillment of new possibilities of human well-being. Our hope frees us to respond creatively to the new possibilities for recreating society because in hope we are empowered by the energy that comes from the conviction that God loves us and accepts us. Knowing that we are accepted by God, and that God will never abandon us, gives us unending courage to take the risks we need to take in order to walk together again—restoring the intimacy and friendship with God as well as restoring the wholeness of the Body of Christ.

TRUST

The daily effect of living by hope is the energy to trust, not only ourselves but also others. Hope correlates with trust in the goodness of God and the power of goodness in life. The trust that is characteristic of a life style of reconciliation is not only a trust that God's gracious acceptance of us, even in our sin, is something we can rely on, but also a trust that God trusts us. God has entrusted us with creation, with each other, and with many gifts which enable us to walk together again and bring life to each other. The challenge to trust in a life committed to reconciliation is to know oneself as entrusted with many gifts, and to draw out the trustworthiness of others by encouraging them to be all that they can be. To draw out the trustworthiness in others is an act of reconciliation which calls to their better selves to act in a new way. This is the style of Jesus.

John Shea has made a brilliant comparison of the Adam and Eve story and the Jesus story that illustrates well this characteristic of trust.[2] His comparison lights up some important dimensions of trust in a reconciling style of life. Shea reads the Adam and Eve story as a symbol of estrangement, and the Jesus story as a symbol of reconciling trust. In brief, it looks like this.

The story of the Fall is a symbol of what we do with our freedom to determine our style of interaction with others and

19

with our environment. We pick up the story of Adam and Eve on the sixth day, when God entrusted the earth to their care and them to each other. This story implies that everything comes to us as a gift from a totally free act of a gracious God. The Adam and Eve story is pervaded with a sense of being trusted with gifts, the gifts of creation and of one another. The serpent enters to sow the seed of distrust. The serpent suggests that trust in God is ill-founded. Adam and Eve choose to believe the snake. They choose to believe God cannot be trusted. With this choice they admit into the world alienation, twisted motives, the need to build protective walls to keep others out and to keep the self secure. By distrusting God, Adam and Eve reverse their basic relationship to life. When dwelling within God's trust and returning that trust, they centered themselves on God as the source and power of fulfillment. Now that they dwell in distrust, they settle within themselves, and move from other-centeredness on God to idolatrous self-centeredness. This is the real root of sin— to have an excessive preference of self over others.

As long as Adam and Eve dwelt within God's trust and returned that trust, they were free. As soon as they dwell within distrust, they only know fear. With distrust there enter into the world fear, manipulation, domination, war. The freedom that comes with trust does not shrink from the demands of relationships, sexuality, friendship, social responsibility. The fear of distrust does. The fear of distrust is suspicious of all that makes up life. Fear builds walls of protection, seeks the control of domination, and the power of manipulation. The moment Adam and Eve cannot trust God, they cannot trust each other either. Estrangement from God yields estrangement from one another. Separation and suspicion become the marks of their lives. This is symbolized in their sewing fig leaves into clothes to hide their nakedness, their vulnerability. Nakedness is the great symbol of trust. To be able to stand naked before another is a way of saying, "I trust you. I am willing to hand myself over to you. I am ready to risk all that I am with you." Adam and Eve are suddenly aware that they are not ready to say that to each other. The result—estrangement and fear.

The Jesus story, on the other hand, brings us back from the fear that tells us not to trust—not to trust God, not to trust anyone. Whereas Adam and Eve used their freedom to become strangers, Jesus used his to make friends. When we say that God reconciled the world in Christ, we are saying that God's trust in humankind has been returned. The reconciling power in the life of Jesus lies in his believing that the Father trusted him. He returned that trust by not abandoning his Kingdom-mission of living for the sake of making everyone a friend of God and of one another. Jesus lived a life of reconciliation not only by trusting the Father, but also by reflecting his relationship to the Father by entrusting others, and eliciting trust from them. Jesus' great acts of reconciliation were those of enabling others to recognize that they had been entrusted by God with precious gifts, of providing for them a safe space of acceptance wherein they might trust themselves, and of allowing them the freedom to release within themselves the gifts with which they had been entrusted. We find notable examples of this style of reconciliation in the interaction Jesus has with Peter. We see this especially in Jesus' commission to Peter at Caesarea Philippi (Mt 16:13–19) as well as in his invitation to follow him at the end of the Gospel of John (Jn 21:15–19). Jesus' pre-eminent act of reconciliation, of course, is in his death-resurrection-sending forth of the Spirit. The Book of Acts testifies to the early Church's living entrusted lives set free by Jesus' great act of reconciliation.

The foundation principle for being able to walk together in trust is found in Jesus' commission to his disciples when he sends them out on mission: "What you have received as gift, give as gift" (Mt 10:8). This is the principle that says the bond of trust which we share with God is to be reflected outward into the affairs that make up the whole of our lives. The parable which most pointedly illustrates this principle is that of the Unmerciful Servant (Mt 18:21–25). The servant who was forgiven a great debt did not forgive even a small debt owed to him. The servant is chastised because he betrayed God's trust in being forgiven by not imitating God and reflecting this trust outward to the one in debt to him. He did not give freely what he had received freely.

Talk of trust as a characteristic of a style of life can be too easy and slick for the kind of world we know. Living in trust is not always contemplating the lilies of the field. Our world is a rough place in which to live. Slick talk of trust recalls the hucksterism of P.T. Barnum: "There is a sucker born every minute and two to take him." Are we to see this challenge to trust as a call to gullibility? No! The trust that is a characteristic of a reconciling style of life is not a call to some sort of unrealism, destructive gullibility or misplaced surrender. Neither is it a call to a passive handing over of responsibility. Nor is this trust blind to evil and deception. While never promising a rose garden, trust simply does not allow these things to dictate the terms of our relationships. Non-violent resistance to evil is an example of this kind of reconciling trust. The trust which pacifism attempts may appear foolish and unproductive, yet this is the kind of reconciling trust that distinguishes the distinctive style of Jesus.

A realistic outlook on trust and entrusting others is espoused by Seward Hiltner. He seems to maintain that a small dose of mistrust might carry a bit of sanity to it. He expresses what he would like to believe and act upon about trust this way:

1. As a realist I know that the world is a rough place, and I shall not be shattered or disillusioned when I find untrustworthiness just where I have least expected it. But the world is also full of potentialities, and I shall not permit my awareness of untrustworthiness to shield my perception away from serious pursuit of those potentials.

2. If I got everything I wanted at any moment of my life, that situation might well land me in worse difficulty than I am in now. I do not distrust all my wants. But I must be constantly self-critical about them. My wants as such are neither to be trusted nor distrusted automatically. I must sort them out to see what among them is to be trusted and pursued.

3. Even though most of life declares its ambiguity in capital letters, I know nevertheless that I have experienced great moments when the unambiguous, the wholly trustworthy, has been a part of my experience. I resolve not to become so suspicious that I shall fail to recognize such gifts, no matter where they may come from. On the other side, I pledge that I shall not concentrate so hard on grail hunting that I shall distort the ambiguities that make up most of my experience.

4. I have no apology for a prudent suspicion that tests out whatever or whoever claims to be trustworthy. But I shall permit this attitude to occupy only a preliminary place in my relationships. With persons I like, such an attitude soon disappears. But even with those I do not like or cannot understand, I shall endeavor to remain open to anything in the other that is worthy of trust.

5. If I can maintain this attitude of paradox, yet with a slant always in the direction of readiness to trust wherever there are partially trustworthy elements, then I shall feel that I am responding to something in the creation itself but in no way being forced or compelled.[3]

This vision of trust reflects a style of life well suited for reconciliation. It is not a romantic vision easily disillusioned by evil, but a realistic insight into possibilities for good. While knowing that distrust abounds, it is not so paralyzed by suspicion that it fails to recognize grounds for trust. And while living with a prudent sense of suspicion, it is ready to trust whenever there are trustworthy conditions at hand.

The stories of the Garden of Eden and the Garden of Olives teach us that we are pursued by a relentless trust of God. God's relentless trust in us never lets our fears and suspicions become so dark and deep that we fail to recognize that we have been entrusted by God, and that we are called to act as God's representatives by entrusting others and eliciting trust from them. Christians are free to trust others because we know we have been entrusted by God, and that we trust in God. If we can let go of fear and suspicion, and come to know the other as gift, we can answer to that of God in the other. This is the way to unlock the power of reconciliation within us. If we are ever to walk together again, the attitude of preliminary fear and suspicion must be slanted in the direction of trust, trusting our own gifts and trusting the gifts of another. The daily effect of walking in trust is to enable a certain fearlessness which allows us to take the risk on our own goodness and on another's. What God has trusted, we must start trusting. What God has been willing to release and take risks on, we must be willing to release and take risks on. Only when someone gives us permission to start trusting ourselves (as God has) will we take ourselves seriously with our gifts (as God does). Only when we start trusting ourselves will we be able to take responsibility for ourselves and our mistakes.

A friend of mine has shared with me a letter he wrote of his personal experience of trust. With his permission, I use it here as an example of unlocking the powers of reconciliation when we discover our own giftedness through the help of others, and become free enough to release those gifts. The letter goes like this:

> When I was a child, my parents used to take us every year to the parish carnival. They would give us a buck to spend on anything we wanted. One time after we got back into our car to go home, they asked me if I had a good time. I sat in silence for a while, then burst into tears, opened my hand and showed them my buck. You see, I was afraid to spend it, afraid to let go of it, because I thought I might make a mistake, get something I didn't want, and never get a buck again.

> Well, what happened to me last year, poetically speaking, was that people at school helped me spend my buck. And it was great, letting go, getting confidence that I had something to spend. And you know what? After spending that first buck, I looked in my pocket and found another and another and another. And God is good, so are his people, and so am I!

This is a touching story of reconciliation with oneself and with others. Reconciliation with oneself is discovering we have a buck to spend; reconciliation with others is being willing to spend it. The life style of reconciliation marked by trust is discovering that we have been gifted by God, and are called to offer these gifts to others.

FORGIVENESS

Forgiveness flows from hope and trust. Forgiveness makes the attitude of reconciliation a reality. Forgiveness corrects any notion that we live separate from each other. Forgiveness allows us to experience at-one-ment with each other. Because forgiveness leads to walking together again, the inability to forgive and to accept forgiveness may be the greatest obstacle to reconciliation.

Forgiving is not easy, at least if my experience is typical. How many times we catch ourselves saying, or hear another say, "Don't tell me to forgive. I can't." What obstacles get in the way of forgiving? Two stand out.

The first is fear. The unforgiving person is generally full of fear. Often this is the fear of being hurt again. The fearful person builds walls instead of bridges in relationships. Bridges make one vulnerable; walls protect by keeping the other separate and apart. Forgiveness will break through this protective wall and bring us closer. But coming closer is precisely what we fear. Coming closer, especially emotionally closer, makes us too vulnerable. After being hurt once, we are too frightened ever to make ourselves vulnerable again. As my friend, Fr. Steve Rowan, once said, "The tree that is withered by a premature frost will only, with difficulty, open up and bud again."

Another obstacle to forgiveness that flows from fear is power. This is the sense of feeling that we need to hold something over someone else. Not to forgive is to assume some kind of position of superiority which says to our offender, "You owe me." The unforgiving person has a strong need to thrive on being right and to be in control of everything. Forgiveness breaks down any kind of superiority and allows the other to be on equal footing with us. The unforgiving person is always trying to get even, and so will never get ahead.

We learn a great lesson about forgiveness from Herman Melville's Ahab in *Moby Dick*. On one whaling voyage Ahab has his leg bitten off by Moby Dick, the great white whale. The wound so maddens Ahab, especially the senselessness of it, that he spends his whole life in mad pursuit of the offending animal. But at the end of the book, when Ahab plunges his harpoon into the whale, he only succeeds in tangling himself up in the rope, and is pulled into the sea where he drowns. The lesson: forgive, or it will drive you mad, and lead to your ultimate destruction.

Three steps are characteristic of the forgiveness that leads to walking together again in a reconciled way of life. The first is that the way we think about our offender must be amended before we can change our pattern of speaking and acting toward him or her. If it is true that how we feel is influenced by how we think, then when two people separate, their reunion will be as good as the thoughts each had about the other while they were apart. The first healing of hurt must take place in the heart. Only then will our words be healing and forgiving.

Next comes letting go. This step, like most early steps, is hard. We hang on. We do not want to let go. Forgiveness that "lets go" is not quite the same as "forgiving and forgetting." The forgiveness that leads to reconciliation is not the forgetting that is like pressing the erase button on our tape recorders, or punching in the "delete all" command on our personal computers. Erasing and deleting may be proper functions for machines, but not for people. For us, the past must be reworked, not erased. To erase memory is to lose a rich source of meaning for one's life. The memory that is a resource for meaning and healing is not a matter of reminiscing that broods over the past. The memory that is a rich source of meaning and healing is more a matter of recollecting, seeing anew, and reintegrating the past into one's self-understanding with an acceptance that sets us free. Forgiving like this is a kind of dying. But we resist dying. We resist with anger, bargaining, and depression. Finally we come to acceptance. Not until we reach acceptance will our forgiving ever be more than tolerating, and our remembering be anything more than reminiscing.

The third step in forgiveness is to awaken the true potential for good in the other. Awakening the good in the other and drawing it out is the clearest sign of reconciliation being accomplished. Not until we are able to draw out the goodness in the other will we be able to walk together in a reconciled way of life. We often miss the power of this step toward reconciliation because we have not yet reached the stage of acceptance in our letting go. Without acceptance, we continue to think that the script of forgiveness reads like this: "I'm OK, but you're not so hot. Even so, I forgive you anyway." This is not the script of mutuality, but of superiority and power. True forgiveness that leads to reconciliation says, "I'm OK, and you're OK. So let's walk together again." This is the script that expresses the attitude that can awaken and restore in the other the great potential for good-

26

ness that is there. Forgiving is the kind of giving which awakens the goodness that is in another, and enables the other to move from self-centeredness and fear to self-forgetfulness and freedom. Forgiveness like this contributes to reconciliation because it restores the other to the dignity of being a self-forgetful lover with the great potential for building bonds of friendship and community.

This is characteristic of the style of forgiveness in the life of Jesus. Jesus was the great reconciler because he was able to break through the sinners' preoccupations with how bad they were. Consider some of the great stories of forgiveness in the Gospels: Jesus receives the anointing of the sinful woman in the home of Simon the Pharisee (Lk 7:36–50); Jesus accepts the Samaritan woman at the well (Jn 4:1–42); Jesus accepts the woman caught in adultery (Jn 8:1–11); Jesus accepts Zacchaeus, the tax collector (Lk 19:1–10). The style of Jesus with these people is not to say that the way they are living is wrong, even if society might think it to be right. The style of Jesus is to enable others to feel accepted in his very presence. Jesus' way with sinners is to enable them to see themselves as accepted by God so that they can, in the confidence of this acceptance, accept themselves, confess their sins, and release the great potential for good that is within them. This is the style of forgiving that marks the style of a life of reconciliation.

CONVERSION

Conversion is what enables us to live by hope, in trust, and to forgive "seventy times seven times." Conversion is the over and over again centering of our hearts on God, and bringing all things into communion with God. Conversion may be a troublesome notion for many of us. First of all, conversion suggests change. After we have spent so much time trying to get our lives together and under control, who wants to face the call to change? Conversion meets with resistance on other scores, too. For instance, for some conversion rings a conservative theological tone which calls to mind revivalistic contexts aimed at moving us to step forward for Jesus and be saved. In such contexts, conversion points to an intensely personal experience often accompanied by so much religious commotion—voices, visions, and demonstrations of emotion. Those who prefer a more subdued approach to religion look askance at such religious commotion and sentimentalism. For others, conversion is more properly applied to the large-scale sinners, the Mary Magdalenes and Augustines of our day. What place could conversion have in the life of an ordinarily ordinary person?

Whether we resist conversion because it conjures up religious commotion and sentimental piety, or because it seems more appropriate for the notorious sinners, or simply because it speaks to us of the need to change, we cannot ignore its central place in the teaching of Jesus. "The time has come . . . and the reign of God is at hand. Be converted and believe in the good news" (Mk 1:15). This is how the Gospel of Mark begins the public ministry of Jesus. This verse summarizes the preaching of Jesus as well as the drama of the people encountering him. What, then, is this conversion to which we are called who have heard the preaching of Jesus, encountered him in the Spirit, and claim him as our Lord and Savior?

Shuv is the Old Testament term for conversion. It suggests physically changing one's direction. *Shuv* implies that a person has been going in the wrong direction and so is moving farther and farther away from his or her goal. An "about face" is necessary to achieve one's goal.

Metanoia is the New Testament term for conversion. It suggests an internal change that shows itself in practical conduct. "Repentance" and "penance" have been used to translate this notion. Repentance suggests the interior renewal that must accompany the forgiveness of sins. Latin Christians used *paenitentia* or "penance" to translate *metanoia* and to express the conversion going on in one's life. While *metanoia* carries the basic meaning of "to turn around," it does not refer exclusively to the radical about face of those who stand in complete opposition to God. Conversion, as a call of the Gospel, is for everyone, not just the notorious sinner who has made a radical choice for evil and selfishness as a way of life.

The turning envisioned by *metanoia* is more than an intellectual changing of one's mind. *Metanoia* calls for something more.

28

Quoting Paul VI's *Paenitemini* (1966), the Introduction to the Rite of Penance says,

> We can only approach the Kingdom of Christ by *metanoia*. This is a profound change of the whole person by which one begins to consider, judge, and arrange his life according to the holiness and love of God, made manifest in his Son in the last days and given to us in abundance (Par. 10).

This is the Gospel vision of conversion. It calls for an interior transformation that comes about through an encounter with the good news that God loves us unconditionally. The change initiated by this encounter with love is heart deep. In the biblical sense, this means the whole of ourselves is engaged in a transformation from the inside out. This interior transformation blossoms out into a change of awareness, vision, attitude, and conduct. A whole new orientation of our lives takes shape. To be converted means to see things we have never seen before, to think new thoughts, to hold to new convictions, and to do new deeds all because we have encountered Love and now orient our lives in the direction of the power of that Love.

Conversion always has an interpersonal quality about it. Relationships have a way of helping us see what is going on with ourselves, and relationships have the capacity to call us beyond the limits in which we think we have confined all possibility for ourselves. Love is what evokes change in us. In the biblical sense, conversion is only possible because God loves us. Because God loves us and lives within all of us through the Spirit, every personal relationship in our lives has within it the capacity to call us to conversion.

Turning to God in conversion is always a response to being loved by God. God's love breaks into our lives to open our eyes and change our hearts. Another way of expressing this truth is to say that God saves us. We do not save ourselves. The primary disposition on our part in this saving action of God is to be open to receive the gift of God's saving love, or "amazing grace." Without an openness to love there can be no conversion. Without an openness to love, we live in the dark, blinded by our own selfishness. Just as "blindness" is a good metaphor for the condition of sin, "seeing" is a good metaphor for conversion. In the process of conversion we begin to see more clearly. We see ourselves more truly, and we see others, and the relationship we have created with them, more honestly. When our hearts are open to love, our eyes see rightly the life-giving and loving dimensions of all our relationships.

Rosemary Haughton describes four aspects of conversion within relationships: conflict, encounter, self-discovery, and transformation.[4] Conversion is not complete until all four have in some way come to term. Two examples of conversion will help us recognize these dimensions and the process of conversion in a reconciling style of life. The first is the paradigm of conversion from the Bible, the conversion of David. The second is from Rosemary Haughton.

David's conversion in the Second Book of Samuel serves as a paradigm of authentic conversion. David is a man richly blessed by God with gifts for ruling the chosen people. In his mission of ruling the people, David demonstrates his fidelity and humility before God (2 Sam 6), and God promises to remain faithful to David's descendents (2 Sam 7). However, conflict enters David's life when he yields to temptation and violates the convenant by taking Bathsheba, Uriah's wife, as his own, and arranges for Uriah's death (2 Sam 11). The passion which motivated him to violate the covenant continues to blind him, and he does not yet see his sin. Then he encounters the word of God through the prophet Nathan. Nathan tells David the story of the rich man's theft of a poor man's lamb (2 Sam 12:1–4). On hearing this story, David shakes with moral indignation. Then comes the moment of self-discovery, for Nathan has only to say, "That man is you" (2 Sam 12:7). David recognizes his sin and confesses himself as sinner, "I have sinned against the Lord" (2 Sam 12:13a). Through his encounter with the word of God spoken by Nathan, David discovers himself to be alienated from God and to be no longer with God in fidelity to the covenant. Upon this self-discovery, David opens himself to God's pardon which is granted to him immediately: "The Lord forgives you; you will not die" (2 Sam 12:13b).

The rest of the story shows the transformation that comes to David after his self-discovery through his encounter with the word of God. Through his confession and conversion, David regains his sense of God which he lost in the blindness of his sin. He knows his God to be merciful, and so responds to God with total trust in his mercy. David opens himself to the pardon which he has received by praying and fasting that his illegitimate son would be spared the punishment of death, which the prophet said would come to the child born of David's sin. So David kept a strict fast and spent every night lying on the ground. However, when he finds out the child has finally died, he rises from the ground, bathes, combs his hair, changes his clothes, and eats. His officials wonder why he is not mourning. David answers:

> When the child was alive ... I fasted and wept because I kept thinking, "Who knows? Perhaps the Lord might be merciful to me and not let the child die." But now that he is dead, why should I fast? Could I bring the child back to life? I will some day go to where he is, but he can never come back to me.

The child is dead; life must go on. David's response to the child's death is immediately to have intercourse with Bathsheba who conceives Solomon (2 Sam 12:24). This is the freedom of authentic conversion. This is the transformation that comes with trust in divine mercy and pardon. David lives with an attitude of total trust in the love which is offered by God, and he continues to live with the freedom of an entrusted person graced with pardon and peace.

Rosemary Haughton tells a story of the experience of conversion which also illustrates the dynamics of the conversion process.[5] A man in his early forties is generally content, easy-going, and undemonstrative. He lives a placid home life, except for the conflict which he experiences with his sixteen year old daughter. She is intelligent and full of fierce, anti-nuclear idealism, and she is contemptuous of her parents' easy acceptance of their comfortable life. He begins to read some of the left-wing literature which she is always leaving around the house. However, he explains away his action as simply "trying to see the other point of view" and being fair to the young visionary idealism.

31

One day he abandons his pride and encounters his daughter directly, asking about her political opinions. With sense and an unaccustomed humility, she answers his questions and takes this opportunity to introduce him to the humanitarian projects carried on by an unofficial club to which she belongs. The club provides a kind of drop-in center for anyone with no place to stay for the evening. He is moved by what he hears. The effort it cost him to abandon his pride and talk with his daughter has made him open to what she tells him, and her response of confidence in him creates a new relationship between them. This new relationship enables him to see himself more clearly. This is a conversion of sorts. In seeing himself more clearly, he becomes aware of that in him which is an obstacle to the new relationship with his daughter. He knows this as his sin and he repents.

This self-discovery lights up the dynamics of other relationships that make up his life. Rosemary Haughton gives a telling description of what happens to the rest of his relationships as a result of the discovery he makes of himself through his encounter with his daughter, the other young people who run the drop-in center, and the people who frequent it:

> . . . he discovers himself as not only lazy and indifferent but smug, conceited, vain, and hard-hearted. His apparent humility, in asking little of life, he realizes as simply cowardice and pride, that would not expose itself to failure. He sees that he has failed in all sorts of ways—in relation to his wife, of whom he required that she should be simply a cushion to protect him from any self-knowledge; in relation to his children whom he has seen as pleasant extensions of himself, blameable when they were unappreciative of the security and comfort he gave them; in relation to his colleagues whom he now sees he has encouraged to find in himself a justification for their own personal attempts at evasion of difficult decisions—just because he is so kind and easy and utterly harmless.

> All this is not, of course realized fully in the moment of encounter and challenge and response. The kind of self that he has discovered is realized gradually, later on, but it is at this

moment that he actually sees, and seeing, repents, and repenting, is reconciled.[6]

The most important part of this conversion process is the
experience of being loved. This man discovered himself as
loved—loved by his daughter, and loved by the people of the
drop-in center. This was his way of finding grace in deed. Practical decisions follow from the transformation which he experiences. He begins to go regularly to the club to help, he sees his
wife and children more as people and less as furniture, and he
tries to be present to his colleagues when they need to discuss
their personal problems. But will this transformation last? Has
conversion really taken hold? No, unless effort is made to bring
the whole of his life into relation with this new vision of himself. For this he needs not only his own effort, but also the context of the supportive community. He needs the supportive
context of a community which has a shared corporate self-
awareness, a shared language, ritual, standards of living, and
common goals to which he can be committed and sustained in
his newly acquired vision and efforts toward transformation. For
Rosemary Haughton such a supportive context is the meaning
and function of the Church in the world.[7]

Both the biblical story of David and Haughton's story of
the middle-aged man illustrate the structure of the experience of
conversion, and point us in the direction of recognizing what is
involved in making conversion a characteristic of a style of life
committed to reconciliation. Conversion is not a once-for-all
moment. Conversion is a continuous appropriation of God's love
in the whole of our lives.

How far does conversion extend? Is the response of openness to the gift of love enough for conversion? Conversion extends as far as human relationships extend. The openness which
is the fundamental attitude of conversion serves as the basis for
the continuous appropriation of God's love, for integrating the
whole of our lives into our love of God, and for continuing to
grow in conformity to Christ by allowing his words and deeds to
reshape our imagination and refashion our conduct. Continual
conversion is the ongoing verification of who we are as persons
committed to love God and neighbor as ourselves.

Lillian Hellman gives a marvelous image for understanding our lives as ongoing conversion in her description of "pentimento," which she uses to begin her book, *Pentimento: A Book of Portraits:*

> Old paint on canvas, as it ages, sometimes becomes transparent. When that happens it is possible, in some pictures, to see the original lines: a tree will show through a woman's dress, a child makes way for a dog, a large boat is no longer on an open sea. That is called pentimento because the painter "repented," changed his mind. Perhaps it would be as well to say that the old conception, replaced by a later choice, is a way of seeing and then seeing again.[8]

A life of ongoing conversion is like that. It is the matter of having old conceptions replaced by new images. It is a matter of seeing, and then seeing again. Like forgiveness, conversion does not forget the past by erasing it, but reworks the past by recollecting it with fresh understanding. This giving way of one image for another, as a canvas being painted and repainted according to the changing perspective of the artist, is repentance, or ongoing conversion. Our lives are full of change, but we often resist seeing anything new. An openness to conversion will keep our lives from getting stuck in worn-out, no longer helpful images of ourselves, others, or the world.

Lillian Hellman underscores two important aspects of pentimento which are integral to ongoing conversion. First, replacing the old conceptions by later images is a matter of seeing, and then seeing again. There is freedom here. There is consciousness and deliberate choice to alter an earlier image that no longer fits the new perspective of the artist. There is a sense of moving on, of creating, of acquiring a new perspective and seeing freshly. The result is a new masterpiece. The old is reworked, not scrapped. And so, too, with a life of conversion. We see the world differently now. We have changed. We want to be in a new way, not as we were before. Conversion demands this; reconciliation cannot happen without it.

Second, in looking back over her life, Lillian Hellman rediscovers the meaning of her life, reappropriates this meaning, and integrates the people and experiences into the whole of her life from a new perspective. This is what conversion does and how forgiveness happens. The process of "repenting" involves sorting out the meanings that were present in old relationships, whether those were with family, friends, colleagues, or God, from the meaning still there or freshly emerging. The "repenting" that is part of conversion is the letting go of what can no longer be experienced as life-giving and the making room for something new. Conversion means reforming our imaginations with fresh images of who we are, of what is happening to us, and of what is possible for us and for the world. Reconciliation cannot happen without these new images and the power they release to recreate not only personal relationships, but also the whole of our social reality.

HOSPITALITY

Up until now we have described a reconciling character as one rooted in hope in God's love, trusting in God and in oneself, forgiving so that all may be at-one, and undergoing continual conversion in order to keep one's heart fixed on God. Over all these, we need to put on love. "Love one another as I have loved you" (Jn 13:34). Only after that comes the demand to celebrate Reconciliation.

Jesus' command of love is tough. People throughout the ages have tried to make it work. Some people have died for it; almost all have known the discouragement of failing to make it work. What does this love demand? Of all the attempts to bring some insight into what love demands, I have found those which explore the notion of "hospitality" to be the most helpful. The New Testament word for this kind of love which is commanded, and which is the love that reconciles, is *agape*. The Greek word, however, does not seem to work for most people today. Who knows what it means? "Hospitality" works. Everyone seems to have some idea of what it means.

Stop here for a moment to think about what hospitality means to you. When you extend hospitality, what do you do? When you have received hospitality, what did you receive?

35

What did it feel like? Now you may want to compare your ideas with mine.

Hospitality has rich biblical roots. Two of my favorite biblical stories of hospitality tell us of the marvelous things that can happen when we create a welcoming space for another. These stories tell us that guests carry precious gifts with them and are eager to reveal these gifts to anyone who would create a safe and sacred space for them.

My favorite Old Testament story of hospitality is that of Abraham's receiving three strangers at Mamre (Gen 18:1–15):

> The Lord appeared to Abraham at the sacred trees of Mamre. As Abraham was sitting at the entrance of his tent during the hottest part of the day, he looked up and saw three men standing there. As soon as he saw them, he ran out to meet them. Bowing down with his face touching the ground, he said, "Sirs, please do not pass by my home without stopping; I am here to serve you. Let me bring some water for you to wash your feet; you can rest here beneath this tree. I will also bring a bit of food; it will give you strength to continue your journey. You have honored me by coming to my home, so let me serve you." They replied, "Thank you; we accept" (Gen 18:1–5).

As the story goes, these strangers revealed themselves as the Lord, announcing that Sarah, even in her old age, would give birth to a son. By welcoming the strangers, Abraham discovers how the Lord's promise to him would be fulfilled. The author of Hebrews points to the moral: "Remember to welcome strangers in your homes. There were some who did that and welcomed angels without knowing it" (Heb 13:2).

In the New Testament, my favorite story of hospitality is the Emmaus story (Lk 24:13–35). The two travelers to Emmaus invited the stranger who had joined them on the road to stay with them for the night. As the story goes, Jesus made himself known to them as their Lord and Savior in the breaking of the bread. In both stories, hospitality to the stranger becomes the opportunity for the strangers to reveal their most precious gifts, and for the hosts to discover something special about themselves. Through hospitality, separations and distinctions evaporate in the unity of being together.

Hospitality, however, should not be limited to the gesture of receiving the stranger. It needs to become a fundamental attitude that we express toward one another. As such, hospitality is a helpful way to interpret the demand of the love commandment of Jesus. As an expression of effective love, hospitality becomes a characteristic of a style of life committed to reconciliation. As such, hospitality has two important dimensions. One has to do with power; the other with presence.

Hospitality and Power

Hospitality does not seek power over others. Cruelty does. Cruelty deliberately causes harm, especially by crushing a person's self-respect. By manipulating a disparity of power, cruelty sets up a relationship wherein the stronger becomes the victimizer of the weaker. As long as the difference in power is maintained, cruelty will be maintained. To the extent that the difference in power is eliminated, to that extent cruelty will be eliminated. Philip Hallie's studies of cruelty led him to discover that the opposite of cruelty is not liberation from the disparity of power. Rather, he found that the opposite of cruelty is hospitality, a sharing of power.[9]

He discovered this when he came upon accounts of the activity of the little French Protestant village of Le Chambon-sur-Lignon. Beginning in 1940, this French Protestant village of about 3,500 saved the lives of about 6,000 people, most of them Jewish children whose parents had been murdered in the killing camps of central Europe. What was the nature of the hospitality that saved and deeply changed so many lives? Hallie recounts a simple story that says it all:

> One afternoon a refugee woman knocked on the door of a farmhouse outside the village. The farmers around the village proper were Protestants like most of the others in Chambon, but with one difference: they were mostly "Darbystes," followers of a strange Scot Darby, who taught their ancestors in the nineteenth century to believe every word of

37

the Bible, and, indeed, who had them memorize the Bible. They were literal fundamentalists. The farm-woman opened the door to the refugee and invited her into the kitchen where it was warm. Standing in the middle of the floor, the refugee, in heavily accented French, asked for eggs for her children. In those days of very short supplies, people with children often went to farmers in the "gray market" (neither black nor exactly legal) to get necessary food. This was early in 1941, and the farmers were not yet accustomed to the refugees. The farm-woman looked into the eyes of the shawled refugee and asked, "Are you Jewish?" The woman started to tremble, but she could not lie, even though the question was usually the beginning of the end of life for Jews in Hitler's fortress Europe. She answered, "Yes."

The woman ran from the kitchen to the staircase nearby, and while the refugee trembled with terror in the kitchen, she called up the stairs, "Husband, children, come down, come down! We have in our house at this very moment a representative of the Chosen People!"

Not all the Protestants in Chambon were Darbyste fundamentalists; but almost all were convinced that people are the children of God, and are as precious as God Himself. Their leaders were Huguenot preachers and their following of the negative and positive commandments of the Bible came in part from their personal generosity and courage, but also in part from the depths of their religious conviction that we are all children of God, and we must take care of each other lovingly. This combined with the ancient and deep historical ties between the Huguenots and the Jews of France and their own centuries of persecution by the Dragons and Kings of France helped make them what they were, "always ready to help," as the Chambonnais saying goes.[10]

Acts of cruelty crush a person's self-respect, and bring the havoc of separation, alienation, and war. Acts of hospitality heal, restore a sense of worth, bring reconciliation, communion, peace. The reconciling power of hospitality lies in its "powerlessness." Hospitality reconciles because hospitality cares enough to create space in one's life to welcome another in. The key to this space is not that it is merely a place, but that it is above all the quality of the environment wherein another can be at home in one's own human existence. This brings us to the dimension of hospitality and presence.

Hospitality and Presence

"Hospitality" has become a favorite notion of liturgist Fr. Eugene Walsh, who finds that it expresses best the kind of love we would hope to find in Christian communities in order to enable good liturgical celebrations to happen.[11] For Fr. Walsh, the phrase that best captures the meaning of hospitality is "to pay attention to." People seem to know what it takes to pay attention. It takes time. It takes deliberate, conscious effort. When we pay attention, we stop being preoccupied with ourselves and make the effort to get out of ourselves and be interested in the other. As Fr. Walsh says,

> To be hospitable, you must pay attention at three levels. First, you have to pay attention to one another, then you have to pay attention to what people are doing all around you and what they are asking you to do. Finally, you have to pay attention to what is going on inside you as a direct result of all that is happening outside and around you.[12]

In this threefold paying attention, we are not only well on our way to having good liturgical celebrations, but we are also well on our way to being reconcilers. Hospitable reconcilers pay attention. By paying attention we touch the possibility of being open to God, to others, and to ourselves. When we bring these three together, we are engaged in reconciling activity.

Henri Nouwen has explored dimensions of the movement from hostility to hospitality to great effect for growth in the spiritual life.[13] "Presence" again is key. According to Henri Nouwen, we live in a world of strangers, estranged not only from neighbors, family, or friends, but also from our deepest selves and from God. In this world we witness a search for a hospitable place where "life can be lived without fear and community can be found."[14] To offer an open and hospitable space where strangers can cast off their fear and become one with their fellow human beings is to do the work of reconciliation. The style of life committed to reconciliation and marked by hospitality is the life that creates "the free and fearless space where brotherhood and sisterhood can be formed and fully expressed."[15]

The life of reconciliation marked by hospitality is well expressed in this extended metaphor which I once heard Fr. James Dunning use to talk about ministry. I use it here with Fr. Dunning's permission.

> Each of us is like a rock with walls and barriers that keep others out and keep us secure. But year after year God keeps carving away at our rock. One day we discover that God's hand has created some empty space in our rock. He has been chipping away at us and now we discover a cave hewn out of stone. We find we have some space to welcome people in, people who are also weary, tired, and in need of some space in which to gather so that they will not feel alone. They come in and say to us, "Oh, I see you have been doing some rock dwelling, too. The carving hand of the Lord has also been chipping away at your grand design and your plans and ambitions. I see you have some empty space. Perhaps I might come in. You know what I have been through. Perhaps you can hear me. Perhaps you won't force your plans on me, manipulate me, or try to control me. Perhaps you will offer a place where I can be me."

In the process of reconciliation, God's carving hand is at work on us, not putting us in our place, but creating some sacred space and asking us to do the same. The empty space leaves room for God to fill us more fully with God's image, and it leaves room for God's people to come in and hear some good news, to experience some new bonds of communion, to feel the gentle touch of one who cares, and to rejoice because they have finally found someone who has room for them and accepts them.

This is living the life of reconciliation—allowing God to be present to us to form us in God's image and welcoming others into sacred space where they can give freely the gifts they have been entrusted by God, and where they can feel hugged by God in the embrace that does not smother but supports and affirms the goodness that has been released by the power of forgiveness and healing.

Now that we have taken a stand on reconciliation in life by sketching some characteristics of a person committed to reconciliation, we can proceed to explore some basic attitudes toward God, sacraments, and the moral life which underlie the renewal of the Sacrament of Reconciliation.

FOURTH MOVEMENT: APPROPRIATING THE CHRISTIAN STORY

How does the above description of characteristics of a style of life committed to reconciliation shed light on your present understanding and practice of reconciliation in life? In what ways did this chapter affirm you? In what ways were you challenged? Complete the following sentences:

I realized that . . .
I relearned that I . . .
I was surprised that I . . .
I wonder if . . .
I wonder why . . .
I wonder when . . .

FIFTH MOVEMENT: CHOOSING A FAITH RESPONSE

What does being committed to a reconciling style of life mean for you in action terms? What does it mean for you at the level of feelings and attitudes? Complete the following sentences:

Next time, I want to . . .
I need to think more about . . .
I hope that I . . .

Suggestions for Further Reading

Donald Evans	*Struggle and Fulfillment*
Thomas A. Harris	*I'm OK—You're OK*
Rosemary Haughton	*The Transformation of Man*
Henri Nouwen	*Reaching Out*
John Shea	*The Challenge of Jesus*

2

God's Forgiving Grace

FIRST MOVEMENT: PRESENT ACTION

Tell about a time you received an unexpected, undeserved gift. What was that experience like? Name one of your personal gifts that is a sign of God's life in you. Who is God for you? What image of God is most prominent in your life?

SECOND MOVEMENT: CRITICAL REFLECTION

What experiences have you had which had the greatest influence on your image of God? How are these experiences still affecting you? How is your image of God affecting you? What gifts can you give to God?

THIRD MOVEMENT: THE CHRISTIAN STORY AND VISION

These years since Vatican II have witnessed the implementation of the Council's mandate to reform the sacramental rituals. We who have lived through these years of experimentation, revision, and renewal know well that we cannot create a sense of worship by changing our ritual books, music, environment, vesture, or gesture. Though all of these revisions are indeed important for encouraging a fuller human response, our awareness of the presence of God is still the all-important matter. The experience of God evokes worship; worship does not evoke God. Therefore, the goal of revising rituals is to mediate God's loving presence more clearly.

Before we can appreciate the revised ritual of the new Rite of Penance, we need to look at some basic attitudes toward God, sacraments, and the moral life. The single and simple thesis which holds our probing of attitudes together is that whether we experience God and how we experience God have a great deal to do with the quality of our sacramental celebrations and of our moral lives. To the extent that we lack a vivid sense of God's loving presence (or "grace"), to that extent our sacramental celebrations become empty, flat, boring, and meaningless. Indeed, worship in word and sacrament is not a self-generating activity. Worship is a response to an experience of God present in our midst. Sacramental celebrations come out of life and express life. If we are going to celebrate we must have something to celebrate. In sacraments, we celebrate our experience already begun and, in this way, deepen that experience by bringing it to a new level of expression. At the same time, we heighten our awareness of God in Christ and through the Spirit in the Church and in the world.

In like manner, to the extent that we lack a vivid awareness of God's loving presence, to that extent the tone and quality of our moral lives become fragile. Morality itself means to ritualize in the actions of our lives the experiences which we have of God's presence. The moral life is like worship. It is a response to an experience of God. The moral life takes place in a different context when an awareness of God is lost: sin becomes the infraction of a rule rather than a turning away from God; moral actions become an increased quantity of moral goodness rather than a grateful response to the goodness of God; moral deliberation becomes a computer-like problem-solving rather than a prayerful discernment of the call of the word of God for this moment. Without an experience of God, sacramental celebrations and the moral life wither.

In these next two chapters we will look at three attitudes which have a strong influence on how we understand the Sacrament of Reconciliation and so have an effect on the way we enter the celebration of it. These are our attitudes toward God, grace, and sacraments. In the fourth and fifth chapters, we will examine sin and conscience as two dimensions of the moral life which also have a significant influence on how we celebrate Reconciliation.

GOD

We are in a new climate these days for talking about God and celebrating experiences of God. After the death-of-God movement of the 1960's, God is "in" again, alive and well on the campus, in the city, the suburb, and now even in the desert. The 1970's search for spiritual odysseys, Christian or not, Eastern or Western, has reawakened religious concerns. God, Jesus, and related religious themes have exploded on the scene in sight and sound, color and fashion, in ways we could hardly have imagined a decade or two ago. People everywhere and of all ages are seeking Him (or Her) with an urgency we have not experienced before in recent decades. In their seeking, people can find God playing in a thousand places. This is true poetically and literally. Jesus plays on Broadway, in parks, and in movie houses. Even George Burns makes a comeback playing God. Jesus makes the cover of *Time* magazine more than once. "God is back" and "Jesus saves" fill our freeways on bumper stickers and billboards; "Smile, God loves you" and "God doesn't make junk" fill our classrooms and recreation centers on buttons, banners, posters, and T-shirts. Talk of God as well as talk to God, though banned in our public schools, is now familiar chatter all around. This yearning for religious experience gives us a fresh opportunity to seize, and a fresh opportunity to share, the Christian experience of God and the Christian ways of celebrating that experience.

Experiencing God

If it is true that whether we experience God and how we experience God have a great deal to do with the tone and quality of our sacramental celebrations, then we need to begin our consideration of Reconciliation by retrieving our experience of God. Take a moment to recall an experience of God. Focus on concrete circumstances and the feelings that accompanied the experience. Where did it happen? Under what conditions? What was it like?

How did you do? Was that brief, blunt request too hard to fulfill? If so, try this one: Recall a time when you were acutely aware of being related to something greater than yourself. Putting the request to retrieve an experience of God this way is not meant as a replacement for the word "God," but it is an attempt to help you get at a base in experience for talking about God. For example, you may want to recall an experience that brought you in touch with values beyond your own. Or you may recall an experience that gave you a sense that life is worthwhile. Or maybe you would recall an experience that brought you a sense of personal healing and wholeness where the conflicts of life seemed to be resolved. Or maybe your experience is one which took you out of the ordinary in wonder, awe, and surrender.

People who have shared their experiences of God with me have told me stories of personal experiences of virtuous people, of moral (s)heroes; they have spoken of great deeds of courage and integrity, of times with friends in good conversation over what each cares about deeply; they have spoken of experiences of death, or birth, of children at play, of a grandfather sitting by the sea fishing; they have spoken as well of Yosemite vistas, of solitary walks through the ocean surf at Carmel-by-the-Sea, and of quiet listening to Debussy. For all of them, God is the "something more" that drew them out of themselves and put them in touch with a sustaining, uplifting graciousness which they could "feel" at the deepest dimension of these human moments.

The "In and Through" Approach

In the Judaeo-Christian tradition, the God who is with us (immanence) is also the God who is totally other (transcendence). When we accept the total otherness of God, we admit that we cannot know God immediately, but only in a mediated

46

way. There is no other way for us who are body-persons. This is the way of sacrament. The pre-eminent mediation, or sacrament, of God for us is Jesus Christ. Edward Schillebeeckx has captured this truth succinctly in the title of his book on sacramental theology: *Christ, the Sacrament of the Encounter with God.* The way of sacrament, the way of incarnation or mediation, occupies the heartland of our Catholic heritage. The sacramental principle says that our experience of God comes *in and through* something else.

The Bible knows this "in and through" approach to God well. Nature, historical events, and people (pre-eminently Jesus) are the primary media in and through which the Bible speaks of experiencing God. The Exodus from Egypt, that formative experience of Israel becoming the People of God, can serve as a good example of how this approach works in the Bible. First comes the experience. A band of slaves are brought to freedom by Moses. After the event comes the sharing of the experience by telling the story over again. Through storytelling, a growing awareness dawns that recognizes not Moses but God as the one who freed the slaves and made them a free people. Then annual celebrations of the event continue to make the presence and action of God in this liberating event alive for each generation. Retelling the story of Exodus as one's own story evokes new experiences of a liberating God which shed light on the present and opened the future to a fresh response to God through liberating deeds. The God who once freed slaves held in bondage continues to call the people of every age who live by this story to a freedom they only dimly perceive.

The Exodus follows the recurring biblical story line: God frees people from a death-dealing situation for a new life which they are free to choose and pursue. This is the story of reconciliation in a nutshell. The Christian people see in and through the life, death, and glorification of Jesus not only the continuation of this story, but also the revelation of new depths of God's loving, sustaining graciousness which gives us the assurance of final victory. The story of Jesus assures us that life is stronger than death, and that grace abounds greater than sin. This is the story we live by.

The pattern of this story is repeated over and over again in the lives of individuals and of the whole community. Notice the pattern. First, experience. Then comes awareness that there is something more to the experience than meets the eye. From awareness comes recognition: "God!" "God is touching me!" "I have seen the Lord!" From recognition comes celebration: God is here! Let's celebrate! From celebration comes a fresh response: Because we have been liberated, we must do liberating deeds! (All this happens, of course, in the context of grace.)

The theology of the "in and through" approach tells us that every human experience, if given a chance, can disclose God. God comes to us in and through our everyday experiences because God is already there. We really have nothing to do with God's being there. The "in and through" approach, the way of sacrament, begins with the presupposition of universal divine presence. We cannot induce it, conjure it, or create it. God's coming is always God's own graciously free and loving action. It is gift. The question for us, then, is not how to make God present, as though God were missing. Our question is: How can we allow God, who is everywhere present, to enter our minds and hearts? God is always everywhere present to us, but we have to want to be present and receptive to God. We cannot do God's part. All we can do is the human part as well as we can. Our part is to be open, to receive, to embrace, then to respond in celebration with joy and thanksgiving. We call this way of responding "faith." This is the pattern that lies behind all sacramental celebrations, and this is the pattern we must enter if our sacramental celebrations are ever to be meaningful. But more on that later. We are getting ahead of ourselves a bit.

The Depth Dimension of Experience

Contemporary theology offers some helpful metaphors that illumine the way we often experience God in the ordinariness of our lives without quite realizing it. Rather than putting God in a box and thinking of distinct realms where we might experience God (Church, sacraments, prayer), contemporary theology advocates a model of thinking of different levels or dimensions of experience. God is experienced in the deepest dimension of every human moment. Paul Tillich, one of the great Protestant theologians of this century, follows this model of thinking by using the metaphor of "depth" where God is experienced in the depth-dimensions of every human experience. Karl Rahner, perhaps the greatest Catholic theologian of this century, uses the metaphor of "horizon." For Rahner, God is experienced as the background against which we see everything else. Both these metaphors tell us that every human experience points beyond itself to something more. These metaphors tell us we must be sensitive to the depths of everydayness, to the larger mystery within which we live. To see "something more" requires a contemplative vision of life, a kind of seeing that does not stop with looking at the appearance of things, but sees through to the depths. This kind of seeing which takes a long, loving look at the real is the vision of faith.

William Luijpen, a philosopher who has studied the way we talk of God, has given some examples of our giving expression to the experience of the "depth" of our existence by calling the name "God."

A child is born and the believer exclaims "God!"
In health or illness the believer shouts "God!"
He sexually unites with another person and in his
    ecstasy the believer calls "God!"
He is dying and his lips whisper "God!"
At the rising and the setting of the sun, in the pale
    light of the moon and the stars, before the roaring
    of the sea, at the undulating of the wheat stalks, the
    threat of a storm and the menace of a flood, at the
    welling up of a storm and the germinating of the seed,
    the believer exclaims "God!"
When he conquers in battle or suffers defeat, when he
    lives in poverty or in prosperity, when he suffers injustice
    or finds justice, the religious man calls "God!"
When he is reduced to slavery in Egypt, rises against
    his oppressors and when he overcomes the terrible
    risk of his revolt against his masters, the believer
    exclaims "God!"
When, while wandering through the desert with his people,
    he meets ethical demands imposing themselves on him as
    inescapable conditions of humanity, the religious man
    shouts "God!"

When he can finally establish himself in a land of his
  own, the believer calls "God!"
When he must go into exile, he complains "God!"
And when he can again return from his exile, he
  joyfully shouts "God!"[1]

Karl Rahner offers a set of questions which point to the horizon of human experience:

> Have we ever kept silent, despite the urge to defend our-
> selves, when we were being unfairly treated? Have we ever
> forgiven another although we gained nothing by it and our
> forgiveness was accepted as quite natural? Have we ever
> made a sacrifice without receiving any thanks or acknowl-
> edgment, without even feeling any inward satisfaction?
> Have we ever decided to do a thing simply for the sake of
> conscience, knowing that we must bear sole responsibility
> for our decision without being able to explain it to anyone?
> Have we ever tried to act purely for love of God when no
> warmth sustained us, when our act seemed a leap in the
> dark, simply nonsensical? Were we ever good to someone
> without expecting a trace of gratitude and without the com-
> fortable feeling of having been "unselfish"?[2]

If we find such experiences in our lives, says Rahner, then we
who live by faith have in fact experienced God, perhaps without
quite realizing it.

Gregory Baum is another leading Catholic theologian who
has also identified some common human experiences in and
through which God is present to us. He names the experiences
of friendship, encounter, conscience, truth, human solidarity,
and compassionate protest.[3] Michael Novak, in a similar way,
speaks of freedom, honesty, community, and courage as experiences in and through which more than ourselves seems to be operating. He names this something more as God.[4] Peter Berger,
likewise, finds "signals of transcendence" within common human situations. He names the everyday kinds of experiences of
order, play, hope, damnation, and humor as pointing beyond
themselves to something greater.[5]

What these thinkers seem to be saying is that while some

50

experiences may be more conducive to experiencing God than others, there is no experience which, if given a chance, could not disclose God to us. This means we should cease trying to confine the presence of God to specifically religious sectors of life. We cannot put God in a box. Psalm 139 captures this ever present reality of a gracious God quite poetically:

> Where could I go from your spirit?
>> From your presence where could I flee?
> If I went up to heaven, you would be there;
>> if I lay down in the world of the dead,
>> you would be there.
> If I flew away beyond the east,
>> or lived in the farthest place in the west,
> You would be there to lead me,
>> you would be there to help me.

The Baltimore Catechism said it more succinctly, but much less poetically:

> Q. Where is God?
> A. God is everywhere.

When we begin to confine God to specifically religious areas of life, we are forced to turn away from the ordinary experiences of life in order to be touched by the gracious reality of God. Yet this is not the way it was for Jesus. The fundamental message of Jesus about God is that human life is the home of God. Do not look anywhere else. All the parables of Jesus are stories about experiencing God. These stories are filled with very human characters and very human experiences. Yet none of them ever mention "God" directly.

What the theologians seem to be saying today, and what so many people searching for God force us to admit, is that if it makes sense to speak of God at all, then we must be able to experience God in the center of our lives where we spend most of our time and expend most of our energy. To realize that God is there in the center of our lives at the deepest dimension of every human moment means that God is never far from us. To experience God in the depths is to be aware that we are related to a

51

larger mystery within which we live. St Paul understood this well when he expressed the following in his speech in the Areopagus of Athens:

> Yet God is actually not far away from any one of us; as someone has said, "In him we live and move and have our being" (Acts 17:27–28).

For this reason, our relationship to God and response to God cannot be relegated to special activities or special moments. Our relationship and response to God are going on all the time, whether we want them to or not.

Let it be understood, however, that this accent on the presence of God in and through the ordinary human moments of our lives is not to denigrate the special moments we call sacramental celebrations. The accent helps us appreciate that the ordinary place of experiencing God is in the ordinary events of our lives. The basic truth of our religious and sacramental tradition is that, if we do not experience God in the midst of our lives, we will not experience God in those specifically religious sectors like Church, sacraments, or prayer. One of the Telespots from the Franciscan Communications Center says it well. The scene is of a woman walking to church. Along the way she meets a black couple and an oriental couple. She gives an uninterested look to each. As the woman reaches for the door to enter the church, a voice speaks the only words of the Telespot: "If you don't see God here, it's not likely you'll find him in there." The Telespot has it exactly right. If religious moments have a role in our lives, they are not for looking away from life, but for looking more deeply into life.

Sacramental celebrations, as we will soon see, become meaningful insofar as these moments bring to our awareness the divine graciousness present throughout the whole of our lives, and in every moment of our lives. As contemporary theology continues to remind us, we experience God at the deepest dimension of our ordinary human experience. We come to sacraments to deepen the experience already going on. Experience comes first, then awareness and recognition, and finally come celebration and response.

Images of God

From experiences of God come images of God. Images in turn evoke and shape ongoing experiences of God. Most of us have picked up our images of God from the way we have been taught about God, especially through the way we have been treated in the name of God and according to God's will. (Pastors, parents, and educators, beware!)

Our images of God are hard to shake, even when we become adults. They seem to have embedded themselves in the elusive corners of our subconscious and continue to influence our convictions and experiences of God and of ourselves. They influence our feeling for what it is like to live in relationship to God, and they especially affect the attitude, or disposition, we bring to those significant moments of encountering God, such as the sacraments. Yet these second-hand images and their power will pale against those to which we come as a result of a first-hand experience of God in the depths of our lives. The attitude we take toward the Sacrament of Reconciliation has a lot to do with the images of God we carry around with us. And, conversely, the experiences we have of Reconciliation can have a lot to do with confirming or changing the images of God with which we live.

So we need to examine our images of God. Just as we tried to retrieve an experience of God, now we need to identify the image of God which is most powerful for us. So before going on, stop for a moment to do this little exercise. This is an either/or forced choice exercise. Which alternative do you choose and why?

God is more summer or winter?
God is more yes or no?
God is more father or mother?
God is more here or there?
God is more sour or sweet?
God is more "No Trespassing" or "Public Swimming"?

Now fill in the blank with the name or title for God which best expresses your experience of God and relationship to God:

For me God is _____ .

In the Judaeo-Christian tradition, God is imaged in a great variety of ways: father, mother, lover, husband, king, judge, cre-

53

ator, potter, rock, fortress, whirlwind, to name but a few images. In the "in and through" approach to God, the imagery we use for God emerges from the medium through which we encounter God. For example, if nature is our primary medium, we may prefer images of God as creator, rock, or whirlwind. If an historical event is our medium, we may prefer images of deliverer, fortress, and refuge. If people are the media for encountering God, we may use father, mother, lover, and so forth. In the "in and through" approach to God, images say something about the inherent quality of God and something about our relationship to God. We cannot talk about God independently of our relationship to God. To say "God is a lover," for example, is to say something about the inherent quality of God as love and also something about our relationship to God as loving. We can never say anything about God without at one and the same time saying something about how we have experienced God. We know God is love, for instance, in and through our human experiences of love. The "in and through" approach keeps the reality of God joined to the reality of the human experiences in and through which we encounter God. This is what allows us to say that in and through our love for one another we become aware of a greater Love sustaining us. In and through our experiences of accepting and being accepted we become aware of a greater Acceptance receiving and forgiving us. We cannot talk about our relationship with God without talking about our relationship with one another. And we cannot talk about our human experiences at any depth without talking about our relationship to God at the "depths." This is going to be very important for understanding sacraments as significant manifestations of God and as our response to God.

While we take our images of God from the medium of encounter, we choose our preferred image on the basis of its being able to convey what we know about our relationship to God. We cannot escape the truth of the image. Images do not lie. We choose the image that is true for us. The images that we use of God are ultimately determined by what is happening in our human lives where we encounter God and respond to God. For this reason, we can learn a lot about ourselves in relation to God, and a lot about our attitude toward the Sacrament of Reconciliation by paying close attention to the images of God we carry around with us, especially the image of God most operative for us.

For example, if we approach Reconciliation as penitents who carry around an image of a vengeful, "gotcha" God who is on the prowl and punishes every act contrary to God's will, then we would probably approach Reconciliation with tremendous fear and a scrupulosity that wants to be sure every sin is accurately confessed in number and kind. If the priest-confessor carries around an image of God as Divine Reason having an answer to every question, then the priest is most likely to project this image by feeling obligated to provide a solution to every problem. On the other hand, if the priest and penitent have an image of God as tender lover, then the penitent does not approach Reconciliation fearing disapproval and rejection and the priest invites and encourages the penitent to realize her or his best possibilities.

Look back now over your responses to that short exercise on images of God. What do your responses tell you about your relationship to God? What do your responses suggest about the disposition you might be bringing to Reconciliation? Remember, whether we experience God and how we experience God have a great deal to do with the tone and quality of our moral and sacramental lives. Did your responses show that you experience the God of Jesus or some other gods? That is, do you carry around images of God which invite you to celebrate an experience of God as forgiving, accepting, reconciling, healing, or is your God forbidding, rejecting, confining, punishing?

Before we can begin to experience the God of Abraham, Isaac, Jacob, and Jesus we must destroy our whole pantheon of false gods and distorted images. We all have them. We have all burned incense at shrines of our favorite gods. An all-time favorite is the legal God, known by a number of images: Commander-in-Chief, Grim Reaper, Resident Policeman. This is the "gotcha" God. This God keeps book on us, waits for us to trip up so we can be marked a loser, and this god threatens to "imprison" us in hell if we get out of line. Then there is God-the-Aspirin to whom we run to make everything better whenever anything goes wrong. There is also the Managing Director God who makes it start raining just when we have our picnic blanket spread out, or who kindly manages to get us a little extra mileage so we can make it to the next gas station. If we are honest, we know these images of God are very hard to shake. But shake them we must if we are to experience the God of Jesus, and if our experiences of the Sacrament of Reconciliation and our moral lives are to be enriched.

Our first task before approaching Reconciliation, then, is to figure out how many strange gods we carry around with us and the ways they affect the tone and quality of our lives. These gods of our pantheon are indeed incredibly powerful, but hardly resemble the God that has fond regard for each of us. Images of God like these nourish fear as the motivating force for giving worship and being moral. Rewards are expected for those who fulfill God's commands and punishment for those who do not. While these images have the potential to keep the distinction between Creator and creature clear, as well as to nurture a sense of the transcendent and the sacred, they often evoke a religious style that is passive, socially irresponsible, and minimalistic. A stress on God's power and dominion discourages personal responsibility and self-determination. This can lead to the failure to confront unjust social structures. Minimalism, the child of the "gotcha" God, tells us just how far we could go before committing a mortal sin, and just how much we need to do to fulfill our Sunday Mass obligation.

Images of God like these collapsed for many people during the 1960's under the influence of high family mobility, television, the civil rights revolution, Vatican II, the Vietnam War, and the birth control controversy. Movements within the Church like charismatic groups, Cursillo, marriage encounter, and others encouraged images of a God closer to us as tender lover, companion, and friend who wanted to be called "Abba"—Daddy—and whom we should try to serve out of love and gratitude rather than fear.

New images of a friendly, loving, close God were bound to affect our understanding and attitude toward sin, guilt, the need for confession, and our style of reconciliation. Changing images of God and a new religious consciousness have enriched the Church with a fresh vitality. These have encouraged prayer and a return to the sources in our spirituality, enhanced personal responsibility over old paternalism, and heightened our social consciousness. But in the midst of the many good things that are happening, we do risk losing some important things. When religious experience is focused so much on the plane of human encounter, we risk losing some reverential awe before the transcendent mystery of God. When God is so much "on our level" we lose sight of the biblical God who is alternately consoling and constantly exposing the illusion of our self-sufficiency. Emphasizing the immanence of God (God "on our level") over the transcendence of God (the total otherness of God) risks creating a relaxed Christianity which fits so well with our American lifestyle. Then sin loses its religious meaning, reconciliation is completed on the horizontal plane, and the sacramental celebrations of forgiveness are replaced by encounter groups. As one person told me quite bluntly, "Why do I need your Sacrament of Reconciliation when I have my T-group?"

We must never find ourselves faced with an either/or forced choice when it comes to God: either the tough God of challenge and judgment, or the loving God of fond acceptance (which in its own right already includes challenge and judgment). The Bible witnesses to a many-sided God. But when it comes to an image of God that serves as a solid foundation for approaching Reconciliation, which image should take precedence? Jesus gives the answer. We know what we know about God in and through Jesus, the primary sacrament of the encounter with God. Jesus is God-with-a-face, the visible image of the invisible God. Look at how Jesus approaches the sinner. Take the sinful woman of Luke 7:36–50 (often thought to be Mary Magdalene), Zacchaeus of Luke 19:1–10, or the Samaritan woman at the well in John 4:1–42 for examples. Only after Jesus affirmed them and helped them to accept themselves was he able to confront them with their sinfulness and call them to something new. Affirmation and acceptance first, then challenge. Affirmation and acceptance imply the challenge to goodness. Being affirmed and feeling accepted do not yield complacency in the story of Jesus. They release untapped power for good.

Are we any better off than Luke's sinful woman, Zacchaeus, or the Samaritan woman? The environment of our lives is filled with pressures and put-downs that make accepting ourselves and acknowledging our goodness difficult. We are shaken by critical voices of judgment, the watchful eye of a superior, and ongoing conflicts with authority. Do we need an image of a tough God to intensify and ratify this shake-up in a divine way? The divine ratification we need is that which comes with the good news that God really does love all people without exception, that God loves "us," and, most importantly, that God loves me! The heartwarming part of the Good News is that we do not have to come to this stunning truth all by ourselves. As we make our efforts to reach out and be open to this loving God, God is already there helping us. This is grace: "I am here; I am with you; I love you; I will never let you go!"

GRACE

In retrieving our experiences of God and images of God, we are forced to confront the basic question that penetrates to the nature of our relationship to God: Is the Mystery within which we live, and to which we are inescapably bonded, ultimately gracious or indifferent? Are we grounded in a reality that cares for us or not? That is for us or against us? The Christian response to these questions is that the hallmark of God is graciousness. God cares for us. God is for us. This takes us to the heart of the reality we call grace.

Some may ask, however, "Why speak of grace before sin? After all, is not the Sacrament of Reconciliation for the forgiveness of sins? Do we not go to the Sacrament to get grace which we lost through sin? Does not grace then come to restore us to what we should be by straightening out our motivation and will?" These are common questions which reflect a certain attitude toward the Sacrament of Reconciliation and grace. These are good questions because they help us focus the relationship between grace, sin, and Reconciliation in a way that will help us appreciate the new Rite of Penance and the place it may have in our lives.

With Augustine, many want to say grace is what it is because of sin, especially original sin. Grace corrects our nature and restores it to what it should be. Yet with St. Paul we can never allow sin to be more powerful than grace. In light of the life-death-glorification of Jesus, the power of sin has been broken in our lives. Grace—the redeeming love of God—affects our lives to the core. This redeeming grace is God's undefeatable love for us. God's unconditional acceptance of us affects our very being before we ever make a free choice. We are graced from the beginning. The only way we know to be human is to be graced. God's love of us is constant and always available. If God were ever to remove this love, we would not be at all. Though never without grace, we are only more or less open and transformed by grace. Just as a gift cannot be given unless it is received, so grace cannot transform us unless we allow it to. The transformation that happens in us when we accept God's self-communication of love is the work of the Holy Spirit.

If grace could have its way, it would be the exclusive energy empowering all our choices. Yet grace does not interfere with our freedom to mess ourselves up. Sin is the exercise of our freedom to act against our positive, loving relationship with God. We can mess ourselves up through sin in many ways that are not in keeping with our dignity of being graced by God. Yet our sin does not destroy grace, for God never withdraws this redeeming love from us. If God's offer of lover were not constant and always available to us, then conversion and forgiveness would not be possible. But the energy for conversion and forgiveness comes from grace in the power of the Spirit. In St. Augustine's powerful phrase, "If we but turn to God, that itself is a gift of God." Once we realize that, we can take Christian delight in ourselves again. We can like ourselves! We can stop messing ourselves up! Our God is a gracious God who, like the merciful father in Luke's famous parable (Lk 15:11–32, often misnamed the Parable of the Prodigal Son), is not out to catch us in sin, but to grab us and hug us, even in our sin.

So in shaping our attitude toward the Sacrament of Reconciliation, and our understanding of it, we are better off hearing the word of grace before the word of sin. To hear the word of sin before grace may so distort our hearing that we will never break through to the clear words of love, acceptance, and forgiveness that are spoken and ritualized in Reconciliation. Furthermore, if we begin with an understanding of grace, we may be able to shape a new attitude toward Reconciliation which will help us understand not only the new Rite, but more importantly the place Reconciliation has in our lives.

In workshops on the Sacrament of Reconciliation, I ask this question: Why do you go to this Sacrament? The three most frequent answers given are: the Church requires it, to get forgiveness, and to get grace. The last response is the one we need to explore at the moment, for it suggests an understanding of grace that gives rise to a certain attitude toward Reconciliation (or any sacrament, for that matter).

A way of understanding grace compatible with the new Rite of Penance is to draw a contrast between where we have been in our understanding of grace and where we are going.

Because grace is a noun, we too easily think of grace as almost physical. Grace appears to be a thing, a mysterious quantity of stuff, like some divine gold stars that can be measured and mechanically handed out. Grace often appears to be something God gives us if we pray, fast, do good works, receive the sacraments, and keep the commandments. If we get enough grace through all these efforts of ours, we will be pleasing to God. Moreover, not only will we be pleasing to God, but we can then make some legitimate claims on heaven as our reward.

This is certainly the kind of understanding of grace with which I grew up. I remember teaching a CCD class during the Baltimore Catechism years in which I used the vivid illustration of the two milk bottles to convey grace and sin. The "sin" bottle was empty; the "grace" bottle was full. Through sin we drained our souls (the bottles) of grace. By going to confession, we got filled up again. This made the sacraments a kind of divine filling station. The Church was the great reservoir with seven heavenly channels through which flowed this divine life. Sound familiar?

Although this notion had the advantage of making grace a reality for generations of Catholics, and expressed clearly the sacraments as a means of grace, it also had many disadvantages. It depended on the impersonal model of grace as a mysterious quantity of stuff. While we are trying to dispose of this impersonal model, we must not lose sight of grace as something real. God's graciousness actually reaches out to us in and through all the people and events of our lives. In this way of thinking,

60

prayer and sacraments do not lose their validity as ways to mediate grace. Rather, they become special moments to heighten our awareness of the grace of God meeting us everywhere. All of created reality, every event of our lives, each moment of interpersonal encounter can be the occasion of grace. For many people, Psalms 19, 95, 104, and 139 speak clearly of the world as the theater of grace. For others, Gerard Manley Hopkins' "God's Grandeur" has more power to bring them to a real breakthrough in appreciating this understanding of grace.

> The world is charged with the grandeur of God.
>   It will flame out, like shining from shook foil;
>   It gathers to a greatness, like the ooze of oil
> Crushed. Why do men then not reck his rod?
> Generations have trod, have trod, have trod;
>   And all is seared with trade; bleared, smeared with
> toil;
>   And wears man's smudge and shares man's smell:
> the soil is bare now, nor can foot feel, being shod.
>
> And for all this, nature is never spent;
>   There lives the dearest freshness deep down things;
> And though the last lights off the black West went
>   Oh, morning, at the brown brink eastward, springs
>   ——Because the Holy Ghost over the bent
> World broods with warm breast and with ah!
> bright wings.[6]

The poetry of Hopkins and the psalms express so well that we live in the ambience of grace because God loves us and touches us in and through every moment of our lives.

From our previous reflections on experiencing God and imaging God, we saw that we do not have to "get" God. God's love has already begotten us. Experiencing God in the depth-dimension of human experience and imaging God in a way that expresses how it feels to be in relationship with God disclose the fact that we are bonded to God as a fundamental condition of being human. To be human is to be graced. We cannot escape it. Experiencing God in and through a world charged with God's grandeur, we recognize that we not only stand in a real relationship with God, but we also recognize the flow of that relationship. God initiates. We respond. We experience our relationship to God as a given, a gift. God touches us; we do not touch God. It dawns on us that God is with us and for us. We do not logically argue to that conclusion. Like Francis Thompson's "Hound of Heaven," God pursues us. In a real sense, then, there is nothing more to "get." Faith, prayer, sacraments, and good works are not things we do to get God to love us (i.e., give us grace). In and through these responses of ours, we heighten our awareness and appreciation of God's love already bestowed on us, and we deepen our relationship with God. This keener awareness and deeper relationship are what we "get" through prayer and sacraments, if we are going to continue to speak of "getting" at all.

If grace is always concrete, but we are not to think or speak about grace as a mysterious quantity of stuff, then what mode shall we use to speak about grace? What language shall we use? Contemporary theology prefers to speak of grace in the mode of the biblical metaphor of covenant, or in the mode of the personal experience of friendship. For example, Peter Fransen begins his great work on grace with a parable which expresses the reality of grace in the mode of the personal experience of love.

Once upon a time there was a young girl, an orphan, who grew up in coarse surroundings. Her foster parents were hard and rough, and had never wanted her. Never as a baby or as a growing child had she known the subtle intimacy of a true home. She had never been loved.

And then she grew into a young woman. Daily encounter with disparagement, egotism and brutality hardened her heart. All she knew was self-defense, daily surly bickering to make sure of a minimum of security and right. To the best of her knowledge, it had always been so in the past, and it would remain so in the future: biting in order not to be bitten—the law of the jungle. She had no faith in man; she had not even faith in herself.

Her whole appearance betrayed the solitude in which the soul of her youth was living. She toiled and moiled, dressed in cheap, graceless attire. Her one means of escape from hopeless emptiness was rough and rowdy amusement. Selfish, suspicious and uncouth, with bitterness distorting her mouth, she was aware that she had no beauty and that what men wanted was her body for a few lustful moments.

There lived in the same city a young man, hale and strong. His sunny youth, spent in the midst of loving parents, brothers and sisters, shone in his gaze and sang in his voice. His step and speech were assured and firm, as is the case with those who have found peace. He was a good man.

One bright morning in spring, the miracle happened. The young man met the girl by chance. Moved in his innermost self, his heart went out to her. With the eyes of love, he saw right through and beyond her shabby vulgarity. He looked out for her, spoke to her with the simplicity of a conquered heart. But she laughed in his face at first, addressed him in crude, unmannered language. She thought he was ridiculous.

But tact, patience and respect found their way at last to a remnant of yearning which lay still unwithered in the depth of the girl's being. For the first time in her life, she was appreciated for her own sake—the greatest need of human nature. Yet the beauty he discovered in her came not from her but from his love.

Love has been a creative power since the beginning of the world. The young man's deference and appreciation stirred up in her a nascent self-reliance, a foretaste of peace and quiet, of inner self-assurance. And timidly, gropingly, the young woman awakened to first love. She shyly began taking care of her appearance, though gaudily still and without elegance. His tenderness and his example refined her taste. Beauty came to her with the first smile.

Soon they became absorbed in each other. They steadily drew together in a selfless exchange of pure mutual love. What had happened really? Or better: what had come into being? That girl had been granted a great favor, a matchless present, a gift she did not deserve: the favor of love.

After the long, barren winter of her youth, a seed had been sown in her innermost self; it was ready to spring into life.

Though still very much herself, she was already another person. She experienced a soothing security, welling up from unsuspected regions within her; she grew steadily in strength and depth, in proportion as her formerly cherished convictions were pulled up by the roots. It was like a painful dying. All the distrust, hatred and vindictiveness she had so far nursed in herself, whatever she had clung to with the despair of a drowning person, she had now to let go; she had to resign herself to the sensation of being stripped bare, bereaved of all. A harrowing agony, indeed, but one of which life is born.

Like a ship tossed on the waves and driven from her course, the girl tried another tack. She steered to the unknown: she made *the leap of faith in another.* The aggressive self-assertiveness, the armor in which she had shielded herself so far, was torn off her. She attempted *the leap of hope in another* who would in the future stand surely for her. Meanwhile, an unsuspected marvel happened: she felt enriched by her new state of bereavement, secure and anchored in her surrender. Faith and hope ripened into *real love,* the final leap, indispensable to anyone who wants both to lose himself and to find himself in another. The girl had lost everything she had, but what she lost was recovered superabundantly. She ceased putting her trust in appearances and now saw more deeply into things. She discovered the beauty of her surrounding world—the setting sun, the violet in the shade, the light in the eyes of a child, the laughter in a voice. She saw everything through the eyes of her beloved. She became another being altogether; for the first time, she was her true self. Her injured youth lived on in her, but it now began to develop along the lines of generosity and disinterested care of others—in a wealth of gratitude.[7]

Fransen finds this parable expressed in the more gripping language of covenantal fidelity in Ezekiel 16. Take a moment to read that chapter. There the prophet describes the drama between God and us. He speaks of the unyielding, undefeatable love of God for the faithless city, Jerusalem, which prefigures the whole of God's people through all times. God's mercy and fidelity (sometimes rendered "grace and truth"), about which the prophetic tradition spoke, became a reality in the New Testament in the person of Jesus the Christ (Jn 1:14).

Fransen's beautiful parable leaves us skeptical about whether there ever was anyone powerful enough to work such a miracle. Only a pure and powerful love could change such bitterness and hatred into a return of love. Not just anyone could do that. Only one who possessed God's own heart could. When that one came in the person of Jesus the Christ, the parable became real. Jesus, the incarnation of God's mercy and fidelity, demonstrated and spoke frequently of God's love for us, especially of the love which forgives and perseveres in the face of betrayal and infidelity. Jesus' parables in Luke's "Lost and Found Department" (Luke 15) emphasizes the reality that God loves us with unceasing fidelity. The parables of the lost sheep, the lost coin, and the lost (prodigal) son express well the drama of grace and challenge us to face anew the reality we often find so hard to believe: God's love for us is an undefeatable love which perseveres and is always ready to accept.

The great Protestant theologian Paul Tillich has left us with another powerful description of an experience of grace and a way of talking about grace. We find it in one of his great sermons, "You Are Accepted," a reflection on Romans 5:20. In response to his own question, "Do we know what it means to be struck by grace?" Tillich writes this:

> Grace strikes us when we are in great pain and restlessness. It strikes us when we walk through the dark valley of a meaningless and empty life. It strikes us when we feel that our separation is deeper than usual, because we have violated another life, a life which we loved, or from which we were estranged. It strikes us when our disgust for our own being, our indifference, our weakness, our hostility, and our lack of direction and composure have become intolerable to us. It strikes us when, year after year, the longed-for perfection of life does not appear, when the old compulsions reign within us as they have for decades, when despair destroys all joy and courage. Sometimes at that moment a wave of light breaks into our darkness, and it is as though a voice were saying: "You are accepted. You are accepted, accepted by that which is greater than you, and the name of which you

do not know. Do not ask for the name now; perhaps later you will do much. Do not seek for anything; do not perform anything; do not intend anything. Simply accept the fact that you are accepted!" If that happens to us, we experience grace. After such an experience we may not be better than before, and we may not believe more than before. But everything is transformed. In that moment, grace conquers sin, and reconciliation bridges the gulf of estrangement. And nothing is demanded of this experience, no religious or moral or intellectual presupposition, nothing but acceptance.[8]

These personal modes of thinking and talking about grace help us interpret the confusing array of grace jargon with which traditional Catholic theology has been filled. Simply put, grace is a theological code word for the gift-dimension of our lives and for the abiding, pervasive presence of God's love in the Holy Spirit. As far as God is concerned, grace is the loving quality of God. The indwelling of the Holy Spirit is the life of God in us. Classical theology called this "uncreated grace." The Spirit dwelling in us forms us in the image of the Son, thereby bringing us in relationship with God the Father. As far as we are concerned, then, the transformation in us which God's Spirit effects is also grace. Classical theology called this "created grace." "Sanctifying grace" is that gracious presence of God in the Spirit which is available to us in and through the mediation of the world charged with the grandeur of God, especially other persons. "Actual grace" is simply a way of specifying that abiding gracious presence in God's Spirit touching us in particular situations. For example, a meeting with a friend whose simple presence or word makes us mindful of the deeper mystery of love and calls us to respond to it is a moment of actual grace. "Sacramental grace" is still another mode of specifying God's ever present graciousness in our world—this time in the community ritual celebrations of that presence. We can speak of ourselves being in the "state of grace" when we are so immersed in God's love for us that this love becomes the central dynamic source of energy for our life of love.

The shift in our understanding of grace is clearly from quantities of grace to the quality of our awareness, acceptance, and appreciation of God's loving presence and relationship with us in the Spirit. When we begin to understand grace through a personal mode of thinking, and from within a relational context of loving, then we can see that grace works the way love works. The effects of grace are like the effects of love. (Recall Fransen's parable.) We know from experience that when we are loved, some dramatic effects come over us—there is a bounce to our step, a zest in our living, a delight in being ourselves, and a freedom to be and to do without fearing our worthwhileness or defending our value. Grace transforms us like that, too, through the power of the Holy Spirit.

The history of the theology of grace has spoken of the effects of grace in ways which reveal the marks of experiencing God's love. The effect of God's love for us has been described as elevating, i.e., a qualitative change comes over us so that we can speak of a "rebirth" or becoming a "new person in Christ"; as forgiving, i.e., the justifying action of love brings us out of our self-centeredness and into fuller communion with God and with others; as healing, i.e., the force of love cures the sickness that is selfishness and enables us to love in return; as freeing, i.e., freedom is a function of the others and includes them. Grace frees us to act without fear, for the presence of God's love in the Spirit assures us of our value before God. This gives us a sense of security and self-possession which frees us to be for others and for the world.[9]

This awareness and this freedom do not come easily. We all need the incarnate, actual experience of transforming love to move our belief in the love of God from our heads to our hearts. Only then will we know God's love in a way that will set us free. All of us have had enough experiences of rejection, and we have a sufficient grasp of ourselves to know we really need healing—healing which only the unconditional love of God can bring. We need it not just once, but again and again, for doubts do linger. But the love of God which can break through those doubts seems so far away. We can often feel very much alone. With our heads we say we believe God loves us, but in our hearts we have no real experience of that love. Is there any "in and through" experience that can open us to the truthful and freeing power of God's love? There is in the love of Jesus and in those who continue to love in the Spirit of the Father and the Son.

The experience of being ministered to by one who shows genuine personal concern, who pays attention, who accepts us beyond what we deserve, and who affirms all that is good in us is the human experience in the Spirit that makes grace actual for us and that makes God very near. With such an experience of being loved, we may believe, perhaps for the first time, that God is love and that we are lovable. When we experience ourselves as being love, we want to make our whole lives respond to it; we want to be more open to it; we want to make some return of thanks for it; we want to extend the range of its influence to the whole world. This is both the power and the summons of grace.

Anyone who loves us makes real the truth of God's love for us. Lighting up the truth of God's love is the work of the sacraments. Lighting up the truth of God's love in life's moments of forgiveness and healing is the work of the Sacrament of Reconciliation. In the next chapter we will explore some of the dimensions of sacramental theology and principles of sacramental celebration which will help us appreciate the power and summons of grace in the new Rite of Penance.

FOURTH MOVEMENT: APPROPRIATING THE CHRISTIAN STORY

How does the above presentation of the mystery of God and grace shed light on your present understanding of these mysteries? In what ways has this chapter affirmed you? In what ways have you been challenged? Share your responses to the "images of God" exercise in this chapter. Complete the following sentences:

I realized that I . . .
I relearned that I . . .
I was surprised that I . . .
I wonder if . . .
I wonder why . . .
I wonder when . . .

FIFTH MOVEMENT: CHOOSING A FAITH RESPONSE

What does being graced by God mean for you in action terms? What does it mean for you at the level of feelings and attitudes? Complete the following sentences:

Next time, I want to . . .
I need to think more about . . .
I hope that I . . .

Suggestions for Further Reading

Peter Fransen	*The New Life of Grace*
Roger Haight	*The Experience and Language of Grace*
J. Norman King	*Experiencing God All Ways and Every Day*
Dermot Lane	*The Experience of God*
John Shea	*Stories of God*

3

Celebrating Sacraments

FIRST MOVEMENT: PRESENT ACTION

What place do the sacraments have in your spiritual life? Which sacraments are most important to you? Why? What do sacraments do for you? Tell about your most memorable experience with sacraments.

SECOND MOVEMENT: CRITICAL REFLECTION

Where did you get your understanding of sacraments? How have your experiences of sacramental celebrations affected your understanding of the sacraments? How has your understanding of the sacraments affected your participation in sacramental celebrations? Why do you celebrate sacraments at all?

THIRD MOVEMENT: THE CHRISTIAN STORY AND VISION

In the last chapter, we could not talk clearly about our experience of God and grace without introducing the principle of sacramentality. Sacramentality is the heartland of the "in and through" approach to God. Now that we have explored dimensions of experiencing God, we can look more closely at what it means to say that to the extent that we lack a vivid sense of God's loving presence, to that extent our sacramental celebrations become empty, flat, boring, and meaningless. Sacraments celebrate our experiences of God in Christ already begun.

Since the time of the Second Vatican Council, and following upon its mandate regarding the sacraments, we have been given new forms for celebrating the seven ritual sacraments. We have revised the rites; now we are in the process of revising ourselves. While it seems fair to say that just about everyone has accepted and implemented the new forms for the Eucharist, we cannot say the same thing about the new Rite of Penance. If this new Rite is ever to be accepted and celebrated effectively, it must be accompanied by the attitudes and thinking of the "new" sacramental theology and those principles of celebration which flow from this theology to support and give life to the new Rite. Too many places still operate on a sacramental theology and on principles of celebration that are inadequate to give life to this revised Rite of Penance. Turning to biblical imagery, we might describe our present situation as trying to pour new wine into old skins. As the Bible testifies, this never works! Since the new sacramental theology is what makes the revised rites have any sense at all, we need to see that these new skins of the revised rites receive the new wine of our sacramental theology. This chapter will first sketch the basic sacramental theology underlying the revised rites, especially the Rite of Penance, and then the fundamental principles of celebration which flow from this theology.

THE NEW SACRAMENTAL THEOLOGY

The Sacramental Principle

First of all, the "new" sacramental theology is not really all that new. It derives greatly from the early Church Fathers. Its "newness" follows upon one of the most significant achievements of contemporary theology: the recovery of what is called

the incarnational principle. Whether we say incarnational principle or sacramental principle, we are saying the same thing. We
are saying that God's way to us and our way to God is in and
through the human, the fleshy, the historical, the particular.
There is no other way for us who are body-persons to experience the invisible except through that which we can touch, or to
hear the inaudible except through that which strikes the ears.

A human story which illustrates this so well is the story of
Helen Keller. Notice the "sacramental" dimensions to this story.
Helen's world was a world of particulars, sensations of odor,
taste, and touch. There was no light or sound. At first the movements of her teacher's hand in her own did not disclose anything
beyond tactile pressure. Then one day a whole new world
opened up for Helen. She learned that a touch can point beyond
itself to something more. That day Helen realized a deeper dimension of reality that was there all the time, but she had never
"seen" it. Here is Helen's account of that eventful day:

> We walked down the path to the well-house, attracted by
> the fragrance of the honeysuckle with which it was covered.
> Someone was drawing water and my teacher placed my hand
> under the spout. As the cool stream gushed over one hand
> she spelled into the other the word *water,* first slowly, then
> rapidly. I stood still, my whole attention fixed upon the mo-
> tions of her fingers. Suddenly I felt a misty consciousness as
> of something forgotten—a thrill of returning thought; and
> somehow the mystery of language was revealed to me. I
> knew then that "w-a-t-e-r" meant the wonderful cool some-
> thing that was flowing over my hand. That living word
> awakened my soul, gave it light, hope, joy, set it free! . . . As
> we returned to the house every object which I touched
> seemed to quiver with life. That was because I saw every-
> thing with the strange, new sight that had come to me.[1]

Helen's experience is a living example of the sacramental
principle—the human, the fleshy, the concrete can point to an
invisible reality. Sacramental faith is like the way Helen "saw"
water. This faith opens our eyes so that we no longer stop at the
appearance of things, but see through them to the deeper reality
in which we live. For persons of faith, the world of experience

72

speaks of God's presence. In and through our human experiences we encounter God and enter into a personal relation with God.

If we really grasped the sacramental principle and the sacramentality of all created reality and every human encounter, we would know that nature is never separated from grace. All that we experience is charged with the grandeur of God's presence and manifests God's saving love. But this presence and saving love must be reawakened and reappropriated in all of us by special moments of manifestation. Christ is the most unique moment; the words of Scripture, the Church, the ritual sacraments are others. Here we will focus on the ritual sacraments as those significant moments of the manifestation of God's love for us.

Sacraments as Personal Encounter

In our treatment of both God and grace above, we saw that contemporary theology has made significant shifts in the model of thinking about each. The same is true with sacraments, too. In 1963 Edward Schillebeeckx's book, *Christ the Sacrament of the Encounter with God,*[2] introduced a new way of thinking about the sacraments. An earlier way of thinking regarded the sacraments as mechanical operations. The mechanical mode of thinking asked the questions one would ask of objects: who made it, what is it made of, what is it made for, who may use it, how does it work? Schillebeeckx spoke instead of sacraments as an encounter with God.

This mode of thinking shifts from the mechanical to the personal metaphors of encounter, interpersonal relationships, and personal communication. The person of Christ is at the center manifesting a personal God in and through the community of believers interacting with one another. The central question of this way of thinking asks what we must do in order to guarantee effective encounter. What is the energy that gives life to encounter and communication? The answer is simple: personal presence. Personal presence means "paying attention to." (We have already met this as a dimension of hospitality. We will meet it again in the second half of this chapter under principles of celebration.) In personal encounters and in personal communication, we pay attention to what we are doing; we pay attention to what is going on inside and outside; we feel beyond the surface into the depth of what is going on.

The Basic Sacraments: Christ and the Church

Along with this shift in our way of thinking about sacraments, contemporary theology has expanded our understanding of sacrament beyond the seven ritual sacraments to embrace the more basic realities of Christ and the Church as sacrament. From these two, the seven ritual sacraments derive their sacramentality, that is, their power to signify, and to effect encounter.

What does it mean to say Christ is a sacrament? Jesus the Christ is a sacrament because he is the incarnation of God, that is, the visible expression of the invisible God. This is the burden of Paul's remarks: "He is the image of the invisible God, the first-born of all creation" (Col 1:15). And "In him all the fullness of God was pleased to dwell" (Col 1:19). Jesus, in short, is God-with-a-face (Jn 1:14). So when we say Christ is the sacrament of God, we say Jesus is God's way to us. Jesus the Christ is the primordial sacrament because in him we find the fullest expression of what a sacrament is: the visible, audible, tangible expression of God's saving love for us and the human response to this love.

After Jesus comes the Church. After Jesus died and rose from the dead, he disappeared from our sight so that we could no longer see him, hear him, or touch him. So, what does he do to keep in touch with us and to help us keep in touch with him? He takes us on as his body. Jesus the Christ is embodied in the community of his disciples through the Spirit. This is the force of Paul's statement: "For just as the body is one and has many members, and all the members of the body, though many, are one body, so it is with Christ. For by one Spirit we were all baptized into one body" (1 Cor 12:12–13). We, the Church, are the body of Christ (Col 1:18). We are his body, his face, his voice. So when we say the Church is the sacrament of Christ, we say: I am God's way to you; you are God's way to me. Think about that. What an awesome responsibility that is!

The Second Vatican Council officially endorsed this understanding of the Church. It did so by moving away from a too heavy stress on the juridical understanding of the Church which tended to create a we/they split between those who are Church and those who belong to the Church, between those who give and those who receive, and between those who sanctify and those who are sanctified. Doing away with the split has significant implications for understanding the dynamics of ritual sacramental action where all give and all receive. No one is a passive spectator. When the Council pulled away from an overstress on organization and authority as its first word about Church, it retrieved the biblical notions of the Church as people. Some of the Council's favorite images of the Church are people images, like People of God and Body of Christ. When Vatican II calls the Church a sacrament, then, it means that all those who are baptized in Christ and are alive in his Spirit make visible that which would otherwise be invisible, the risen Christ.

In this light, then, we may enhance our approach to the sacraments by retrieving St. Paul's image of the Church as the Body of Christ. This image discloses that we share a common existence as Church. The life of each Christian makes sense only in relation to the whole body of which Christ is the head. We experience the love of God (grace) in and through the life of the graced body which is the Church. As something happens to the celebrating community in the sacraments, it happens to each member. For this reason, celebrating sacraments brings us closer to one another in the Church.

Contemporary approaches to the sacraments tell us that sacraments happen first to the whole community. The community is the starting point for understanding what happens to the individual. When we lose a sense of being community, when we lose a sense of the Church as sacrament, then we too easily privatize the celebration of the sacraments. We make the individual the starting point and end point for understanding the effectiveness of the sacraments. Perhaps in our own day we can retrieve the significance of community for sacraments through an effective implementation of the Rite of Christian Initiation of Adults. The vision of the RCIA is that all members of the Church are gifted by the presence of God and are empowered to share their gifts and experiences of God.[3] Through the rites of initiation, we may come to appreciate the fundamental truth about the communal dimension of all the sacraments.

This understanding of the Church as sacrament undergirds

the great emphasis given today on the need for communal celebrations of the sacraments. This is especially apropos to the Sacrament of Reconciliation. As the early history of this Sacrament
shows, reconciliation is the responsibility of the whole community. When speaking of offices and ministries in Reconciliation,
the Introduction of the new Rite of Penance speaks first of the
ministry of the whole community:

> The whole Church, as a priestly people, acts in different
> ways in the work of reconciliation which has been entrusted
> to it by the Lord. Not only does the church call sinners to re-
> pentance by preaching the word of God, but it also inter-
> cedes for them and helps penitents with maternal care and
> solicitude to acknowledge and admit their sins and so obtain
> the mercy of God who alone can forgive sins (Par. 8).

The sense of communal responsibility in reconciliation has been
lost in our day because too many people live without a sense of
being part of a community. The involvement of others in sin and
reconciliation is alien to many people's experience. The real absence of community makes it difficult to effect the real presence
of reconciliation as a communal responsibility. The experience
of the Church as a healing community of life and love lies at the
heart of helping people appreciate the full meaning of reconciliation in life or in sacrament.

The meaning of the Church as sacrament has had a wide
ranging effect not only on the meaning and celebration of Reconciliation, but on all the ritual sacraments. These give expression to the twofold dimension of the Church as sacrament. One
dimension pertains to modeling, the other to serving. As model,
the Christian people are to manifest what all people, transformed by God's saving love, are called to be in the Kingdom of
God. As servant, the Christian community's attitude and action
toward all peoples is to make visible and tangible God's attitude
of accepting, saving love toward sinful human persons. Through
Christians, collectively and individually, everyone ought to experience God's gracious acceptance reaching out to him or her.
This is what it means for the Church to be sacrament. The seven
ritual sacraments make explicit this basic sacramentality of the
Church in different ways.

Toward a Definition of Sacraments

Now that we have looked at these two fundamental truths of sacramental theology—Christ as the Sacrament of God, and the Church as the Sacrament of Christ—we can proceed with an understanding of the ritual sacraments. Within the context of these fundamental truths, our common definition of sacraments proves to be inadequate: an outward sign instituted by Christ to give grace. This definition too easily makes the sacraments mechanical instruments of grace (seen as a material, packaged thing), rather than personal encounters with Christ in the Church. Contemporary theology has not settled on a single uniform definition of the sacraments, but a description which seems faithful to the general thrust of contemporary sacramental theology might run something like this:

> Sacraments are symbolic actions manifesting the offer of God's saving love for us in Christ and through the Spirit in the Church. In the sacraments, we respond to God's self-giving and draw closer not only to God but also to one another in the Church.

We need to explore the dimensions of this description in order to understand the sacraments in light of contemporary theology.

Sacraments: God's Self-Giving

The first part of this description tells us that Christ is the fundamental sacrament and all ritual sacramental action flows from Christ as their source. Jesus the Christ is God's greatest gift to us. As Schillebeeckx would have it, he is "the" sacrament of encounter with God. This makes the action of Christ through the Spirit in the Church foundational to all ritual sacraments.

Moreover, to say "sacraments are symbolic actions" means that, before we have ritual sacramental action, we must have something to ritualize or celebrate. Sacraments do not create for us something out of nothing. This comes from the fact that sacraments, like all prayer, are first and foremost a response to the action of God in Christ and through the Spirit within us, around us, and for us. God initiates. We respond. The experience of God evokes worship; worship does not evoke God.

This puts us squarely into contact with the general thesis of the previous chapter: whether we experience God and how we experience God have a great deal to do with the tone and quality of our sacramental celebrations. This says clearly that sacraments are a function of religious experience. That they are so is deeply rooted in our liturgical tradition which understands all liturgical action to be expressive of the community's faith experience. The Second Vatican Council's *Constitution on the Liturgy* says it more formally: "The sacraments not only presuppose faith, but by words and objects they also nourish, strengthen, and express it; that is why they are called 'sacraments of faith'" (*S.C.* #59). For this reason, sacraments are for believers. The sacramental ritual celebrates our experience of God in Christ and through the Spirit in the Church.

Because an experience of God is already in progress we do not go to the sacraments to get something we do not already have to some degree. What, then, do the sacraments do? The sacraments enlarge the richness and the reality of an experience of God already going on, and bring that experience to a new level of expression and awareness in our lives. This is what "sacramental causality" is all about. This is possible because of what we have seen in our prior discussion of grace. There we saw that God's saving love in Christ and through the Spirit is already present in all moments of our lives.

For example, the healing and reconciliation that take place over the kitchen table when neighbors gather to encourage and support one another, or in support groups when friends gather to review life and challenge and support one another in faith, are instances of the loving and welcoming God present through the Spirit in the Church. Christians paying attention to one another in love are mediating God's loving presence. So, what more does the Sacrament of Reconciliation do, then? It brings to solemn expression in a community act of worship the experience of healing and reconciliation already going on in the Church. In the sacramental action, Jesus the Christ, in the power of the Spirit and through the human signs of the sacrament (especially the sign of a sinful people gathered together), reveals his healing presence. Through the sacramental action, we enter into the center of God's healing and forgiving love, we are helped by others

78

to discern and awaken to God's forgiving love in the ordinary moments of our lives, and we are enabled to respond to this love with a renewed energy of thankfulness and praise by making clear signs of our own conversion and commitment to reconciliation.

Therefore, we ought not to look to the sacraments to insert God's loving presence into the ordinary course of our lives, but to bring us from being less aware of this presence to being more keenly aware of it in our lives. The sacraments proclaim and enable us to appropriate the love of God already present and offered to us. In our celebrations of the sacraments, we need to focus on taking this love home again in order to live with a fresh awareness of being loved and being able to love. In this way, we might say the sacraments become "light up" times for us. In the vast ensemble of manifestations of God's love for us, the sacramental moments "light up" or unveil, deepen, and enlarge our ongoing experience of God in Christ and through the Spirit to bring us closer together as the Church.

Without this prior experience of God in Christ and through the spirit to "light up," sacramental ritual would be mere pretense, empty, flat. This principle applies across the board of sacramental action. With Reconciliation, for example, it goes like this. Rather than saying, "We go to confession to get forgiveness," we ought to say, "We experience the forgiving acceptance of God's saving love in Christ and through the Spirit in and through the community. We go to confession to deepen our awareness of being forgiven, and to draw closer to God and to one another." If the sacramental moment of Reconciliation has not been preceded by an experience of God's loving acceptance in and through the community and by our conversion from the depths of our hearts to that love, then sacramental absolution is putting the cart before the horse. Our conversion and reconciliation are enlarged and deepend by the sacramental celebration of Reconciliation. The ritual action of this sacrament lights up both the presence of God forever reaching out to us in love, and the deeper meaning of all those times when we reach out to others in sorrow and forgiveness as being moments of encounter with God's saving love in Christ.

Now apply this principle of the sacraments as "light up"

times to the other sacraments. What religious experience of God in Christ and through the community lies behind each sacrament? What prior religious experience of God's love ought to be present before we can truly speak of a sacramental baptism, confirmation, Eucharist, marriage, ordination, or anointing?

Another implication of our description of the sacraments has to do with the significance of the "for us" aspect of sacramental action. This is the communal dimension of sacraments. We have already hinted at its significance above. We have seen that out of our understanding of Church as sacrament comes the emphasis of sacraments as community affairs. Sacraments happen first to the community, and then in and through the community to the individual. The community is the starting point for what happens to the individual. Christian existence is always co-existence. God's love for us is made visible and tangible in and through the community.

Contemporary sacramental theology tells us that effective sacramental action presumes a community wherein the symbols of our ritual actions have already been enfleshed. There's the rub! Some Catholic charismatic communities, along with some programs for the catechumenate (RCIA), are perhaps our best contemporary examples of respecting this dimension of sacraments. The community which the sacraments presume is not just a collection of individuals assembled for a short time, nor is it just a physical unity; rather, it is a unity of ideals and values, a common pattern of feelings about all sorts of things, a sense of belonging, of caring and being cared for. The lack of a vital sense and experience of community may be the greatest demon of our sacramental catechesis and celebrations.

Our age of pluralism has fragmented our sense of community and our value of community. Pluralism is a complex product of aggressive individualism and adoration of the ego, political and cultural freedom, increasing mobility of peoples, and an increasing sense of the inadequacy of any one position trying to comprehend all points of view, or any one way of doing things as being the only way. We are so influenced by this pluralism that when we begin our sacramental catechesis with the assumption that we value community, and that community is a desirable goal to achieve and live by, we are met with confusion and sometimes hostility. This was certainly my experience one evening in an adult education program on Reconciliation. When I began to talk about the communal dimension of this sacrament, I was interrupted by a frustrated woman. "Father," she shouted from the back row, "you are talking about community being necessary for good sacramental celebrations as though we know what you mean. How long have you been around here? There ain't no community here! We come here because it is geographically convenient. Nothing more than that holds us together." (Unfortunately, the pastor was not attending the sessions to hear this challenging statement and strong indictment of her parish experience.) What this woman seemed to reflect to me was what Walter Burghardt once portrayed in a caricature of a parish gathering to pray:

> A number of individuals (ten or a thousand) unknown to one another, uncaring of one another, come in and out of the cold and, in quavering song and stilted prose, petition an absent God to become really present so that they may receive Him bodily and return each to his or her isolated home convinced that they have been nourished spiritually.[4]

Sound familiar?

The revised Rite of Penance calls the whole community into the ministry of reconciliation. That is what is so exciting about this new Rite. This is also what causes so much depression. Where are these communities which the Rite presupposes? As yet, the new Rite is thoroughly incongruous with the lives of too many people. The real absence of community does not effect the real presence of reconciliation. Either the new Rite will remain wholly irrelevant, or the Church will have to change itself in some radical ways. Until we have some vital experiences of community in our day, sacramental catechesis will continue to meet bewilderment, and maybe even the hostility born out of frustration. As long as we continue to be inattentive to the communal dimensions of our lives, we will continue to encourage an understanding of sacraments as a private "me and God" affair. Such privatism will destroy communal worship and any sense that the sacraments send us back into the community to expand the love we have received.

Sacraments: Our Response to God's Self-Giving

This brings us to the second half of the description of the sacraments: our response to God's offer of love by which we draw closer to God and to one another in the Church. This describes the effect of the sacrament, or "the increase of grace," if you will. The effect of the sacraments, simply put, is to light up the presence of God's love forever reaching out to us in the ordinary routine of our lives. Sacraments also bring us to live in greater unity with God and with one another.

As we saw in the last chapter, grace is a relational reality. The sacraments effect a deeper relationship with God in Christ and through the Spirit, and with others in the Church. The dynamics of sacramental action call us to live more completely and richly than we might otherwise. This is due to the fact that sacraments bring us to a new level of reality by expanding and deepening our experience and awareness of God and of one another. The grace of the sacraments is tied up with growth in awareness and in our capacity to respond.

From this perspective on the effects of the sacraments, we touch upon the real reason for sacramental celebrations. Sacraments are our need, not God's. The whole point of celebrating sacramentally is to provide human situations in which we can respond in a tangible and visible way to our experiences of God in Christ and the Spirit, and to our belonging to one another in community as the Body of Christ. The sacraments provide a concrete way to express our communal faith and experience our Christian co-existence. We are Christians because through the Christian community we have met Jesus, heard his word of invitation, and responded to him in faith. We gather in sacramental celebrations in order to speak this faith over again in community, and, by speaking it, to renew and deepen it.

The Bishops' Committee on the Liturgy has expressed the need to celebrate sacraments well when it says,

> People in love make signs of love, not only to express their love but also to deepen it. Love never expressed dies. Christians' love for Christ and for each other, Christians' faith in Christ and in each other, must be expressed in the signs and symbols of celebration or it will die.[5]

This statement expresses clearly the precise role of sacramental celebrations in our lives. They give bodily expression to our love for each other and for Christ. They also express our faith in each other and in Christ so that we will be able to experience more deeply, nourish more fully, and cherish more dearly this love and this faith.

The next time we hear the questions "How often should I go to confession?" and "Why should I go to confession?" we might remember this statement of the Bishops' Committee. How often do we need to express our love? How often do we need to hear and feel that we are loved by God and by others in a visible and tangible way? This is "how often" and this is "why" we need to celebrate Reconciliation.

A further dimension of the sacraments as a "response to God's love" is that our participation in the sacraments has the power to stretch our behavior, our values, and our working images of life, of God, of ourselves, of people. Through our participation in sacramental action we live our selves into a new way of thinking about all these, and we live our selves into a richer way of experiencing them. Celebrating sacramental moments has the power to transform our images, affections, and behavior so that our experiences of being loved open out into ways of loving that will extend the range of love's influence in the world. This brings us to the heart of a sacramental spirituality. Sacraments, in their fullest sense, do not stop with the ritual action, but extend into the world to reshape our religious experiences and our world.[6] The experience of being forgiven and accepted, for example, summons us to be forgiving and accepting in turn.

The energy for responding to God's love of us can be intensified or reduced by the ways we celebrate the sacraments. For this reason, we need to look at some of the implications of this new theology of the sacraments for celebrating sacramental moments.

PRINCIPLES OF CELEBRATION

This sacramental theology implies some important principles for governing our sacramental celebrations. Fr. Eugene

Walsh, a leading American pastoral liturgist, has summarized these principles succinctly in his booklet, *Theology of Celebration.*[7] There he identifies three principles which flow from the new sacramental theology. The first is that *sacraments should not be treated as things but as actions.* This means we ought not to regard sacraments as existing in themselves as if we could "give" them to one another. Sacraments are actions done by persons. They are the actions of Christ and the Church (the entire assembly celebrates them) at one and the same time. In the sacramental action, we cannot do Jesus' part. Only Jesus can do his part of entering our lives to help us see and feel how much God loves us. Our part is to make clear the signs in and through which Jesus enters our lives.

The second principle is that *in the sacramental celebration all give and all receive.* We saw this principle grounded in an understanding of the Church as sacrament. In the sacramental celebration, we have no split between the active agents who do the sanctifying (bishops, priests, deacons), and the passive receivers (everyone else) who are sanctified. Everyone is important. Everyone has a vital function to fulfill. This is not to say that everyone can do anything, or that anyone can do everything. The different levels of ministry and responsibility still prevail. In the Sacrament of Reconciliation, the priest has his role, and the penitent has his or hers (Pars. 9–11). How well each does his or her part makes a difference in the effectiveness of the celebration. We will look more closely at the responsibilities of each in the Sacrament of Reconciliation in the last chapter.

The third principle is that *sacraments are forms of personal communication which occur by means of human signs.* The signs must be clear, simple, and humanly attractive if the full import of the celebration is to shine forth. In order for this to happen, all who celebrate must pay attention to what they are doing. An older theology led to a minimalist way of thinking about signs and sacraments. It tended to think that as long as the intention was there, the right words were said, and the gestures were made according to form, then the sacraments could not fail. In the end, it did not really make much difference how well or poorly we did them. However, this kind of minimalist thinking led to the mechanical and careless performance of our sacramental rituals that has in fact turned so many people off and away from any further engagement in the sacraments.

In the sacraments we reach each other through the signs we make: creating space, speaking, listening, reading, singing, gesturing, etc. Through these signs Christ is trying to reach us and we are trying to reach Christ. Poor signs can interfere with his work. Good signs enhance it. Or, we might say, good signs increase and nourish our faith; poor signs weaken and destroy our faith. The effectiveness of the sacramental celebration depends in large measure on how well we make the signs. This is so because our sacramental moments are subject to the laws of communication. If we heed these laws, we make good sacramental celebrations and will foster and nourish faith. If we violate these laws, we make poor celebrations and will weaken and destroy faith.

Fr. Walsh uses an example and a story to capture in a creative and effective way two laws of communication that bear on sacramental celebrations. These illustrations are so good that they deserve repeating in full.

Fr. Walsh calls the first law "the law of parties." It looks like this:

> If you go to a party and you have good drinks, good food, excellent and stimulating conversation, you have a good and enjoyable time. The time passes swiftly; you come away with the feeling that you would really enjoy going back again. When you get an invitation again, you jump at the opportunity. Then, there's the other kind of party: dull and boring people primarily, plus tasteless refreshments and food, or none at all. You feel trapped. You want to leave as soon as possible, and you get away as soon as you can. When you get another invitation to this kind of party, you shamelessly and brazenly tell any lie necessary. I really can't come because my mother-in-law . . . my farm . . . my child is sick . . . I promised my boss . . .[8]

The point is clear. Good signs are life-giving. They open us to one another. Bad signs are death-dealing. They close us off from one another. To use the idiom of a former decade, "If you turn 'em on to one another, you turn 'em on for God. If you turn 'em off from one another, you turn 'em off from God." The theological truth is hard to miss. If we are brought to life by the signs we make and the way we make them, Jesus the Christ has a chance to get in and do his transforming action. If we are bored to death, then Jesus the Christ does not have a chance to get in and do anything.

The second law Fr. Walsh calls the "law of Frankenstein." He describes it with this story:

> In the story we encounter two Arabs, religious and pious Moslems. One owns a camel, and the other wants to buy it. They bargain for quite a while and at last come to terms. The seller of the camel tells the new owner that there are certain signals to which this camel responds. He responds to no others. If you say, Wow," the camel gets up and trots in whatever is first gear for a camel. If you say, "Wow, Wow," the camel goes into full gallop. If you want to stop the camel, you must say "Amin." The seller demonstrates. The new owner is satisfied and pays. He mounts the camel and says "Wow." The camel rides and trots toward the desert.
>
> In the open desert, the rider ways "Wow, Wow," and they gallop away in the distance. After some hours of travel, the rider suddenly sees they are approaching the edge of a great canyon. An instant drop of thousands of feet through the chasm to the rocks below. There is no way around. He realizes that the joy of riding the new camel distracted him from the main route. He must stop. In a panic, though, he realizes that he has forgotten the signal for stopping the camel. The animal speeds closer to the edge. The good Moslem's instinct is to immediately pray to Allah. His prayers become louder and louder as his camel races closer and closer to the edge. He concludes his prayer by shouting the traditional "Amin!" The camel comes to a struggling halt just at the very edge of the drop. . . . In profound relief, the rider draws himself forward and peers into the depths of the great canyon. With widened eyes, he cries out "WOW". . . . .[9]

Again the point is hard to miss. Signs do their work whether we want them to or not. Once we release a sign—speech, reading, gesture, vesture, etc.—we cannot call it back or redirect it with new intentions. We will have, in effect, created a "monster" which is out of our control. Fr. Walsh summarizes these two laws succinctly:

> Making signs of human communication is our own very proper business. We know the laws, and we know how to make the laws work. Good human signs make good human experiences. Good human experiences attract us and make us open to persons and to fertile personal relationships. Poor human signs make bad human experiences. Bad human experiences repel us and make us closed to one another and to personal relationships. Open persons live and grow. Closed persons shrivel and die. The law is inexorable. It works whether or not we are aware of it, and whether or not we like it.[10]

In our sacramental celebrations we need to pay attention to these laws of human communication. Religious experiences and sacramental celebrations are subject to them as much as any other human experience is. We must pay attention to them for the stakes are high. As the Bishops' Committee on the Liturgy declared, "Good celebrations foster and nourish faith. Poor celebrations weaken and destroy faith."[11] We must work to make effective celebrations. We will see the practical consequences of these principles when we comment on ways of preparing for and celebrating the Rite of Penance in the last chapter.

FOURTH MOVEMENT: APPROPRIATING THE CHRISTIAN STORY

How does the above presentation of the "new" sacramental theology affect your understanding of sacraments? In what ways has this chapter affirmed you? In what ways have you been challenged? Complete the following sentences:

> I realized that I . . .
> I relearned that I . . .
> I was surprised that I . . .
> I wonder if . . .
> I wonder why . . .
> I wonder when . . .

FIFTH MOVEMENT: CHOOSING A FAITH RESPONSE

What place might the sacraments have in your spiritual life now? How have your attitudes toward sacraments been affected by the "new" sacramental theology? Complete the following sentences:

Next time, I want to . . .
I need to think more about . . .
I hope that I . . .

Suggestions for Further Reading

William J. Bausch	*A New Look at the Sacraments*
Regis Duffy	*Real Presence*
Tad Guzie	*The Book of Sacramental Basics*
Joseph Martos	*The Catholic Sacraments*
James F. White	*Sacraments as God's Self-Giving*
Eugene Walsh	*Theology of Celebration*

4

Sins to Confess

FIRST MOVEMENT: PRESENT ACTION

What are the most significant relationships in your life? How do you live responsibly within those relationships? How would you recognize responsible behavior? Selfish behavior? What is "sin" for you? What kind of confession are you accustomed to making?

SECOND MOVEMENT: CRITICAL REFLECTION

What has contributed to your present understanding of sin? How does your understanding of sin shape your approach to confession? How would you answer the question, "Whatever happened to sin?" What do you think is the root cause of sin in our lives? What do you need in order to break from the power of sin?

THIRD MOVEMENT: THE CHRISTIAN STORY AND VISION

"What's there to confess? We are all human. Everyone has faults. What's a sin, anyway?" This does not represent a facetious attitude. Many adults express it who are sincerely interested in making the Sacrament of Reconciliation more than a routine recitation of faults, but a healing encounter with the undefeatable love of our forgiving God, which the Church professes Reconciliation ought to be. Identifying sin is a necessary step before we can properly enter into this sacrament. Where there is no sense of sinfulness and the need for reconciliation, how can there be authenticity in the sacrament? Many adults simply do not know what to confess because they do not have a sense of sin. We will never get anywhere in our efforts to renew the Rite of Penance unless we can be much clearer in our understanding of sin.

The understanding of sin for many of us came from the need to have something to say that would be appropriate as a "confession" so that we would be given absolution and be permitted to receive Communion at Mass. Since we had to have our confession ready when the institutional programs said we should be ready, our understanding of sin had more to do with satisfying the regulations of authority in our institutions than it did with our sense of personal responsibility and our need for reconciliation. No wonder, then, that adult confessions sounded so much like childrens' confessions. When the adults no longer felt bound by programs and institutional expectations of authority, they no longer had anything to confess. Many commentators on the Sacrament of Reconciliation claim that the loss of a sense of sin has contributed to the increasing decline in the use of this sacrament.

At this moment in the Church we are very much in need of some good adult conversations about sin. What might adults talk about in such a conversation? An adult notion of sin is a tough one to work out. It is even tougher to appropriate. "Sin" is such a battered word, wounded and brutalized by so many misunderstandings. One tragedy today is that too many priests and too many people are still willing to settle for childish ideas about sin. For too many, sin readily suggests moral taboos which fix our attention solely on what was done without giving due regard to the roots of action, to the why behind the what. Moreover, seldom does sin denote sexism, racism, elitism, or other violations of justice. No surprise, then, that many adults make

90

the same kind of confession now as they did as children. Apart from adding sex and alcohol to the list of taboos, nothing seems to have changed in their approach to sin and confession. Yet much has changed in the Church.

A dramatic sign of change in the Church's thinking about sin is reflected in the move from the dark confessional box to the well-lighted, welcoming, gracious reconciliation room. Many adults want to know the understanding of sin that is an essential part of this external change. They already sense that something different ought to go on in their confession when they move from the dark box to the inviting room, but they are not quite sure what. One thing is certain, however, and that is that more and more people are growing ever more resentful of Church people who want to keep them in the dark and treat them as children forever. These adults are letting it be known, loudly and clearly, that they are not children and will not tolerate being treated as children any longer. Along with the new light in the reconciliation room, they want some new light and plain speaking on sin. This does not mean they necessarily want all the compexities of human living wrapped neatly in one little package. Yet they do want some understanding. They want some tools for thinking. They are capable of making their own decisions, and they are determined to do so. The one thing that distinguishes adults from children is this capacity to make free, responsible decisions and live with the consequences. Many adults are ready to do that, and so are looking for some clear notions of how to think about sin which represents their freedom and responsibility.

What do we need to know about sin so that we can begin to act like grown-up people and stand accountable for the sort of persons we have become and for the sort of decisions and actions we have made before God and other people? Is there a way to think about sin without retrieving childhood guilts or inflicting paralyzing humiliations on adults? Answering these questions is the task of this chapter. Fulfilling this task does not mean we need to come up with a new catalogue of sins for adults only. The task, rather, is to provide a way of understanding the reality of personal sin which will enable adults to enter the new Rite of Penance in a way that will enhance their experience of the healing and conversion which they seek in and through this sacrament.

WHERE WE HAVE BEEN

Our "confession" already reflects our living understanding of sin, morality, and the moral life. Before we take a detailed look at where we are going in our understanding of sin, we ought to take a synoptic look at where we have been. Analyzing a typical confession of an adult will help us do that. This sample confession and its analysis may be a bit of a caricature. But, as caricatures will, it sums up, magnifies, and focuses the main features of the understanding of sin, morality, and the moral life reflected in the lives of many adult Catholics today. Does a confession like the following sound familiar?

Bless me Father, for I have sinned. It has been four weeks since my last confession. I said my penance and went to Holy Communion. The following are my sins.

I was angry three times; I gossiped twice; I lied four times; I lost my patience three times; I missed Mass once due to my own fault, and once because I was sick; and I entertained impure thoughts and desires three times.

I am sorry for these and all the sins of my past life. I ask pardon of God, penance and absolution from you, Father, please.

What understanding of sin, morality, and the moral life lies behind a confession like this?

Such a confession reflects an approach to the moral life that focuses largely on bits of behavior taken in isolation from the larger context or overall pattern of one's life. This approach too easily breaks up the moral life into neat compartments. Each compartment is well-defined by laws. Morality, in fact, is largely a matter of law, and the moral life a matter of obedience. Laws define moral obligation. What is morally right and wrong is defined by what is allowed and what is forbidden. The challenge to the moral life is to discover the appropriate law for each situation and assess how far it binds in the circumstances. The primary questions we need to ask in making such an assessment are "What am I doing? Is it allowed? How far can I go?"

According to this view, sin is primarily a transgression of law. Where there is no clear-cut law, there is no question of sin. If we want to know whether a certain kind of action is sinful or not, we only need to know whether it is commanded or forbidden by law. Once we know the laws, then we can judge the sinfulness of our actions on the basis of whether they fall within the limits of these prescribed laws. Using this understanding of sin, we would normally examine ourselves against well-established laws that define our moral obligations. Among the laws regulating our moral life, a few are singled out and given a somewhat disproportionate consideration. This is what seems to have happened, for example, to the precepts of the Church pertaining to the obligation to attend Mass and to observe the appointed times of fast and abstinence. From the Ten Commandments, special attention seemed to fall on the fourth with its concern for obedience and respect, the sixth with its focus on sexuality, and the eighth with its prohibition of lying, backbiting, slander, gossip, and the like. The actions that we do which are outside the limits of law can easily be counted up over a short period of time. This gives us a quantitative picture of our moral life and leads to the laundry-list type of recitation of sins as the matter for confession.

A confession like this seems to reduce the complexities of morality to the simplicities of a list of isolated, individual acts of commission or omission. This type of confession also reflects a highly individualized notion of sin. Sinful actions are not only isolated from the overall pattern of our lives, but also from the multiple relationships that make up our lives. Also, in the past, preoccupation with law and measurement, coupled with a highly individualized notion of sin, left many of us with a weakened (or absent) sense of moral responsibility for the quality of life and love in our communities. Without a sense of responsibility for the quality of life and love in our relationships, we approached the sacrament by making too much of the past and too little of the future. We used the Sacrament of Reconciliation primarily as a private guilt-shedding process, and gave little attention to the moral life as a process of ongoing conversion, or to the Church as a community of reconciliation.

This, in brief, is where we have been: act-centered, law-oriented, individualistic. Where are we going? The remainder of this chapter explores significant dimensions that ought to be part of an adult conversation on sin. Retrieving a sense of sin begins with recovering a sense of responsibility. Within this context, we can approach a contemporary understanding of the kinds of sin to confess. This will be an analysis of actual sin: mortal and venial. The chapter closes with an example of a confession that would reflect this contemporary approach to sin, and then provides a brief analysis of that confession in order to clarify its main features.

A SENSE OF SIN: A SENSE OF RESPONSIBILITY

What do adults need to grasp in order to retrieve a sense of sin in a grown-up manner? I would say a "sense of responsibility." "Being responsible," "responsible decision-making,"and "owning responsibility" sum up the qualities of character and action which mark Christian moral living.

The roots of our sense of responsibility lie in our grasp of the fundamental fact about being human: *to be human is to be in relationship.* A widely held view in contemporary philosophy and in modern science is that all reality is fundamentally dynamic and relational rather than static and individual. The whole of the created world is basically a field of ongoing interactions and interrelations. A metal placard at the beginning of a trail in Yosemite National Park reminded me of this truth with a quote from John Muir: "When we try to pick out something by itself, we find it hitched to everything else in the universe." In short, the discussion of modern philosophers and the discoveries of modern science tell us that nothing exists by itself; everything exists in dynamic interrelationship.

The fundamental insight we need to grasp is that "relationality" pertains to the core of being human. The "self" is inherently relational. We are who we are by virtue of the relationships that make up our lives. To be human is not to be an "I" living in isolation. To be human is to be "I" and "you" in mutual relationship. Personal relationship is the only way for the human person to grow and mature. Personal relationship gives us the chance to open up, to go out of ourselves. To the extent that we deny this possibility, we do not grow. We remain closed in and shrivel up inside. When we fail to open up and go out to others, we destroy other people and ourselves in the process.

From this fundamental condition of being in relationship, we discover that the fundamental capacity for being human is the capacity to enter into relationships. To be able to enter into relationships requires the *capacity to give love and to receive love.* This giving and receiving of love is what makes life worth living. This capacity is foundational to the moral life. It is what being responsible is all about. It is what being moral is all about; for being moral, after all, is a matter of love. The quality of our moral life is reflected in the quality of the giving and receiving that make up our relational life.

From the Judaeo-Christian point of view, the meaning, substance, and consummation of life is summed up in our love of God and love of neighbor. These two loves are not separable. This is the force of the Great Commandment of Jesus:

> "Love the Lord your God with all your heart, with all your soul, with all your strengh, and with all your mind"; and "Love your neighbor as you love yourself" (Lk 10:27; cf Mt 22:37–39; Mk 12:29–31).

In commenting on the Great Commandment, one of our leading biblical scholars, Rudolf Schnackenburg, says,

> If we are to understand Jesus' purpose in laying down the double commandment of love, we must realize that in it Jesus linked the two commadments and put them into mutual relation. According to Jesus' mind, love of God is to find expression and give practical proof of itself in the equally important brotherly love (Mt 22:39) and, conversely, brotherly love receives as its foundation and support, the love of God.[1]

95

The First Letter of John expresses the inseparability of these two loves this way:

> If someone says he loves God, but hates his brother, he is a liar. For he cannot love God, whom he has not seen, if he does not love his brother, whom he has seen. The command that Christ has given us is this: whoever loves God must love his brother also (1 Jn 4:20–21).

All this seems to be saying that our love of neighbor is in some very real sense our love of God. If this is true, then in the Judaeo-Christian perspective, the meaning, substance, and consummation of life is found in human relationships and in the qualities of justice, respect, concern, compassion, and support that should characterize them. To be able to give and receive love in relationships is what being human is all about. This is what living the Christian moral life is all about. This is what it means to be responsible.

Christian theologians find in "responsibility" the essential theme of Christian faith and the central characteristic of the moral life. A leading American theologian of this century, H. Richard Niebuhr, has done much to give impetus to the "responsibility" motif in Christian morality. For him responsible moral action includes at least these four elements:

Response
This means the action we do is not a reflex reaction, but a deliberate action which we initiate with knowledge and freedom.

Interpretation
Our response is made to interpreted action upon us. We respond to what we perceive to be happening.

Accountability
This means we own our actions as coming from our own interpretation of what is happening. It also includes staying with our actions in their consequences and looking forward to the ongoing interaction which our actions stimulate.

Social Solidarity

Ongoing interaction recognizes that we are part of a community of interaction and that we never stand in isolation from a whole set of relationships which we help fashion by our ongoing responses, and they in turn help fashion us.[2]

H. Richard Niebuhr summarizes these elements in his idea of responsibility by describing an agent's action as

response to an action upon him in accordance with his interpretation of the latter action and with his expectation of response to his response; and all of this is in a continuing community of agents.[3]

Sin: The Biblical Perspective

"Responsibility" as a motif for the moral life has found its way into Catholic moral thinking with the strong support of the biblical renewal in the Catholic Church. The great Catholic moral theologian Bernard Häring, who has been instrumental in renewing Catholic moral thinking, has used this notion of "responsibility" with great success in restructuring Catholic moral thought. Bernard Häring, along with Charles E. Curran and other Catholic theologians committed to the renewal of moral theology, has found in the biblical renewal a fresh theological framework and orientation of understanding the moral life.[4]

From the Bible we see that Christian morality is primarily a "vocation." This means that our life is a response to the Word of God spoken to us pre-eminently in Jesus, but also in and through all the people and events of our lives. From the point of view of vocation, wherein God calls and we respond, responsibility replaces obligation as the primary characteristic of the moral life. Also, the relationship that we establish with God in and through our responses to all things becomes the focal point for examining the moral life and understanding the needs for growth in the moral life. From this point of view, practicing the presence of God becomes essential for Christian responsibility, Christian moral growth, and our awareness of sin.

We have already seen in our first chapter that God is present to us in and through all that makes up our lives. We are never not in the presence of God. How we respond to all actions upon us reflects our response to God. As Niebuhr asserts, "Responsibility affirms: God is acting in all actions upon you. So respond to all actions upon you as to respond to his action."[5] (Here is where we can understand the convergence of the moral life and spiritual life. Moral growth and spiritual growth happen together. The confession of sins followed by a style of life marked by reconciliation is part of our spiritual development as well.)

The biblical context for understanding the moral life this way is the covenant between God and Israel. The covenant is an act of pure love, a grace. The biblical notion of covenant tells us that God has taken the initiative in love to call us into communion, as was done with Moses and Israel on Mount Sinai. Our relationship to God is marked by God's freely giving and our freely accepting the covenant. God continues to call us into communion in and through all the people and events that make up our lives. As gifted by God in this covenant, we express our gratitude to God by living in response to God in and through all our choices and actions. This means there is never a time when we are not responding to God. The whole of our moral lives is an expression of thanksgiving. We live morally because we are grateful for the love and life we have been given and which we can give in return. Since we live the whole of our lives in the presence of God, we express our love and gratitude to God in and through all the responses we make in our lives.

The covenant is also the proper context for understanding sin in the Bible. *Sin, in the fullest religious sense, is personal rebellion or separation from God.* This is dramatically symbolized by Moses breaking the tablets of the covenantal laws before the people when he sees they have turned away from God by making an idol (Dt 9:16–17). Breaking the tablets symbolized the break in the covenantal relationship which gave the whole meaning to the Ten Commandments. Idolatry is a sin not merely because it fails to fulfill the first commandment, but because it breaks the personal bond of which the commandment is but an external expression. Idolatry is the greatest of sins, for it refuses to accept the God of the covenant and the claims which a covenantal relationship makes on us. Because we are a covenantal people, all our sins are in some way an expression of idolatry. This means that in and through sin we set up something else (self, power, prestige, wealth, etc.) as the center of our loyalty and the goal of our hearts' desire.

The most common expression for sinning in the Old Testament is *hatt'ah,* which can be translated "missing the mark." The basic meaning of "missing the mark" points to an existing relationship which has been ruptured. The "mark" that is missed is not the letter of the law, but covenantal love. To sin is to fail to respond in love to the personal love which is offered in the covenantal relationship. To sin is to be disloyal to the covenantal relationship with God and with other members of the covenantal community.

If sin is basically the failure to love God, it is not surprising that sin is frequently associated with the "heart" in the Bible. For the biblical authors, the response to God is rooted in the heart. To sin is to harden one's heart to God's love. For this reason, the psalmist beseeches God to create a clean heart for him (Ps 51:12), and Jeremiah and Ezekiel speak about the law of the new covenant that God will write in the people's hearts so they will know, almost instinctively, right from wrong (Jer 31:33–34; Ez 36:25–27).

In the New Testament, the word *hamartia* carries the sense of "missing the mark" to convey both the sense of the condition of being separated from God, as well as the additional sense of the interior quality of the heart from which springs the rebellion causing the separation. No wonder, then, that we frequently find sin spoken of in the context of conversion, which is the call for a renewed heart. This is clearly illustrated in the prodigal son's coming to an awareness of his sin and wanting to be converted and to return to his father (Lk 15:11–32).

The covenantal context and the primary words for sin stress clearly that a relationship of love is violated by sin. This context, furthermore, lifts the notion of sin out of a legalistic framework to set it on a level of a personal relationship with God. In the worship of the golden calf (Ex 32), Israel missed the mark of convenantal love, or sinned, not so much because Israel broke one of the laws of the covenant, but because she broke the personal bond of love of which the law was an external expression. The law was not to be the final object of Israel's fidelity. God was. Sin in the Bible is not breaking a law. Sin is against people, not against concepts or structures. Sin is breaking or weakening the God-given bond of love. The dynamic of Israel's response to God and the place of law in this response can be diagrammed like this:

Israel————Law————→ God

The law was an aid to Israel's fidelity and pointed to the responsibilities of being in relationship to God. But to make the law the end of Israel's loyalty would be to make an idol of the law, or to commit sin. Perhaps the legalism of the Pharisees, their making the law an end in itself, contributed to the loss of the fundamental biblical insight into the nature of sin as personal rebellion and estrangement from God.

To say sin is "missing the mark" does not specify the precise content of sinful actions. But it does indicate that sin is whatever contributes to rupturing the personal bond of love in covenantal relationships. The covenant binds us to God and to one another at one and the same time. In the Bible, even offenses which seem to find their evil in being harmful to one's neighbor are seen as involving one's relationship with God. For example, David sinned against Bathsheba, but confesses, "I have sinned against the Lord" (2 Sam 12:13). In Ezekiel 18:3–32 the evil of the offense against the neighbors is that it implies a rejection of God. In the Parable of the Merciful Father, the prodigal son confesses, "I have sinned against God and against you" (Lk 15:18). As we have already seen the Great Commandment of love binds the love of God and neighbor into an inseparable bond so that to sin against either is to involve the other.

Jesus the Christ is the new covenant. In him we find the most complete expression of living faithfully as a covenantal person. We turn to him to know what it means to live responsibly in the covenant. This brings the themes of discipleship and the imitation of Christ to the forefront of our reflection on the

100

moral life. To use these themes in our moral reflection means to make Christ our primary referent for what it means to be human and to be moral. To say this is to say that we need to think along with Christ and his words and deeds. To do this we need to form our consciences by letting our imaginations be shaped by his parables and his deeds. The good shepherd, the good Samaritan, and the merciful father of the prodigal son stand before us as models of the sorts of persons we ought to be. Forgiving the sinful woman, having compassion on the crowds, washing the disciples' feet, going the extra mile, and the self-sacrifical love of the crucifixion are models of the sorts of actions we ought to perform.

When we examine our lives in light of the life of Christ, we come to understand the meaning of the Christian moral life and the Christian meaning of sin. But what does all this have to do with the actual decisions we make from day to day? In short, it has to do with being and doing what Christ was and did. This does not mean being a first century Palestinean Jew who died on the cross. But it does mean manifesting God as love. What does this mean? It means something more than simply "being nice." The call to love strains our energies to discover those actions which will build up the goodness in another, receive another's qualities as gifts, and promote the well-being of self, others, and of all creation so that we can live in communion with dignity, freedom, justice, and peace.

The deliberate refusal to participate in creating a humanly livable world is to act irresponsibly. This is actual sin, pure and simple. When we find ourselves resisting or refusing opportunities to contribute to life and love in community, or when we find ourselves engaging in a way of life that has destructive consequences for our own lives and for others, or when we find ourselves grasping at something to gratify ourselves at another's expense, we are in the realm of irresponsible behavior. We are in the realm of sin. To act against the well-being of human persons and of all creation is to act against God whom we experience in and through persons and creation. Living with a sense of responsibility is living with awareness and in freedom the summons to be lovers in the way Jesus was. This is the goal of the Christian life.

Summary: Sin as Selfishness

Now we are ready to summarize the understanding of sin which emerges from this sense of responsibility and its biblical context. Above all, sin is fundamentally a religious reality. This means that sin makes no sense apart from the presence of God in Christ and through the Spirit, and our awareness of being in relationship to God. If an action is not against God, it is not sin. If we use sin in any other way than to refer to this fundamental relationship to God, we are using "sin" only analogously (as in the phrase, "giving up that diet is simply sinful"). We can grasp the biblical meaning of sin only within the interpersonal relationship of covenantal love. Without a belief in God to whom we can be personally and intimately related in love, and from whom we can choose to be separated, sin makes no sense. If we are to understand sin at all, we must understand ourselves as being loved and being able to love. We must understand that God loves us first, and that this love enables us to love in return. Sin enters in our failing to love or to accept love.

To say sin is primarily a matter of our relationship to God through Christ and in the Spirit suggests a transcendent and immanent dimension to sin. The transcendent dimension expresses a break in our relationship to God. This is the "No" we answer to the invitation to live with God in love. But from our discussion of the "in and through" approach to God in the second chapter, we can see that we do not experience or express this relationship to God from our relationship with all things, especially other persons. Our sin is our way of rebelling not only against God (which we rarely, if ever, do directly) but also against the living images of God, one another.

This accounts for the immanent dimension of sin. We understand the immanent dimension of sin when we see the importance of the human community as the place in and through which we receive love and give love. Sin in its immanent dimension is the "No" we answer in our relations with our neighbors to love and to be loved. We sin when we choose to turn inward and cut off the dynamics of receiving and giving love. In this sense, sin is always a type of self-absorption. Whenever loving, life-giving relationships are weakened or destroyed, sin is pres-

102

ent in some form. Whether that form be lying, gossip, stealing, abusing, ignoring, or whatever is not as important as the result, a life-giving relationship is weakened or broken.

Only when we can understand both the transcendent and the immanent dimensions of sin will we be able to grasp the full significance of the American Bishops' definition of sin which they have first offered in their pastoral letter on the moral life, *To Live in Christ Jesus* (1976), and then repeated in the National Catechetical Directory, *Sharing the Light of Faith* (1979). From their pastoral letter, we read:

> [Personal sin] is different from unavoidable failure or limita-
> tion. . . . It is a spirit of selfishness rooted in our hearts and
> wills which wages war against God's plan for our fulfillment.
> It is rejection, either partial or total, of one's role as a child of
> God and a member of His people, a rejection of the spirit of
> sonship, love and life.[6]

We need to be clear about what this statement says and what it does not say. It does *not* say that sin is a matter of being inadequate, weak, or limited. How often we mistake human limitations for sin. Limitations and unavoidable failures come with the territory of being human. We all share human weakness in varying degrees depending on how we have developed our own interior resources. This statement also does *not* say that sin is first and foremost the breaking of a law. In fact, law, once so readily associated with identifying sin, is not even mentioned. While law may help us recognize sin insofar as law serves to promote and preserve life-giving relationships, sin is not against the laws themselves. Sin is against people, and therefore against God.

Now we can put our finger on what personal sin is in all its ugliness. *Sin is selfishness,* pure and simple. Sin as selfishness is first a matter of the heart, before it ever becomes manifest in external actions. No wonder, then, that the new Rite calls for the sinner to be "converted to God with his whole heart" (Par. 6) and to make an "inner examination of heart" (Par. 6b) before confessing sins. We become sinful to the extent that we turn inward, refuse to respond, and so cut off the dynamic of giving and receiving love. This is to "harden one's heart" in the biblical sense. In sin, we cease to pay attention to, or care about, anyone outside ourselves. Selfishness is self-absorption. It is the failure to love and to accept love. All sin springs in some fashion from a love turned in on itself. Several metaphors, drawing upon several types of relationships, have been used to convey this meaning of sin. Principal metaphors used about sin today are rebellion, isolation, alienation, and estrangement. Each expresses a different nuance of love turned in on itself.

Sin as selfishness is ultimately irresponsibility. Selfishness separates us from life-giving and loving relationships. Selfishness weakens or breaks the God-given bond of love we have with one another. Our responsibility is to care for and to serve one another. This is what it means to be bound together in covenant. Jesus' great commandment of love makes this all clear. When we do not act as a person bound together in covenant with God and with others, we sin. When we sin we destroy other people and ourselves at the same time. We bring about those consequences of personal sin which we have come to know as "social sin." We destroy bonds of peace and justice, and spread conditions of fear, hatred, violence, and bring havoc into the lives of other people and into our own.

Selfishness separates us from life-giving relationships because it prevents us from seeing others as they are. We have already said that part of what it means to live responsibly is to perceive accurately. We respond to what we see; it is that simple. In the spirit of selfishness, we begin to see other people as we desire them to be to satisfy our needs. We look on our children as a "burden" for they do not give us the freedom to do or have all that we wish. We look on our students as "lazy" for they do not satisfy our need to achieve. In short, in the spirit of selfishness we see what we need to see in order to protect and to promote our self-interests. The result of our seeing is to act in response to what we see. If we look on our students as lazy, we refuse to affirm them. Not only do we look on other people falsely, but we look on events falsely, too. Abortion becomes contraception when we are no longer able to care for children. A bombing raid becomes a "surgical" air strike when we are not

104

able to see our nation as capable of mass destruction. The peculiar thing about these deceptions is that they happen so subtly and unconsciously. Often only a rude shock can awaken us to the reality of our false vision.

James McClendon has it exactly right when he uses Matthew's judgment-parable to show that we do not always show ourselves for who we truly are through deliberate choices:

> Jesus, according to Matthew's judgment-parable of the sheep and the goats, tells his hearers that the actions by which their final destiny is judged are not the result of their deliberate choices, but are instead ones in which they act unknowingly, and yet showed themselves for what they truly were: it is "unconscious" acts of charity and mercy (or their absence) which are the true harbingers of our last estate, these and not our informed "decisions" (Mathew 25:31–45).[7]

From this point of view, virtue enters upon noticing human need and responding to it even without due deliberation. Sin enters in the not noticing.

Selfish actions follow upon selfish vision. Sins which do the greatest damage are those with the highest content of love turned in on itself or the deepest commitment to a "me-only" attitude. Our greatest sins are those which make fellowship with others and their proper treatment impossible. We become reconciled to the degree we see more clearly, open up, go out of ourselves, and enter into positive life-giving relationships. This is the only way to grow. This is the only way to be healed.

Since sin is a religious reality primarily, the root answer to breaking through our selfishness is a religious one. Sin as selfishness arises out of the attempt to guarantee that our need to be loved is met. We break the dynamic power of sin in our lives when we realize that we are in fact profoundly loved. Only God's love is so permanent and profound as to release us from our sin. The Sacrament of Reconciliation becomes the concrete sign that God's love is being offered us and cannot be defeated. Through Reconciliation, the dialogue of love, the dynamic of giving and receiving love, is renewed and the life-giving relationship we share with God and with others is strengthened.

ACTUAL SIN

We have long recognized that sin is a wide-ranging reality with various degrees of gravity. We are familiar with the common distinctions of actual sin as *mortal* and *venial*. The Introduction to the Rite of Penance wisely avoids using these categories for reasons I hope will be clear as we progress. The Introduction simply speaks of "sin" or "grave sin." Where did we get our distinctions for actual sin, and how might an adult understand mortal and venial sin today?

The Bible shows that the biblical communities were aware of degrees of sin, but not in the sense of the distinction between sins that must be confessed (mortal sins) and sins which may be confessed (venial sins). The Bible does not even support reducing all sins to two categories, and does not offer any quantitative measurement for distinguishing kinds of sins. We have already seen that sin is primarily and always an offense against God. The greatest sin is the direct rejection of God. This is idolatry. The direct rejection of the true God and setting up idols are the first offenses mentioned in the Ten Commandments. One of the great missions of the prophets was to call Israel away from idolatry and back to fidelity to the one true God of the covenant.

In the New Testament, Paul lists those sins which can exclude one from the Kingdom of God (1 Cor 6:9–10; Gal 5:19–21). There is the famous saying of Jesus about blasphemy against the Holy Spirit that will not be forgiven in Mark 3:28–30, Matthew 12:31–32, and Luke 12:10. This sin will not be forgiven because the person who commits such blasphemy is closed to the power of the Spirit to save. The clearest reference to degrees of sin is found in 1 John 5:16–17. There John does not tell us what he means by "deadly sin," nor does he give an example. But John does indicate a distinction in the degrees of seriousness of sin: some are "deadly" and some are not. Theologians today continue to try to bring precision to what this distinction might be.

The terms "mortal" and "venial" came into usage as a result of efforts to be precise about the distinction in degrees of sin. Tertullian, a north African apologist of the late second and early third centuries, was the first to refer to some kinds of sins as "mortal sins." For him this meant sins for which the Church

106

should refuse forgiveness. We must understand that Tertullian and his Montanist party at the time were reacting to the mild manner in which the Church was receiving sinners back after serious sin. Tertullian and the Montanist party felt that while the Church can forgive sins, the Church should not grant forgiveness to some sins lest this be an invitation for others to sin. The unforgivable sins he called *mortalia* (deadly). On his list of deadly, or mortal sins were idolatry, blasphemy, murder, adultery, fornication, false witnessing, fraud, and lying.

During the era of canonical penance from the fourth to sixth centuries, a fundamental principle guiding penitential discipline seemed to be that canonical penance was required for mortal sins, while private mortification was sufficient for venial sins. However, we have no uniform listing of what were regarded as mortal or venial sins since the distinction was not easily made, nor made on the basis of the same criteria.

When the law was established at the Fourth Lateran Council (1215) making annual confession obligatory for those who had committed a mortal sin, the distinction between mortal and venial took on juridical importance. The distinction of sins becomes important at this point because this law of the Church makes it necessary to know the difference. Once the law is established, there must be some way of determining who is subject to the law. Moralists soon began to turn to quantitative and objective measurements to distinguish mortal and venial sin. As soon as the quantitative thinking came into the morals game, the question "How far can I go before committing a mortal sin?" was not far behind.

Moralists soon settled on the three conditions which traditional Catholic moral theology has maintained as necessary for mortal sin: *serious matter, sufficient reflection,* and *full consent of the will.* While prominent moralists of our tradition took all three conditions for mortal sin seriously, the popular mind gradually came to identify serious matter alone as enough for mortal sin. By focusing on matter alone, ready catalogues of sin could easily be devised to aid an examination of conscience. With these examination aides, the personal factors of knowledge and freedom often got lost. In approaching sin from the point of view that focuses on personal responsibility, as contemporary moral

107

thinking does, we need to retrieve these personal factors of knowledge and freedom in order to appreciate the moral significance of the action. In looking further, then, at how contemporary theology would speak to adults about sin, we will focus primarily on what constitutes mortal sin, because personal sin which deserves the name "sin" is mortal sin. St. Thomas himself claimed as much (ST I–II, q. 88, a. 1). Venial sin derives its meaning by analogy to mortal sin.

MORTAL SIN

Sufficient Reflection

The traditional requirement of "sufficient reflection" has to do with knowledge. Theologians speak of two kinds of knowledge operating in our moral life: speculative and evaluative.[8] We need to understand what theologians mean by each if we are ever to understand this condition for mortal sin. What kind of knowledge is required for acting virtuously or mortally sinfully? The accompanying chart gives an overview of the key points at stake in speculative and evaluative knowledge.

Speculative knowledge is fairly easy to grasp. It is head knowledge. This is the kind of knowledge we have when we have the right information and have mastered the facts. Speculative knowledge is also fairly easy to verify for we only need to double check our observations, our facts, our logic. We can easily communicate this kind of knowledge through preaching, teaching, and sharing since we can detach the facts from the knower and the circumstances to make them readily available to anyone who wants them. In matters of morality, speculative knowledge is knowledge about values. This comes with a knowledge of moral rules and strategies for doing what the rules prescribe. This is the kind of knowledge we use in our moral arguments to communicate values and our reasons for or against a position. While this kind of knowledge is important and necessary for the moral life, it is not the only kind of knowledge we need either to be virtuous, or to act in a personally sinful way. We also need evaluative knowledge.

108

Feature	Speculative Knowledge	Evaluative Knowledge
Symbol	Head	Heart
Content	Right information; "master the facts."	Quality or value of someone or something.
Verifiable	Easily verified since the facts can be observed and the logic demonstrated.	Difficult to verify since quality or value escapes easy demonstration and logical exposition.
Acquired	Can be easily learned, for right information is ripe for teaching, preaching, and sharing.	Quality and value must be caught through personal interaction and encounter.
Communicated	Information or facts are easily detached from the knower and the situation, so are easy to pass on.	Since quality and value are not easily detached from knower and situation, communication is difficult and must be discovered to be appreciated.

Feature	Speculative Knowledge	Evaluative Knowledge
Morality	This is the knowledge of the rules and the strategies for achieving what the rules prescribe; this is knowledge *about* values.	This knowledge is a personal grasp of value. This is what makes our actions truly our *own* for with this knowledge we act on the basis of what we truly value. Moral growth and conversion happen through the experience of value and acquiring evaluative knowledge.

Moral knowledge, properly so called, is evaluative knowledge. This is a little more difficult to understand. Consider this example. I recall my brother's efforts to get me to know the young lady he had recently met and eventually married. I was in the seminary at the time, and he was in graduate school. The geographical distance between us, as well as our different schedules, prevented us from being together very often. So he did the best he could with letters, phone calls, and even pictures to get me to know this love in his life the way he did. But nothing satisfied. He finally said, in frustration, "You'll just have to meet her!" That is it, exactly! I would have to discover for myself through personal encounter what he already knew by heart. When we meet someone whom we truly love, we want all our friends to know this loved one as well. Excitedly we can give all the descriptions of our love that we like, and even show pictures of our loved one, but nothing satisfies like personal encounter or substitutes for it. Not until there is an occasion for personal encounter with this person will anyone else ever be able to know what we know by heart. That is how evaluative knowledge works.

Evaluative knowledge is a lover's knowledge. It is knowledge "by heart." This is the kind of knowledge we have when we are "caught up" in someone or something through personal involvement or commitment. Evaluative knowledge is more personal, more self-involving than conceptual knowledge of facts or ideas, for it has to do with grasping the quality of a person, object, or event. Evaluative knowledge is a felt knowledge that we discover through personal involvement and reflection, rather than something that can easily be passed on through statements, formulas, or rules. Evaluative knowledge is evoked and caught in our experiences; it is not easily taught in a detached way. The most we can hope for in trying to communicate evaluative knowledge is to occasion similar experiences of this value for another so as to draw out of another the value experienced. In matters of morality, evaluative knowledge is the deeply personal, self-involving knowledge that makes our actions truly our *own*. Without this knowledge we act merely by hearsay, by what we are told is right, rather than on the basis of what we have discovered to be valuable. This kind of knowledge is not acquired nor altered through rational argument alone, but by personal experience, discovery, and appreciation of value. The requirement of "sufficient reflection" is fulfilled when we have reached evaluative knowledge. Only then is mortal sin possible.

Full Consent of the Will

The traditional requirement of "full consent of the will" implies personal freedom. Freedom, as a fundamental condition for sin or virtue, is a tough notion to grasp. We want to be sure to avoid two common dangers in understanding freedom. One has to do with selling out to determinism: attempting to escape from freedom by claiming that we are forced to act as we do by heredity or environment. This leads to claims that we are not responsible for anything we do. But if we deny freedom, we deny the possibility of sin. Though we are subject to some powerful influences, we can still freely choose to do good or evil.

The other danger is to avoid being short-sighted in our consideration of freedom. We can too easily limit ourselves just to freedom of choice as the only kind of freedom that matters. This leads to forgetting the connection between the choices we make and the sort of persons we are becoming through these choices. The freedom of self-determination is basic to freedom of choice. We need to say more about each of these. First let us consider the issue of freedom and determinism.

We know that we are very much the product of what is not ourselves. Yet we also know that we are not entirely determined by heredity or environment. We fall somewhere on the continuum between absolute freedom and absolute determinism. We are neither completely free nor completely unfree. Our freedom is not a matter of all or nothing. It is always a matter of more or less. If this were not so, I suspect we would not have the experience of being unsettled or indecisive about choices. We would never have to deliberate about anything if we were completely free or completely determined.

We are free within limits. Our lives are subject to some uncontrollable features which we must simply accept as givens. Our genetic endowment, unconscious motives, and social-cultural conditioning are three uncontrollable features of ourselves. While we cannot be held morally accountable for these givens, they nevertheless constitute something of who we are, and have some influence on what we do. These givens, along with other determinants like peer pressure, fears, blind habits, and other hidden persuaders that pervade our lives, continue to constrict our freedom. Yet the more aware we become of these determinants and their influence on us, the freer we can be to live within the limits which they set. The more we are able to become aware of ourselves and possess ourselves, including all the determining influences, the more we will experience ourselves as responsible for what we do and who we become.

A powerful scene from *One Flew Over the Cuckoo's Nest* brings this home very graphically. It demonstrates what we should all be about in our moral striving to live as responsible adults. In this novel, McMurphy fakes insanity to escape a penal farm for the softer life of a mental institution. He comes to a head-on collision with Big Nurse, the tyrant of the ward who has psychologically emasculated her patients so that they can no longer have freedom to choose. McMurphy begins a one-man campaign against tyranny and for freedom. In one scene he stages a showdown with Big Nurse by calling for a vote which would allow the patients to watch the World Series on TV. He is one vote short of a majority. It is up to Chief, the big Indian who, to escape the pains of tyranny, has retired into a fog where he cannot hear and cannot speak. McMurphy pleads with him to raise his hand, Chief finds his hand going up, and he says to himself:

> It's too late to stop it now. McMurphy did something to it that first day, put some kind of hex on it.... McMurphy's got hidden wires hooked to it, lifting it slow just to get me out of the fog and into the open where I'm fair game. He's doing it, wires.... No, that's not the truth. I lifted it myself.[9]

This is the goal of moral striving. We need to cut short our attempted escapes from freedom so that we can responsibly claim, "I did it myself!" Freedom and responsibility go hand in hand. Responsible freedom says, "I choose to do this because, as a responsible person, I *want* to do it." This is quite different from the familiar, "I really should ..." or "I had better ..." or "I must...." These all indicate motivation from without. Whenever we find ourselves saying "Actually I should ..." chances are that we really *do not* want to, but we feel some external pressure to; there are possible rewards if we do, or punishments if we do not. A cuckoo's nest may be an extreme image for the world in which we live, yet the neurotic is a clear image of the determined conditions which we all share. The neurotic suggests that the tyranny of determining influences over which we seem to have no control has made powerlessness our chief neurosis. We all have a Big Nurse in our lives. That is inevitable. With Chief we often retreat into the fog and attempt to escape from freedom.

The freedom of our moral striving is not doing anything we want to do. The freedom of our moral striving is *wanting to do what we do*. We cannot do everything. Determining factors prevent that. But we can pour ourselves into what we do, make it truly our own, chosen as a genuine expression of ourselves which asserts our integrity. Our freedom to choose this or that is

113

fundamentally a freedom to choose an identity, to become a certain sort of person. Moral freedom, then, refers most profoundly not to choosing this or that value, but choosing, through all the pathways of particular choices, who we want to be, persons either open or closed to the mystery of our lives and of all life.

This brings us squarely in touch with what theologians call basic, or *core freedom.* This is the freedom of self-determination by which we dispose ourselves to become this or that sort of person through exercising freedom of choice. Freedom of choice is that smorgasboard kind of freedom of choosing one from a number of possible options.

To understand "freedom of the will" for moral decision-making, we need to appreciate the difference between freedom of choice and basic, or core freedom. Consider these examples. At our seminary we take our meals in a cafeteria which always has at least three options for dessert. To illustrate freedom of choice with my students, I ask them if they can remember which dessert they chose for lunch on a certain day of the previous week. Only those who choose jello every day remember! The rest do not. One of the reasons they do not remember their choice of dessert is that such a choice does not demand a very deep involvement of their persons. Smorgasboard freedom, the freedom of choice, is like that. It does not demand very much from us.

On the other hand, basic freedom, the freedom of self-determination, involves more. For example, I recently met up with a friend of mine whom I had not seen for six months. At our last meeting together I learned from him that he had begun to see this certain girl on a regular basis. When we met six months later, I asked him if anything significant had happened in his life since our last meeting. He said nothing had. Everything seemed to be moving along, but nothing outstanding had happened. Then I learned from a mutual friend of ours that he had gotten engaged just three weeks ago. This surprised me since it did not make much of an impact on my friend who had gotten engaged. How could he have gotten engaged and not considered that a significant happening in his life? To commit oneself to another in marital engagement demands a great deal more personal investment than choosing a dessert. Is it that he thought of his fi-

ancé and his commitment to her as nothing more than a dessert?
I hope not! The choice to be engaged and eventually marry demands something of us that gets closer to basic freedom than
choosing jello over cookies in the cafeteria.

This approach to freedom rests on an understanding of the
human person as a complex multi-leveled being. To illustrate
this I like to diagram the human person as a moving spiral. Others prefer to use the food metaphors of an onion, artichoke, or
cinnamon roll. The spiral illustrates better our having a common
center for each of the levels of our being. Furthermore, with the
spiral we cannot tell clearly where one level ends and the next
begins. This is closer to real life, I think. With a spiral, too, we
know that each level shares a common center and moves out
from there without ever being disjointed from the whole. The
spiral is "moving" to capture the temporal dimension of being
human and the developmental orientation of the moral life. My
diagram looks like this:

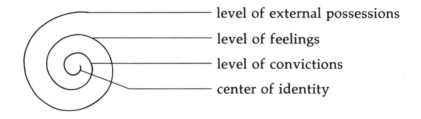

This diagram shows that our actions can spring from different levels of our being. Not everything we do springs from the
deepest core of our being to embody ourselves in a clear and
complete way. Some actions might be rooted there, but most of
our actions spring from a more peripheral level. This cautions us
from concluding on the basis of isolated actions alone that anyone has embodied the full meaning and commitment of himself
or herself. What seems more likely is that we come to actualize
who we are through a whole series of actions which, when taken
together, express the basic character or dominant direction of
our lives. Theologians call this basic direction of our lives, which
manifests a rather consistent personal identity, our *fundamental
stance.* Those significant moments of choice in our lives, which

establish or affirm more strongly than others the character and direction of our lives, are called *fundamental options.*

The Theory of Fundamental Option

Bernard Häring has gone to great length in the first volume of his *Free and Faithful in Christ* to show how a proper understanding of the theory of fundamental option overcomes a shallowness with regard to sin, how it restores an adequate sense of personal sin, how it aids our appreciation of the differences between mortal and venial sin, and how it has strong implications for understanding the need for ongoing conversion in the moral life.[10]

I have found that audiences give mixed reactions to the fundamental option theory and its approach to sin. For some this is a liberating theory, for it "rings true" to their own experience of the complexity of the human person and human choice, and the relation of the individual actions to the person. For others this theory seems to water down a sense of sin by not giving enough attention to external actions. Still others are suspicious of this theory for catechesis, because they believe it has been repudiated by papal documents.

A look at a recent papal document which has explicitly commented on this theory can put this latter suspicion to rest. The 1975 document, *Declaration on Certain Questions Concerning Sexual Ethics,* issued by the Sacred Congegation for the Doctrine of the Faith makes explicit reference to this approach to sin in Paragraph #10. This paragraph shows that the document accepts at least the essence of this theory when it says, "In reality, it is precisely the fundamental option which in the last resort defines a person's moral disposition."[11]

The thrust of this paragraph's treatment of the fundamental option theory is to rein in and correct those exaggerated forms of the theory which unreasonably minimize the significance of individual actions in assessing sin. Responsible use of this theory would not accept this minimizing. In fact, fundamental option properly understood can help us take sin more seriously by showing how sin is truly a corruption of the person. It can also help restore a balance between the three necessary requirements for mortal sin by showing that actions are in the context of the person if we are to determine sin properly.

What, more precisely, does this theory of fundamental option tell us? First let me offer a general comment, and then a more specific, close-up look at its major features. In general, this theory assumes a fundamental Christian conviction about being human: we are born graced. That is, we are created by God out of love for love. We are the good creation of a gracious God. God's love for us has so affected us in our innermost being as to make a claim on us, and to give us an orientation toward love and life. This basic condition of being human demands to be lived out in our freedom. Yet we must live out this condition in a broken world—a world where original sin and social sin abound, and a world where many temptations and bad influences arise to contradict the very orientation of our innermost being, our hearts.

Though more deeply marked by grace than by sin, we always stand in need of purification and conversion. This gives a dynamic character to a life of constant growth. Traditional moral theology understood this basic condition of being human. The classic moral manuals began with attention on our ultimate end and the necessity to make decisions for that end. From a theological point of view, this end is God calling us into communion with God's self. Our basic decision is whether we will live our lives responding to God in and through all our choices.

Now that we have made a general comment about the fundamental option theory, we can take a close-up look at its major features. If we are going to understand mortal sin properly from the perspective of this theory, as many theologians are doing today, we need to make a clear distinction between fundamental stance and fundamental option as Timothy O'Connell does in his book, *Principles for a Catholic Morality.* [12]

Fundamental Stance

When theologians today speak of our fundamental stance, they are speaking of the fundamental direction we have chosen for our lives. Fundamental stance expresses the sort of person we have chosen to be. It brings a stable direction, perduring quality, and personal meaning to our actions. Bernard Häring has aligned this notion of fundamental stance with Erik Erikson's notion of identity.[13] By this he means we cannot lay claims to having achieved a fundamental stance until we can lay claims to having achieved a stable identity. For neither identity nor stance arises all at once. Both come into being through committing oneself to a way of life that is stable enough to sustain a perduring quality of life, and in this way to give personal meaning to actions.

Actions taken by themselves are ambiguous. Situating actions in relation to the fundamental direction of a person's life enables us to discover the personal meaning of actions. Our actions embody, to a greater or lesser degree, the fundamental direction of our lives. They are signs more or less expressive of our interiority. In this sense, our actions are like the tip of an iceberg. They are held above the surface by our attitudes, convictions, and the fundamental direction of our lives which seek external, concrete expression. To get to the true meaning of our actions as expressions of ourselves, we need to look beneath the surface of observable behavior to those attitudes and convictions which give expression to the fundamental direction of our lives and seek concrete embodiment in particular actions. Taking this in-depth kind of look at our actions is what we need to do before making a confession. Only by looking beneath the surface of our actions will we be able to get to the roots of the moral conversion, healing, and growth which we seek through the Sacrament of Reconcilation.

When we take such an in-depth look at our actions, we discover that they may be more or less consistent with the fundamental direction of our lives. This is because our actions arise from different levels of our being. Not all our actions spring from the deepest center of ourselves wherein lies the core of our identity. In the biblical sense, this is the "heart"—the deepest source from which we commit ourselves to God and to others. The truest expression of ourselves as moral persons arises from there; it does not lie in our extenal actions alone. Our hearts give expression to what we most care about, and most value. This gives full force to the biblical prayers which beseech God for a "pure heart," and this gives power to Jesus' sayings, "Where your treasure is, there will be your heart" (Mt 6:21), and "Of what the heart is full, the mouth will speak"(Mt 12:34). The goal of moral growth is to become beatitude people who are pure of heart, people who live single-heartedly so that actions are consistent with who we have chosen to be in our commitment to God.

Fundamental Option

However, we know that our actions, more often than we care to admit, contradict the sort of person we have chosen to be even if they do not involve a complete surrender of the most basic direction of our lives. For example, I know myself to be a person who has chosen to be a good person, caring for others, searching for ways to be faithful, honest, true. Yet, in a frustrating sort of way, not all of my actions exhibit this care and these virtues. Such actions, however, do not rise from the deepest core of myself, but from a more peripheral level. Though these actions do not reverse the fundamental direction of my life, they can weaken my fundamental commitment for good.

There are, however, certain actions which arise from such personal depth that they can significantly reverse or reinforce the fundamental stance or direction of our lives. These are what theologians call fundamental options. A fundamental option arises from a deep knowledge of self and a freedom to commit oneself. Through a fundamental option we express our basic freedom of self-determination to commit ourselves profoundly toward a certain way of being in the world.

Bernard Häring speaks of some special moments in life which are expressions of a fundamental option as the "great decisions." These are decisions appropriate to those who have reached the necessary stage of identity and are able to commit themselves in knowledge and with freedom to a community or to a person. Without any claim to completeness, Häring says this:

> I want to point to such fundamental decisions as personal choice of faith in Jesus Christ and in the role and mission of

119

the Church, made by an adult or an adolescent who has already reached the necessary stage of identity. I would list among such choices: adult baptism as sign of personal commitment to Christ and covenant with the Church—and since adult baptism is the exception in the West, I would note confirmation as a mature ratification of what God offers us in baptism; marriage vows; the vows of celibacy for the kingdom of God; a decision that is the test of deep and true friendship or of self-giving love; the deliberate choice of a profession such as that of a physician or of a politician with a firm commitment to the positive ethos.[14]

Pope John Paul II has used the notion of fundamental option in a similar sense in his document on catechetics, *Catechesi Tradendae,* in 1979. When speaking about youth, he writes:

With youth comes the moment of the first great decisions. Although the young may enjoy the support of the members of their family and their friends, they have to rely on themselves and their own conscience and must ever more frequently and decisively assume responsibility for their destiny. Good and evil, grace and sin, life and death will more and more confront one another within them, not just as moral categories but chiefly as fundamental options which they must accept or reject lucidly, conscious of their own responsibility (Par. 39).[15]

These statements of theologian Bernard Häring and of Pope John Paul II suggest that those fundamental decisions which affect the basic direction of our lives are not made quickly or easily. We must be truly ready for them on all levels of our personality. These statements also show that fundamental choices are deeply rooted in the relational character of our lives. Our basic decisions have to do with our commitment to our own integrity and identity, our commitment to others, and our sense of responsibility to the world around us. If these basic decisions are made soundly and not precipitously, they can well establish the direction of our lives so as to resist those strong determining forces which are constantly warring against us fighting to make us someone else. The condition "full consent of the will" is fulfilled when we exercise our basic freedom of self-determination through a fundamental option.

Serious Matter

Only now are we ready to understand the meaning of serious matter. The important implication of fundamental stance and fundamental option for the moral life are that they help us see that our actions are not disconnected from, but are part of moral growth or deterioration. Also, individual actions have a meaning within an entire pattern of actions. To understand this more sharply, think of the moral life as an ongoing conversation. Individual actions are like the words in that conversation. Like words spoken in a conversation, no action has its proper meaning in isolation from the conversation. Since all moral action is interaction, each individual action finds its proper meaning from within the total conversation that is our moral life. Our individual actions have moral significance as the embodiment of the fundamental direction of our lives to be radically open or closed to God, life, or other persons.

In this context, we can understand "serious matter." The basic question of "serious matter" is not how much of a "big deal" the action is in itself, but how deeply invested we are in the action. The most important feature in the moral life is the sort of person we are becoming by the choices we make and the actions we do. Actions are indeed important for this. But when it comes to determining "serious matter," we need to see our actions in relation to the full development of our knowledge and freedom. Bernard Häring has captured the meaning of "serious matter" well in this statement:

> This approach in no way negates the importance of the object of the act or the gravity of the matter; but gravity or relevance assumes moral meaning only in proportion to the actual development of a person's knowledge and freedom, and to the extent that the deep self-determination that we call fundamental option can be evoked.[16]

121

Mortal Sin: A Synthetic View

Some theologians speak of mortal sin in a shorthand way as a negative fundamental option. This means that mortal sin is a conscious decision to take a radical action in and through which we assume for ourselves a way of life that turns us away from relating to God, others, and the world in a positive, life-giving way. In mortal sin we no longer build up and promote wholesome relationships, nor do we contribute to the well-being of the human community and all creation. This description of mortal sin captures both the importance of particular acts and the larger context of interaction in which these individual acts occur.

The 1975 document on *Sexual Ethics* states its understanding of mortal sin this way:

> In reality, it is precisely the fundamental option which in the last resort defines a person's moral disposition. But it can be completely changed by particular acts, especially when, as often happens, these have been prepared for by previous more superficial acts. Whatever the case, it is wrong to say that particular acts are not enough to constitute mortal sin (Par. 10).

This description shows us two extreme ways of committing mortal sin. One way is for a person, who has a sharp awareness that a particular act contradicts the love of God, nevertheless to decide in favor of that act in a way that reaches into the depths of one's heart and shapes one's whole being. The other way is that mortal sin comes as a result of frequent failures to love and to do the good within one's reach so that this increasing laxity deadens the person's sensitivity to the good and responsibility to others. A point finally comes where a particular act embodies more clearly than others the erosion of bonds of love. This approach to mortal sin shows that all our decisions participate in our process of development either for good or for evil. This does not deny that there are moments when a concrete action makes the complete reversal of our fundamental commitment for good. But it does show why we should become concerned with the pattern of our decisions and actions rather than with individual actions taken in isolation.

Actions that we judge as sinful must never be taken as abstractions, i.e., as being separated from persons and from an ongoing process of interaction. Properly understood, all actions fit into a relational context. Single actions are the product of interactions, deliberations, and desires over a period of time. Two examples can illustrate this approach to mortal sin. Consider adultery. The sinfulness of adultery does not reside simply in its being the physical action of intercourse with someone other than one's spouse. Even this physical act takes its meaning from the larger context of marital interaction, and the experiences of daily neglect, plans to meet someone else, frequent meetings, etc. The action that we call adultery is the accumulation of ongoing rejection and unconcern. We realize the gravity of this action in the context of the general direction of the person's life and the larger context of moral growth or decay.

For another example, recall the movie, *The Godfather: Part I.* Michael Corleone, the son of the Don, does not at first want to have anything to do with the family's business. Gradually he begins to associate directly with the hit-men of the family until he no longer disapproves of their action and their way of life. This pattern of actions and associations becomes the context for his conscious decision to avenge the attempt on his father's life. The actual act of murder which Michael performs is the embodiment of his decision to seek vengeance and change his way of life. In *The Godfather: Part II,* Michael becomes the new Don of the family. This shows that once the basic sin that involves a fundamental choice is committed, all other decisions share in the underlying malice of that basic choice to partially confirm and solidify it.

These two examples try to show that while mortal sin can and does happen through particular actions, we want to assert clearly that for these actions to be mortally sinful, in the proper sense of this term, they must be the expression of the person from the deeper levels of freedom and knowledge. For an action to be a mortal sin, it must really belong to the person as his or her own, and be expressive of the sort of person he or she has become and wants to be. Mortal sin, as an individual act, sums up a deteriorating commitment to life and love so as to identify and seal the selfishness that has already been developing.

This way of understanding mortal sin should caution us from naming as "mortal sin" physical actions in themselves apart from the person and the fuller context of personal interaction. An older Catholic theology appreciated this, too, with its distinction of *formal* and *material* sin. Formal sin is the only true sense of sin. It is precisely the action for which we are personally responsible because it proceeds from knowledge and freedom and so carries a significant degree of personal involvement. Material sin, on the other hand, is "sin" only in an analogous way. A material sin is an act of objective wrongdoing, an act which may even cause a significant amount of harm. But the objective wrongdoing itself does not automatically make doing such actions subjectively sinful. Not until we consider the significant degree of self-possession and self-determination that goes into an action are we truly able to name it sin, or more especially "mortal sin," in its most complete sense.

Contemporary theology's desire to emphasize the reality of sin in its proper sense, as expressing the involvement of the person in actions, would argue against using the term "sin" to describe external acts alone when viewed apart from the subjective involvement of the person. For this reason, the only possible answer to the straightforward question, "Is it a sin to do x?" (when "x" is any action taken in itself, and "sin" is understood to be formal sin), is to say, "It depends." What does it depend on? It depends on the subjective involvement of the person in doing the action. The most we can say about an action in itself is that it is objective wrongdoing (material sin) or objective rightdoing. Not until we consider the degree of involvement of the person can we claim sin, in its truest sense, to be present.

For this reason we should be careful with the way we read and use those actions traditionally listed as "mortal sins" in our catalogues of sins. To say an action is a "mortal sin" presumes that the action is done with evaluative knowledge and basic freedom. Unless this presumption can be verified, we ought to understand these designations of actions by themselves as "mortal sins" in a limited way. These are warnings for us which say that these sorts of actions are so potentially disruptive of the development of positive human relationships that we should want to avoid them. Also, if we find ourselves engaging in these sorts of actions, we ought to take a close look at the sort of person we are becoming. Bernard Häring, with his characteristically pastoral sensitivity, offers this advice:

> Sensible moralists have always realized that their categories regarding gravity of matter can serve only as a rule of thumb. They could be understood as a form of warning. "Danger." But they become senseless if they are used as criteria by a confessor-judge who wants to control the consciences of the faithful in accordance with these determinations of border-line.[17]

Above all, we need to be careful about ever judging another person to be committing mortal sin. No one holds such a privileged point of view so as to be able to judge, as an outside observer, the degree of subjective involvement in knowledge and freedom which goes into a particular action. Again, Bernard Häring offers some keen pastoral advice:

> No human being can give an accurate definition of how much freedom and awareness is necessary for a mortal sin that always means a sin proportionate to eternal damnation by an all-holy and all-merciful God. It is my conviction that there can be no mortal sin without a fundamental option or intention that turns one's basic freedom towards evil. And we have at least approximate criteria for determining whether a person lives with a fundamental option against God. That is, to presume that the person has no such option if, soon after the fall, he or she has genuine sorrow for the sin and continues to strive to please God and to do what is right.[18]

In this light, we should be very careful with the way we respond to the straight-on question, "Is this a mortal sin?" In answering, remember what it takes to make a mortal sin. Mortal sin says that this action in itself, or as the summation of a series of actions, is hopelessly destructive. In this action, the sinner closes oneself from a commitment to life and love. So when I am asked this straight-on question, my answer is cautious: "I don't know. Let's look at it." Then I want to explore questions like these: "In this action, and as a result of this action, is your relationship with God and neighbor still alive? Are you in fact still trying to love and serve?" Questions such as these try to reach the true meaning of the action, and the person's relationship with God and others. Mortal sin radically disrupts the person's relationship with God to turn the person away from an openness to life and to love. In short, if sins of such a radical closedness or destructiveness are not evident, then perhaps we can say that the sinner has not yet destroyed a basic commitment to love God and others. Perhaps we are seriously in the realm of venial sin.

VENIAL SIN

Only now that we have taken such an extensive look at mortal sin are we ready to understand venial sin. Venial sin is analogous to mortal sin. We have seen above that mortal sin demands a significant degree of self-awareness, self-possession, and self-determination so as to be an expression of one's whole life in a way that radically reverses one's positive relationship to God. The classic requirements for mortal sin which we explored above tell us that we enter into mortal sin with a clear head, open eyes, and committed heart. When we examine ourselves for the hallmarks of mortal sin by asking what have we done that is so monstrously evil, contemplated soberly, and then deliberately committed with the intention of making a personal affront to God, what do we find? Probably not much. Most of our selfish neglect takes less spectacular forms, is less clear-headed and open-eyed. These less spectacular forms put us in the realm of venial sin.

Venial sins represent those many free and not so free and open-eyed actions which do not embody the whole of our lives in such a radical way before God. Why does not every act carry such weight as to change radically the direction of one's life? For one reason, many of our choices and actions are not done with the open eyes of clear vision. We often do not see what is before us rightly, and so do not respond to what is really there. Furthermore, many of our daily choices do not appear to our consciousness as being so important as to demand the expression of full freedom. Most of our daily choices are not relevant enough to alter in a radical way our whole life plan. Most often these choices and actions spring from a more peripheral level of our being, and are not rooted in our hearts.

Another reason that not every choice is an exercise of fundamental option is that even after sincere reflection on more important decisions, tendencies remain in us which are not fully transformed by a heartfelt desire to express ourselves in a way that will transform the fundamental direction of our lives. We continue to be influenced by impediments to our knowledge and freedom, which prevent our actions from penetrating to the deepest core of our selves.

Simply put, then, venial sin is acting inconsistently with our basic commitment to be for life and love. Venial sin does not spring from the deepest level of our knowledge and freedom so as to change our fundamental commitment to be open to God, others, and the world. For example, while I may be fundamentally a caring person, my occasional acts of aloofness and causing harm do not radically change the sort of person I am, though they may weaken my commitment to goodness and love. This gives the serious character to venial sins. Even though they do not carry the weight of radical malice in the way mortal sins do, venial sins cannot be dismissed as being of no account.

If a pattern of actions that we judge to be venially sinful can weaken our commitment to goodness and love, can we objectively determine the borderline between mortal and venial sin? Determining this line is the goal of the legalistic mentality which wants to know: "How far can I go?" Theologians today generally agree that there is no possibility of giving an exact determination of where venial sin ends and mortal sin begins. The reason seems to lie basically in realizing that sin is not in the action itself, but primarily in the person. As the American Bishops have put it in their pastoral letter on the moral life, *To Live in Christ Jesus,* "We sin first in our hearts, although often our sins are expressed in outward acts and their consequences."[19] Because of the great diversity of genetic endowment, moral and psychological growth, and environmental influences, we are not able to draw clear objective lines that mark off without ambiguity when we are acting from the depths of our hearts to reverse radically the fundamental orientation of our lives to be for life and love.

These claims, that sin is primarily in the person and that we have no clear objective borderline between mortal and venial sin, in no way suggest that actions are of no account. They are. Actions, whether a "big deal" or not, have consequences not only for others but also for ourselves. The daily inch and quarter-inch decisions we make contribute to the sort of person we are becoming. We are always actively pursuing a way to be by the individual choices we make. Somewhere in the future lies the realization of the sort of person we have become by the small decisions we have already made. Bernard Häring summarizes well the issues pertaining to having no clear objective borderline between mortal and venial sin, and the seriousness with which we ought to take even our venial sins:

> My conviction is that an objective border-line, valid for all, between mortal and venial sin can never be determined. We can, however, say that a relatively small matter normally cannot be the object of a mortal sin. The emphasis is on *relative,* which means in proportion to the moral level, the maturity, the awareness and full use of freedom of the individual person. What one person does not consider as a grave matter can, for a very sensitive person, appear to be absolutely irreconcilable with God's friendship. A relatively small act of goodness will normally not turn a bad fundamental option into a good one, although it can be a first step in that direction. Similarly, each sin, if not soon repented, has the frightening possibility of being a first step or next step towards downfall.[20]

Another factor we need to appreciate about venial sin has to do with the degrees of freedom and knowledge which go into it. Mortal sin, as we have seen above, is a clear, conscious choice for evil. Venial sin, on the other hand, is not so clear and not always so conscious. In fact, most of the time we do not step into venial sin as a result of conscious rational deliberation. Rather, we *awaken* to the fact of venial sin in our lives. If we were to claim that we can sin only when we are consciously and deliberately choosing it, then we would be flying in the face of common observation.

Who among us truly consents to doing evil on a regular basis? Truer to our experience is that we find ourselves in sin when we examine our consciences and look back over what has happened and how it has happened. The significance of this for understanding venial sin is that focusing exclusively on deliberate choices is neither the best nor the only justifiable way of recognizing our sin. A more complete evaluation of the quality and direction of our moral lives will require a much more subtle examination of our basic commitment and the fundamental orientation of our lives.

To help make this examination, and to help understand our sin as more than deliberate rational choice, I want to suggest that we think of the moral life as a kind of story. Individual actions are like the incidents which make up the story. No action has its proper moral significance in isolation from the whole narrative. Since all moral action is interaction, each individual action finds its proper meaning from within the total narrative that is the moral life. The plot of our story is the fundamental orientation that flows from our basic commitment which gives shape to the stable identity of our moral character. We discover the plot only after we are well into the story. The plot is unveiled by looking back over what has happened and how it has happened. From the point of view of looking back, we are able to draw from the collection of continuous incidents a panorama that sets the background for each detail. Yet this panorama grows in quality and scope as the story unfolds. Once discovered, the plot yields a sense of integrity to the narrative that in the end penetrates each particular incident with meaning and significance that goes beyond the immediate context. In this way, we see what makes each incident in the story continuous with others and not just an isolated vignette.

This is what happens in the moral life as well. The moral significance of an action, or whether we are involved in sin or not, is often disclosed in retrospect. The examination of conscience is often the occasion for this awareness of awakening to sin. By looking back over our lives, we discover the true moral significance of individual actions. Often there is significance we did not fully realize at the moment of its happening, but which the unfolding history of our action and the ongoing story of our lives finally disclose to us.

We awaken to our being in sin by recognizing how particular incidents of our lives fit, or do not fit, into the integrity of the fundamental direction of our lives. For this reason, we can say that we have sinned even though there was no conscious, deliberate intention to do evil at that particular moment. The vantage point of looking back over the panorama of our lives to notice what happened, and how it happened, enables us to discover the sin which we have committed and are now living. The more clearly we become aware of God's love for us, and the more deeply grateful for that love we become, the more clearly we awaken to our venial sins and the more seriously we will take them. Our venial sins are what weaken the rootedness of our fundamental commitment to God and to being a loving person.

Furthermore, the more clearly we become aware of God's love for us and the more seriously we take our venial sins, the more attuned we will become to the call to conversion in our lives. The ongoing need for moral growth, the ongoing conversion that ought to mark our moral lives, is the movement bringing us back in line with our fundamental orientation of being committed to life and love. Entering into the Sacrament of Reconciliation regularly can help us maintain the clear direction of our fundamental commitment to be loving, especially when these sacramental moments are accompanied by a sincere examination of conscience. Before examining conscience in the next chapter, we need to draw out some of the implications of this analysis of sin for the confession we make in the Sacrament of Reconciliation.

WHERE WE ARE GOING

The approach to sin outlined in this chapter has some wide-ranging implications for the way we understand ourselves as moral persons, the way we make judgments about what is sinful or not, and the way we confess our sins. I would like to close this chapter by examining a sample confession of sins that is in line with the understanding of sin presented in this chapter. This sample confession needs to be seen in contrast to the one with which I began this chapter. There we saw "where we have been"; here we get a glimpse of "where we are going."

The personal, or covenantal, approach to sin developed in this chapter gives rise to an approach to confession which pays more attention to a revelation of the person than to detailing objective acts in number and kind. The new Rite of Penance calls for this:

> The sacrament of penance includes the confession of sins, which comes from true knowledge of self before God and from contrition for those sins. However, this inner examination of heart and the exterior accusation should be made in the light of God's mercy. Confession requires in the penitent the will to open his heart to the minister of God . . . (Par. 6b).

This means that personal revelation is being called for to a greater degree than material integrity of sinful acts in our confessions. We are being asked to share the patterns of relationships in our lives so that the healing and peace made visible in the ministry of the Church may restore and strengthen our relationships. Such a confession may go something like this:

> Father, I am a married man with three children. I work as an executive for a large computer firm.

> Today I come to confess before God and you that over the past month I have been responsible for allowing love to grow cold in my home and at the office. I have done this by making it difficult for some of our junior executives to have all the data they need to design a new program for the company. I am just so envious of their talents. They represent for me all that I have hoped to become. I resent their accomplishments. I have been so preoccupied with this that I have been inattentive to simple needs of my wife and children at home. I know I am generally a very caring person and I value what my family needs. I regret that I have become so self-centered this month.

131

I want to be able to give my junior partners the encouragement they need, and to give my family more time and attention. This week I am going to spend a full day with my
family and will be sure to affirm my junior partners in the
work they are doing.

Contrast this confession with the one which began this
chapter. What differences in the understanding of morality, the
moral life, and sin do you see there?

A confession like this focuses on an understanding of the
moral life that is largely concerned with promoting positive human relationships which allow the full potential of one's own
and others' gifts to be expressed. Within the context of these relationships, the moral life is seen as the process of constant
growth and conversion to becoming a certain sort of person in
and through the pattern of responses that make up our relationships. From this point of view, no longer is it enough to ask,
"What am I doing?" We must now ask, "What is my doing doing to me? What sort of person am I becoming?" Our moral lives
are reflected more in the quality of our characters and our relationships than in the thoroughness of our deliberations or in the
quantity of actions we do. Living morally is more a matter of appropriating the values which promote positive moral character
and life-giving human relationships than it is living within the
limits of law. Values are primary; laws are secondary.

Sin in this type of confession reflects the awareness of freedom to refuse to respond in love to love. Sin is selfishness pure
and simple. Sin ruptures or weakens the bonds of love which
sustain life-giving relationships. Sin is the failure to be who we
are and to do what we can to contribute to the growth of positive, life-giving relationships.

This confession of sins also recognizes that sin is not an isolated individual matter, but a social affair. Sin has an impact on
the total relational context of our lives. This confession recognizes that we belong to God and to others, and that our actions
have consequences. Our actions reflect a deeper reality that
gives the tone, quality, and direction to our lives. This deeper reality is our attitude which needs to be healed not only by chang-

ing the way we look upon those whom we love and who love us, but also by doing something positive to bring our behavior in line with the drift of our deepest desires for love and for life.

In this light, we approach the Sacrament of Reconciliation as a significant moment in the process of conversion. Through the sacrament, too, we experience the healing power of love welcoming us back into the fullness of the life and love of the community of reconciliation that is the Church.

The accompanying chart capsulizes some of the main features of the shift from where we have been to where we are going in our understanding of the moral life, morality, sin, and matter for confession. *(See chart on pp. 134–135.)*

FOURTH MOVEMENT: APPROPRIATING THE CHRISTIAN STORY

How does the above presentation of sin affect your understanding of sin? In what ways has this chapter affirmed you? In what ways have you been challenged? Complete the following sentences:

I realized that I . . .
I relearned that I . . .
I was surprised that I . . .
I wonder if . . .
I wonder why . . .
I wonder when . . .

FIFTH MOVEMENT: CHOOSING A FAITH RESPONSE

How might you recognize sin in your life now? What kind of confession might you be able to make now? Complete the following sentences:

Next time, I want to . . .
I need to think more about . . .
I hope that I . . .

ISSUE	WHERE WE HAVE BEEN	WHERE WE ARE GOING
Moral Life	Understood primarily in terms of what is allowed and what is forbidden. Being moral is a matter of avoiding bad actions.	Understood primarily as a matter of constant growth and conversion toward a life of love. Being moral is a matter of appropriating and expressing values which promote positive human relationships.
Morality	Morality is prescribed by law and measured by the quantity of actions obedient to law. Primary question: What am I doing?	Morality is the quality of our character and actions which promote a community of life and love. Values are primary over law. Primary question: What sort of person am I becoming?
Sin	A transgression of the law. Individualistic. Isolated, individual actions. Gravity of matter. How far can I go?	Selfishness: failure to respond in love; violation of a relationship. Communal consciousness. Rooted in attitudes and dispositions affecting relationships. Degree of freedom and awareness. Who should I be? Recognizes my failure to be who I am and to do what I can.

ISSUE	WHERE WE HAVE BEEN	WHERE WE ARE GOING
Matter for Confession	Complete list of sins.	What is happening in one's relationships.
	External actions seen in isolation from the whole of one's life.	Gets to the roots of external actions; focuses on attitudes, trends, the direction of one's life and the actions which express that direction.
	Kind and number.	Individual actions seen in the total context of one's life; actions express a pattern reflecting the fundamental direction of one's life.

Suggestions for Further Reading

Charles E. Curran	*Themes in Fundamental Moral Theology*
Sean Fagan	*Has Sin Changed?*
James Gaffney	*Sin Reconsidered*
Eugene Maly	*Sin: Biblical Perspectives*

135

Conscience to Examine

FIRST MOVEMENT: PRESENT ACTION

What is the "moral conscience" for you? How do you examine your conscience? What does the advice which says "Let your conscience be your guide" mean for you? How do you form your conscience? What place does the voice of authority have in your judgment of conscience?

SECOND MOVEMENT: CRITICAL REFLECTION

What has been the most significant influence on your understanding of conscience? What would a mature moral conscience look like for you? What have been the most important voices shaping your conscience?

THIRD MOVEMENT: THE CHRISTIAN STORY AND VISION

"Conscience" is another one of those words like "sin"—often used but little understood. This is really no surprise. Trying to explain conscience is like trying to nail jello to the wall. Just when you think you have it pinned down, part of it begins to slip away. We all know we have a conscience, yet our experiences of conscience are ambiguous and confusing. We struggle with conscience when facing those great decisions of life, such as the choice of a career, or of conscientious objection to war, or whether to pay our taxes which support defense projects. Yet we even feel the pangs of conscience over petty matters like jaywalking or taking cookies from the cookie jar. We are told that conscience enjoys inviolable freedom, yet we are often given rules so absolute in character that we wonder whether conscience matters at all. What is this thing called conscience? Which is the true conscience? What is it that we are to examine in preparation for the Sacrament of Reconciliation?

Try this exercise: draw a picture which depicts your understanding of conscience. Think about that for a moment. Now you may want to sketch your picture, or at least imagine it as vividly as you can in your mind.

I have begun adult education sessions on conscience with this exercise and have had some delightful and telling results. One person pictured conscience as a large head with a quizzical look on its face; another drew a picture of herself with her mother standing behind her speaking into her ear; a popular picture that often occurs is that of a little bird sitting on one's shoulder; someone else drew a picture of the shadow of herself; another drew a large finger pointing down through the opening in the clouds; one drew a picture of two cartoon figures, one in her head and the other in her heart, who were in constant dialogue; another drew a picture of a large lake reflecting the world around it. Are any of these familiar to you? What is the meaning of conscience that each represents? Which best depicts your sense of the "moral conscience"? What kind of picture did you draw or imagine?

This chapter will be a slow, long walk through some of the intricacies of moral conscience. After recalling the dignity of personal conscience upheld by the Catholic tradition, we will explore the meaning of personal moral conscience in our theological tradition. After establishing this understanding, we will be able to appreciate the important distinction between moral

137

conscience and the superego, a psychological notion of conscience. Only then will we be ready to take a long look at the issue of the formation of conscience, and the relation of personal moral conscience to the authoritative teachings of the episcopal magisterium. Finally, we will take a brief look at one method of examining conscience in preparation for celebrating the Sacrament of Reconciliation.

MORAL CONSCIENCE IN THEOLOGICAL TRADITION

We need to be clear about "moral conscience," since the Catholic tradition has long attested its primacy, dignity, and inviolability. According to the Catholic moral tradition, no one is to be forced to act contrary to his or her conscience. Here are a few "quotable quotes" from different moments in the Catholic tradition which point out the inviolability of conscience:

Fourth Lateran Council (1215):
"He who acts against his conscience loses his soul."

Thomas Aquinas (IV *Sent.*, d. 38, a. 4):
"Anyone upon whom the ecclesiastical authority, in ignorance of true facts, imposes a demand that offends against his clear conscience, should perish in excommunication rather than violate his conscience."

John Henry Newman (Letter to the Duke of Norfolk):
"Certainly, if I am obliged to bring religion into after-dinner toasts (which indeed does not seem quite the thing), I shall drink—to the Pope, if you please—still to Conscience first, and to the Pope afterwards."

Vatican II (Declaration on Religious Freedom #3)
"On his part, man perceives and acknowledges the imperatives of the divine law through the mediation of conscience. In all his activity a man is bound to follow his conscience faithfully, in order that he may come to God, for whom he was created. It follows that he is not to be forced to act in a manner contrary to his conscience. Nor, on the other hand, is he to be restrained from acting in accordance with his conscience, especially in matters religious."

Vatican II (Pastoral Constitution on the Church in the Modern World #16)
"In the depths of his conscience, man detects a law which he does not impose upon himself, but which holds him to obedience. Always summoning him to love good and avoid evil, the voice of conscience can when necessary speak to his heart more specifically: do this, shun that. For man has in his heart a law written by God. To obey it is the very dignity of man; according to it he will be judged.

"Conscience is the most secret core and sanctuary of a man. There he is alone with God, whose voice echoes in his depths."

While the dignity and inviolability of conscience in our tradition is incontestably clear, the meaning of conscience in the minds of many is not so clear. What does the Church intend to uphold when speaking of the inviolable dignity and freedom of conscience, as well as when referring to conscience as our "most secret core and sanctuary"?

The Roman Catholic tradition ascribes to three dimensions of conscience: (1) *synderesis,* the basic tendency within us toward knowing and doing the good; (2) moral science, the ability to know the particular good that ought to be done or the evil to be avoided; (3) conscience, the specific judgment of what we ought to do in a particular situation. In trying to simplify matters, Timothy O'Connell refers to these as conscience/1, conscience/2, and conscience/3 respectively.[1] By doing this, O'Connell is not proposing three different realities, nor three distinct stages through which conscience moves in developing from infancy to adulthood. He is simply expressing the three senses in which we can understand the one reality of conscience. We need to explore each briefly.

The accompanying chart summarizes briefly the main characteristics of each sense of conscience in our theological tradition. You may want to take a glance at this chart before proceeding with the more detailed analysis of the theological tradition.

Conscience/1 *(synderesis)* is a given characteristic of being human. This is the capacity for knowing and doing what is good

THREE SENSES OF CONSCIENCE

Conscience/1 (Synderesis)	Conscience/2 (Moral Science)	Conscience/3 (Conscience)
The sense of the fundamental characteristic of being human which makes it possible to know and do the good.	The sense of our way of seeing and thinking.	The concrete judgment of what I must do in the situation based on my personal perception and grasp of values.
Our general sense of value and fundamental sense of responsibility which makes it possible for us to engage in moral discussions to determine the particular moral good.	The realm of moral disagreement and error, blindness and insight.

The proper realm of the formation and examination of conscience. | The primary object of this judgment is not simply this or that object of choice, but being this or that sort of person through what I choose. |
| The fundamental condition which serves as the presupposition to moral agreement or disagreement on a particular issue. | Follows moral truth which it seeks to grasp by making use of sources of moral wisdom wherever they may be found.

The goal of its tasks is to reach "evaluative knowledge," personally appropriated, interiorized knowledge.

Searches for what is right through accurate perception, and a process of reflection and analysis. | This act of conscience makes a moral decision "my own" and the moral action expressive of "me" by realizing and expressing my fundamental stance.

This is the conscience which I must obey to be true to myself.

This is the "secret core and sanctuary" of our self which must not be violated (*G.S.* #16). Each "is bound to follow his conscience faithfully in all his activity so that he may come to God, who is his last end. Therefore he must not be forced to act contrary to his conscience" (*D.H.* #3). |

140

and avoiding what is evil. The very existence of this orientation to the good makes possible the lively disagreement over what is right or wrong in each instance of moral choice. The great array of moral disagreement which we experience in our lives does not negate the presence of conscience/1, but affirms it. Because we have *synderesis,* we share a general sense of moral value, and the general sense that it makes a difference to do what is right and avoid what is wrong. We cannot live morally without conscience/1, yet it is not sufficient in and of itself to enable us to choose what is right in each specific instance. What else do we need?

We need conscience/2 (moral science). The force of conscience/1 empowers us to search out the objective moral values of each specific situation to discover the right thing to do in each instance. Discovering the operative moral values and the right thing to do is the work of conscience/2. Its primary tasks are accurate perception and right moral reasoning. For this reason, conscience/2 receives a great deal of attention in moral education and in moral debates. Conscience/2 is the realm of moral blindness and insight, moral disagreement and error. Conscience/2 needs to be educated, formed, informed, examined, and transformed. In a word, conscience/2 is subject to the process called "the formation and examination" of conscience.

Since we will explore the formation and examination of conscience in more detail later, only a brief sketch of what is at issue here is necessary. In the realm of conscience/2 we learn how to see and how to think. In fact, we might say the goals of the formation and examination of conscience are correct seeing and right thinking. In its accountability to moral truth, conscience/2 is illumined and assisted in many ways to perceive and appropriate this truth. This means that conscience/2 is formed and examined in community. Only through dialogue with many sources of moral wisdom do we come to know what it means to be human in a truly moral way.

A more thorough exploration into the formation of conscience would need to consider at least the following sources of moral wisdom. As *humans* we consult our own experience as well as the experience of family, friends, colleagues, and experts in the field that pertains to the area of judgment at hand. We ana-

141

lyze and test the stories, images, language, rituals, and actions by which the various communities in which we participate live the moral life. As *Christians* we turn to the testimony of Scripture, the religious convictions of our creeds, the lives of moral virtuosos, and the informed judgment of theologians past and present who help interpret the traditions of Christian life. The Christian community lives by the stories of Christian faith which we need to penetrate and appropriate in order to live with a Christian awareness. As *Catholics* we have access to a rich heritage of stories, images, language, rituals, devotional practices and spiritual disciplines which nurture our moral vision and practice. We pay attention to these and to the official teachings of the Church which are pertinent to our areas of concern. We listen carefully to all these sources of wisdom and vision to inform our consciences.

Conscience/3 (conscience) moves us from perception and reasoning to action. The final judgment of what I must do and the commitment to do it is conscience/3. The general orientation to the good (conscience/1), and the specific grasp of what is right in this instance (conscience/2), converge to produce a judgment of what I must now do (conscience/3). The characteristic of the judgment of conscience/3 is that it is always a judgment *for me.* It is never a judgment of what someone else must do, but *only what I must do.* The quintessence of the dignity and freedom of conscience comes here in conscience/3: I must always do what I believe to be right, and avoid what I believe to be wrong. Conscience/3 is the sense of conscience which the Catholic tradition says cannot be violated, and it is what the Vatican Council called our "most secret core and sanctuary" (*G.S.* #16) where we are alone with God.

I find one of the best ways to illustrate conscience/3 at work is to refer to Sir Thomas More as portrayed by Robert Bolt in *A Man for All Seasons.*[2] In that play, Thomas More faces up to his conscience and the call to love God above the prestige of his service to the king. The whole play can be seen as a vivid study of living according to conscience and exercising the freedom of conscience, i.e., the freedom to think only what we believe to be true and to do only what we believe to be right. Three short excerpts illustrate dramatically the power and dignity of personal

142

conscience, especially the judgment of conscience/3. The first is a scene in which Thomas More defends his loyalty to the Pope against the charges of the Duke of Norfolk:

Norfolk: All right—we're at war with the Pope! The Pope's a Prince, isn't he?

More: He is.

Norfolk: And a bad one?

More: Bad enough. But the theory is that he's also the Vicar of God, the descendant of St. Peter, our only link with Christ.

Norfolk: *(Sneering)* A tenuous link.

More: Oh, tenuous indeed.

Norfolk: *(To the others)* Does this make sense? *(No reply; they look at* **More***)* You'll forfeit all you've got—which includes the respect of your country—for a theory?

More: *(Hotly)* The Apostolic succession of the Pope is—*(Stops; interested)* . . . Why, it's a theory, yes; you can't see it; can't touch it; it's a theory. *(To* **Norfolk,** *very rapidly but calmly)* But what matters to me is not whether it's true or not but that I believe it to be true, or rather, not that I *believe* it, but that *I* believe it. . . .[3]

In another place Thomas More again speaks to the Duke of Norfolk about the real roots of his opposition to the King's divorce of Queen Catherine and marriage to Anne Boleyn, and his refusal to sign the Act of Succession. In this scene he says,

More: And what would you do with a water spaniel that was afraid of water? You'd hang it! Well, as a spaniel is to water, so is a man to his own self. I will not give in because I oppose it—I do—not my pride, not my spleen, nor any other of my appetites but *I* do—*I*.[4]

In a third place Thomas More demonstrates the true freedom of conscience and the moral obligation to do only what one believes to be right. Here, too, we see that the judgment of conscience/3 does not extend to anyone else, and, with it, one stands alone with God.

> **Norfolk:** I'm not a scholar, as master Cromwell [the prosecutor] never tires of pointing out, and frankly I don't know whether the marriage was lawful or not. But damn it, Thomas, look at those names. . . . You know those men! Can't you do what I did, and come with us, for fellowship?
>
> **More:** *(Moved)* And when we stand before God, and you are sent to Paradise for doing according to your conscience, and I am damned for not doing according to mine, will you come with me, for fellowship?
>
> **Cranmer:** So those of us whose names are there are damned, Sir Thomas?
>
> **More:** I don't know, Your Grace. I have no window to look into another man's conscience. I condemn no one.[5]

These excerpts also serve to demonstrate the truth of the maxim, "Let your conscience be your guide." This maxim causes endless debate and confusion. We need to be clear about its proper implications.

To follow this maxim uncritically would be to inject the personal nature of conscience with a strong dose of individualism. Such individualism effectively cuts off the judgment of conscience/3 from other centers of moral wisdom. Yet we have seen that genuine conscience is formed in dialogue with other centers of moral wisdom. The work of conscience/2 is to carry on this dialogue. Daniel C. Maguire, moral theologian from Marquette University, explains well the personal yet communal sense of authentic formation and exercise of conscience in this statement: "The individual and supremely personal nature of conscience does not mean *me* against *them;* it means *me* distinct from *them* but intrinsically *with them.*"[6]

The proper implication of "Let your conscience be your

guide" follows understanding it as referring to conscience/3. When conscience/2 has done its moral homework well, it yields to conscience/3. In the last analysis, conscience/3 is the only sure guide for action by a free and knowing person. By following conscience/3 we express and realize our fundamental stance. We act true to the "self." Violating conscience/3 would be violating our integrity. If we have done all we could possibly do to inform ourselves of what would be the most responsible thing to do, then we will not be entering the realm of sin even if we do something which we later discover was the objectively wrong thing to do. This is the force of the integrity and inviolability of conscience.

To review the main features of our theological tradition on conscience, look over again the chart at the beginning of this chapter. There you can see in a schematic way the main characteristics of each sense of conscience in our tradition.

SUPEREGO AND MORAL CONSCIENCE

Psychology, too, has helped us greatly in our efforts to be clear about the meaning of conscience. The work of psychologists helps us understand the development of a mature conscience which is subject to all the vagaries of the human experience of growth and development. The various theories of conscience development can be telescoped into the following framework: the normal pattern of growth is from a conscience subject to external control (what we are told to do by someone in authority, or what we see others do) to a more internal, self-directing conscience (what we ourselves perceive to be right and want to do).

In other words, the one criterion of mature moral conscience is making up one's mind for oneself about what ought to be done. Note: the criterion says *for* oneself, not *by* oneself. The mature conscience is formed and exercised in community in dialogue with other sources of moral wisdom. The point also being made is that if a person spends his or her whole life doing what he or she has been told to do by some authority, or because it is expected by the group, then that person has never really made moral decisions which are his or her *own.* For moral maturity one must be one's own person. It is not enough merely to follow what one has been told. The morally mature person must be able to perceive, choose, and identify oneself with what one does. On the moral level, we perceive every choice as a choice between being an authentic or an inauthentic person. Or, as some would put it today, we act either in character or out of character. In short, we give our lives meaning by committing our freedom. The morally mature adult is called to commit his or her freedom, not to submit it. As long as we do not direct our own activity, we are not yet free, morally mature persons.

We can appreciate this goal of committing our freedom, or developing our character, as a morally mature person if we clear up the confusion between moral conscience and superego which contaminates so much of our thinking and conversing about the moral conscience. One of the most common errors and sources of confusion in talking about conscience, or in examining conscience, is to mistake what the theologians mean by "moral conscience" with what some psychologists mean about conscience when speaking of the "superego."

The conscience/superego mixup causes confusion about what it is we must form, follow, examine, and whose freedom we must respect as morally responsible adults. So many confessions in the Sacrament of Reconciliation are more clearly expressions of an overactive superego producing unhealthy guilt than they are the witness of an adult moral conscience renewing itself so that the moral person can serve God more lovingly and faithfully. But the moral conscience is not the superego. What then is the difference between them?

Psychologists of the Freudian school tell us that we have three structures to our personality: the *id*—the unconscious reservoir of instinctual drives largely dominated by the pleasure principle; the *ego*—the conscious structure which operates on the reality principle to mediate the forces of the id, the demands of society, and the reality of the physical world; and the *superego*—the ego of another superimposed on our own to serve as an internal censor to regulate our conduct by using guilt as its powerful weapon. The superego is like an attic in an old house. Instead of furniture, it stores all the "should's" and "have-to's" which we absorb in the process of growing up under the influence of authority figures, first our parents but later any other authority figures—teachers, police, boss, sisters, priests, pope, etc. Its powerful weapon of guilt springs forth automatically for simple faults as well as for more serious matter. The superego tells us we are good when we do what we are told to do, and it tells us we are bad and makes us feel guilty when we do not do what the authority over us tells us to.

To understand the superego we need to begin with childhood. As we develop through childhood, the need to be loved and approved is the basic need and drive. We fear punishment as children not for its physical pain only, but more because it represents a withdrawal of love. So we regulate our behavior so as not to lose love and approval. We absorb the standards and regulations of our parents, or anyone who has authority over us, as a matter of self-protection. The authority figure takes up a place within us to become the source of commands and prohibitions. Gordon Allport tells a delightful tale that illustrates graphically the way an authority figure takes up a place within us so that not only the context, but also the voice and formulation of the external person, arises from within.

> A three-year-old boy awoke at six in the morning and started his noisy play. The father, sleepy-eyed, went to the boy's room and sternly commanded him, "Get back into bed and don't you dare get up until seven o'clock." The boy obeyed. For a few minutes all was quiet, but soon there were strange sounds that led the father again to look into the room. The boy was in bed as ordered; but putting an arm over the edge, he jerked it back in, saying, "Get back in there." Next a leg protruded, only to be roughly retracted with the warning, "You heard what I told you." Finally the boy rolled to the very edge of the bed and then roughly rolled back, sternly warning himself, "Not until seven o'clock!" We could not wish for a clearer instance of interiorizing the father's role as a means to self-control and socialized becoming.

> At this stage the external voice of authority is in the process of becoming the internal, or propriate, voice of authority. The parents' task is to enlist the voice in behalf of virtue, as the parents themselves conceive virtue.

147

To illustrate the prevailing theory at a somewhat later age, let us say the parents take their son into the woods on a fam ily picnic. Under their watchful eyes he picks up the litter after lunch and disposes it. Perhaps a firm warning on a printed sign, or the sight of a passing constable, may also act as a monitor of neatness. Here still the moral backbone is on the outside.[7]

A simplified way of thinking about the difference between superego and moral conscience is to distinguish between the "should's" or "have-to's" and the "want's" as the source of commands directing our behavior. "Should's" and "have-to's" belong to someone else. "Want's" belong to us. As a friend of mine once reminded me, "Don't 'should' on me. I don't *want* to be the way you think I *should* be." He had it exactly right.

The commands of the superego that tell us what we "should" do come from the process of absorbing the regulations and restrictions of those who are the source of love and approval. The commands of the moral conscience, on the other hand, come from the personal perception and appropriation of values which we discover in the stories or examples of persons we want to be like. The moral conscience is the key to responsible freedom of wanting to do what we do because we value what we are seeking. Whereas the "should's" and "have-to's" of the superego look to authority, the "want's" of the moral conscience look to values involved which have become personalized and internalized. For this reason, a person with an overly developed, or overly active, superego has a difficult time distinguishing what God is really saying and calling him or her to do from what "mother said I should do."

Furthermore, the superego acts out of fear of losing love, or out of the need to be accepted and approved. The moral conscience, on the other hand, acts in love to the call to commit oneself in love. The commands of the superego do not emerge from the perception of value, but from the desire to be loved, or from the fear of losing approval.

John W. Glaser gives a more sophisticated contrast of the differences between superego and moral conscience in his valuable article, "Conscience and Superego: A Key Distinction."[8] In

148

the accompanying chart I have reconstructed Glaser's nine contrasting characteristics of the superego and moral conscience. This listing is not intended to be exhaustive. I have added emphasis to the points of contrast in Glaser's list, and I have slightly reworded his characteristics to bring his language into line with what I am using here.

Glaser points out in his article that the failure to distinguish between superego and moral conscience can cause some serious pastoral confusion. Some of this confusion is already evident in the way many adults approach and experience the Sacrament of Reconciliation, and in the way many priests use this sacramental moment as an opportunity to shape the penitent's moral life.

One area of confusion he points out is in the belief that we can make a transition from grace to serious sin and back to grace again easily and frequently. Such a belief leads to the phenomenon of mortal sin on Friday, confession on Saturday, Communion on Sunday, and back to sin again on Monday. However, the approach to serious sin that respects the dynamics of the theory of fundamental option which we explored in the last chapter, together with an understanding of the difference between superego guilt and genuine moral guilt, challenges such a belief that one can sin seriously, repent, only to sin seriously again—and do all this within a matter of days! The nature of genuine moral conscience which we are exploring in this chapter, together with the dimensions of human freedom, growth, and grace which we explored in the previous chapters, does not support such an easy and frequent transition.

Another area of pastoral confusion pertains to the appropriate form of confessional practice and confessional counseling. A confessional practice that services superego needs would be oriented primarily toward naming individual actions as sinful apart from their total context in one's life and would seek a penance as a form of punishment to guarantee acceptance and forgiveness. The priest's counsel in such an orientation would insist on a thorough confession of the number and kinds of past actions before they could be erased. Such an orientation too easily prevents both penitent and priest from seeing these individual actions as part of a larger future-oriented growth. Confessional counseling sensitive to moral conscience and moral growth

149

SUPEREGO	CONSCIENCE
1. *Commands* us to act for the sake of gaining approval, or out of fear of losing love.	1. *Responds to an invitation* to love; in the very act of responding to others, one becomes a certain sort of person and co-creates self-value.
2. *Turned in toward self* in order to secure one's sense of being of value, of being lovable.	2. *Fundamental openness* that is oriented toward the other and toward the value which calls for action.
3. Tends to be *static* by merely repeating a prior command. Unable to learn or function creatively in a new situation.	3. Tends to be *dynamic* by a sensitivity to the demand of values which call for new ways of responding.
4. Oriented primarily *toward authority:* not a matter of responding to value, but of obeying the command of authority "blindly."	4. Oriented primarily *toward value:* responds to the value that deserves preference regardless of whether authority recognizes it or not.
5. Primary attention is given to *individual acts* as being important in themselves apart from the larger context or pattern of actions.	5. Primary attention is given to the *larger process* or *pattern.* Individual acts become important within this larger context.
6. Oriented toward the *past:* "The way we were."	6. Oriented toward the *future:* "The sort of person one ought to become."
7. *Punishment* is the sure guarantee of reconciliation. The more severe the punishment, the more certain one is of being reconciled.	7. Reparation comes through *structuring the future* orientation toward the value in question. Creating a new future is also the way to make good the past.
8. The transition from *guilt to self-renewal* comes fairly easily and rapidly by means of confessing to the authority.	8. *Self-renewal* is a gradual process of growth which characterizes all dimensions of personal development.
9. Often finds a *great disproportion* between feelings of guilt experienced and the value at stake, for extent of guilt depends more on the significance of authority figure "disobeyed" than the weight of the value at stake.	9. Experience of *guilt is proportionate* to the degree of knowledge and freedom as well as the weight of the value at stake, even though the authority may never have addressed the specific value.

would pay attention to the larger context of the penitent's life and to the values that deserve preference in this context. Penance would be seen as a stage of conversion and would contribute to healing by restructuring one's future toward the important values at stake.

What would this distinction between superego and moral conscience look like when dealing with a pastoral problem? Glaser offers some illuminating pastoral approaches to certain issues of sexuality (an area notoriously susceptible to the tyranny of superego) which respect the difference between superego and moral conscience. For example, the following is a frequently made comment about the need of a superego: "Maybe an individual needs the dynamics of the superego to help himself avoid doing what he really wants to avoid, but cannot—e.g., masturbation. If we take this away, we may be robbing him of real help."[9] To this Glaser responds:

> First, there is the question of what such "support" is doing to his whole conception of God and his life of partnership with God. Second, the superego is far more infallible as a tormentor of failure than as a source of effective motivation. Hence the question: What is such support doing to his own self-concept? More often than not the superego will be ineffective in overcoming the urge to masturbate; but it will, with inexorable certainty, provide a self-devouring gloom following such an act. The disproportionate guilt will set up the very situation which immerses the individual in even deeper depressions, sense of failure and frustration, fixation on this matter, etc.: in short, the very situation which is most conducive to further masturbation.[10]

An actual case dealing with masturbation that was resolved by refusing to be based on the dynamics of superego went like this:

> A counselor told me of a case in which a happily married man with several children had been plagued by masturbation for fifteen years. During these fifteen years he had dutifully gone the route of weekly confession, Communion, etc. The counselor told him to stop thinking of this in terms of serious sin, to go to Communion every Sunday and to confes-

sion every six weeks. He tried to help him see his introversion in terms of his own sexual maturity, in terms of his relationship with his wife and children. Within several months this fifteen-year-old "plague" simply vanished from his life. By refusing to follow a pattern of pastoral practice based on the dynamics of superego, this counselor was able to unlock the logjam of fifteen years; by refusing to deal with the superego as if it were conscience, he freed the genuine values at stake; he allowed them to speak and call the person beyond his present lesser stage of sexual integration. We can pay rent to the superego but the house never becomes our own possession.[11]

Even though the superego is basically a principle of censorship and control, it still has a positive and meaningful function in our personalities. In children, the superego is a primitive stage on the way to genuine conscience. In adults, the superego functions positively when integrated into a mature conscience to relieve us from having to decide freshly in every instance those things which are already legitimately determined by convention or custom.

Yet the development from the superego of the child to the personal value perception of the adult moral conscience does not take place automatically. One of the tasks of moral education and pastoral practice in moral matters is to reduce the influence of the superego and allow a genuinely personal way of seeing and responding to grow. We can examine our pastoral practice on this score by asking, "Have I 'should' on anyone today? Or, have I drawn out of another what he or she perceives to be going on and wants to do?" One of the great temptations of confessional counseling is to "should" on the penitent. Yet the goal of adult moral education and adult moral development is to act more out of a personally appropriated vision and personally committed freedom and less out of superego.

The difference between the working of the superego in the child and the adult is one of degree and not of kind. In concrete cases, the superego and moral conscience do not exist as pure alternatives in undiluted form. We experience a mixture of these in our deliberations. Fr. Frank McNulty provides an illuminating example of this mixture in his account of the interior dialogue

152

he experiences in trying to decide whether to attend a wake service or not. The issue emerged when he did not think he would be able to go to the wake because of a meeting he already had to attend. But the meeting broke up early, and thus the need for the decision. Here is the account of his interior dialogue:

"Good. I will have a chance to attend that wake." (Conscience at work, saying, in effect: Frank, my friend just lost his father. Go to the wake; it will mean something to him.")

"Wait a minute. I can't go to that wake. I'm not wearing clerical clothes. Priests don't go to wakes dressed like this." (Superego warning about making a "bad" appearance, facing disapproval.)

"Why not? The important thing is consoling the bereaved. It's an act of charity. Look at Jesus and his example in Scripture, at how good he was to Mary and Martha when Lazarus died. Did he worry about what he was wearing?" (Conscience back again.)

"What will people think? Remember I was taught that a priest should even carry a hat to a wake. I don't have to do that, but at least I have to wear my clericals." (Superego)

"But I gotta go. I have the time. The family would like to see me there. It will mean a lot to them. I'll probably be the only priest there, since they don't know priests in the parish too well. Go to the wake." (Conscience)

"Well, if I go, maybe no one will recognize me. I can sneak in, say a quiet prayer and sneak out, without declaring myself as a priest." (Superego making a concession, but hanging in there.)[12]

(As it turned out, the family asked Frank to come forward and lead the rosary.) Attaining a mature moral conscience is the result of ongoing moral growth and development. For the Christian, this development happens in the context of the Christian community and under the influences of specifically Christian sources. This brings us to the issue of the formation of conscience, which is crucial to any thorough catechesis on the Sacrament of Reconciliation, and to the development of a mature moral conscience.

FORMATION OF CONSCIENCE

In the moral education of adults, the pastoral priority is to enable people to make their own moral decisions in light of the guidance of Scripture and the teaching of the Church. This means not so much providing answers to moral questions as encouraging the process of arriving at a moral decision. This brings us squarely into the domain of the formation of conscience.

The Range of Interest in Forming Conscience

What is the formation of conscience? We have already seen that this is the realm of conscience/2. Often, discussions about the formation of conscience are preoccupied with answering the practical moral question, "What ought I to do?" The emphasis then is necessarily placed on what we need in order to make a proper moral choice. In this sense, the formation of conscience becomes synonymous with doing our moral homework: acquiring right moral information by gathering pertinent data and appealing to relevant moral rules. In short, the formation of conscience becomes largely a matter of increasing a person's knowledge of facts and values. This is largely a rational matter of being properly informed so as to find the most adequate way to solve a moral problem.

This approach to the formation of conscience implies a particular view of the moral person. The moral person is primarily a judge, or decision-maker, whose principal task is to choose right. When the right "choice" becomes primary, the formation of conscience becomes a matter of acquiring the necessary skills for making right judgments. These are such skills as the ability to acquire accurate data dispassionately, the ability to consider all sides of an issue, the ability to provide sound reasons for a moral judgment, and the ability to have a decisive will to execute a judgment.

Certainly, the natural law tradition of Catholic moral theology encourages this kind of thinking. According to the natural law tradition, to be moral is to be reasonable. The Catholic tradition of natural law has been very optimistic about reason and has placed a premium in the moral life on developing the capacities for exercising reason rightly.

Following this approach to the formation of conscience, the examination of conscience would be largely act- or rule-centered. This means the examination of conscience would focus on "what I did." The process of the examination would entail checking the individual actions to be sure they are in line with moral rules, and reviewing the reasons and motives for acting to be sure they are valid and pure. In short, the examination of conscience would be primarily concerned with the actions done and with the justifications that have been given for them.

Our approaches to moral education and the moral development of conscience in recent years have been dominated by such a point of view. Craig Dykstra rightly calls it "juridical ethics."[13] A prime example of this point of view with its implications for moral education and the development of the moral conscience can be found in the theories of the Harvard social psychologist Lawrence Kohlberg. According to his theories, the moral life is primarily a matter of making choices about how to act in situations of conflict. Moral development is a matter of acquiring the ability to provide increasingly more principled reasons to justify those choices.

One of the dangers of this approach is that it can too easily split the intimate connection between religion and morality in our lives. Religious beliefs, for example, too easily become dispensable baggage in the moral life, since moral choices can be defended on grounds other than religious ones. Another danger with Kohlberg's approach is that, if we limit the formation of conscience to the development of moral reasoning for decision-making, we are placing a severe restriction on what is involved in the Christian conscience and are oversimplifying it. Conscience is concerned as much with "seeing" as with "choosing," and Christian beliefs have a great deal to do with shaping what we see.[14]

155

While decision-making and action are indeed important interests in the moral life, that is not all there is. What else is there? The range of interest in morality includes not only decision-making and action, but also the character of the moral person. We have already seen this wider range of interest operating in our discussion of sin. There we indicated that the determination of sin is not simply a matter of examining isolated actions against a set of moral rules. Determining sin involves the fuller orientation of the person. So we can expect the formation and examination of conscience to involve more than discrete actions and strategies for decision-making, but to include also the fuller texture of the person's moral orientation. As long as we can remember that morality is interested in *who we are,* as well as in *what* and *how we choose,* then we will not separate character and action from our consideration of the formation and examination of conscience.

The task of the formation of conscience is to answer not simply the practical moral question "What ought I do?" but also the prior moral question, "What sort of person ought I become?" This means that the aim of the formation of conscience is not simply to increase a person's knowledge of facts and values, but it is also to help that person become "virtuous."

Conscience and Character

Perhaps the most serious danger in concentrating on choosing and acquiring more principled reasons for the choices we make is that we fail to deal adequately with the formation of the sort of *character* we think it is important to acquire. The very way we describe a situation and the kinds of choices we make follow from the kind of character we have. Character gives rise to choice. Choices confirm or qualify character, for choices are self-determining. In choosing to adopt one or another course of action, we make ourselves into certain sorts of persons. Heroes and saints illustrate this most vividly when they refuse to compromise on matters which seem to others of little practical importance. Once again, Robert Bolt demonstrates this well in his portrayal of Thomas More. The scene takes place in the jail cell when Thomas More's daughter Margaret comes to persuade him to swear to the Act of Succession:

More: You want me to swear to the Act of Succession?

Margaret: "God more regards the thoughts of the heart than the words of the mouth." Or so you've always told me.

More: Yes.

Margaret: Then say the words of the oath and in your heart think otherwise.

More: What is an oath then but words we say to God?

Margaret: That's very neat.

More: Do you mean, it isn't true?

Margaret: No, it's true.

More: Then it's a poor argument to call it "neat," Meg. When a man takes an oath, Meg, he's holding his own self in his own hands. Like water. *(He cups his hands)* And if he opens his fingers *then*—he needn't hope to find himself again. Some men aren't capable of this, but I'd be loathe to think your father one of them.[15]

This scene emphasizes that any choice which really involves free self-determination includes one's whole self with it. Thomas More shows that when we do not act according to our character, our very self can be lost. Moral choices, at base, are matters of integrity: we act in character or out of character.

What is this "character" that is so important in the moral life? When we "size people up" to get a glimpse of their character, what do we attend to? We pay attention to patterns of actions which reflect attitudes, dispositions, the readiness to look on things in certain ways, and to choose in certain ways. These are indices of character, since character is not available for direct observation. Character identifies the responsive orientation of a person: seeing the world as a hostile or friendly place; being a person who loves and helps or one who is fearful and selfish. Character shows itself in its fruits—choices, actions, ways of being in the world and looking on the world.

157

We acquire character by directing our freedom to loyalties outside ourselves. Christian character is formed by directing our freedom to the person and message of Jesus as the ultimate center of our loyalty. In short, we become what we love. Character is what results from the values we make our own. When a value has woven its way into the fabric of our being, we delight in doing what pertains to that value. The just person "justices," and the loving person loves with such ease that we say such actions are "second nature" to these people. Character pre-disposes us to choose in certain ways, even though it does not predetermine every choice. We can act against character, and by making new choices we can change our character.

Attention to character has been the sorely neglected side of the formation of conscience. Some theologians today are encouraging greater attention to character as the more important side of the moral life.[16] These theologians are saying that who we are matters morally. We need to explore the moral import of "who we are." What is there in the nature and function of character that we ought to notice for its importance in the formation and examination of Christian conscience?

Conscience, Character and Vision

We need to notice "vision." *Vision* and *choice* are two key concepts that pertain to conscience and character. The contention of this approach to the formation of conscience is that vision is prior to choice in the moral life. After all, we choose what we do on the basis of what we see, and we see what we see because of who we are, our character. Think for a moment: What really makes us morally different? Is it the specific choices we make? Many of us make the same choices: to pay taxes, to resist violence, to visit the sick. We are morally different because of the underlying vision which provides the foundation for attitudes and choices.

Philosopher Iris Murdoch, who has contributed some foundational ideas to today's interest in vision and character, explains exactly what makes people morally different:

When we apprehend and assess other people we do not consider only their solutions to specifiable practical problems, we consider something more elusive which may be called their total vision of life, as shown in their mode of speech or silence, their choice of words, their assessments of others, their conception of their own lives, what they think attractive or praise-worthy, what they think funny: in short, the configurations of their thought which show continually in their reactions and conversation. These things, which may be overtly and comprehensibly displayed or inwardly elaborated and guessed at, constitute what, making different points in the two metaphors, one may call the texture of a man's being or the nature of his personal vision.[17]

From this we can conclude that the first task of the formation of conscience is the attempt to help us see. And so, the task of the examination of conscience is becoming aware of our vision.

The model of responsibility outlined in the last chapter already suggested that we respond to what we see. Before we can answer the question "What ought I to do?" we need to ask "What is going on?" This is the question of vision. Different visions lead to different choices. In fact, most of what appears in our decisions and actions is the result of what we see going on, rather than the result of conscious rational choices. Recall some examples from above: if we look on our children as a burden, we refuse to carry them, etc.

The "seeing" that is an expression of our character is more than taking a look. Seeing is interpreting and valuing as well. What we regard as worthy of our response depends on our "view" of things. What we see sets the direction and limits of what we do, generates certain choices rather than others, and disposes us to respond in one way rather than another. What is a choice for someone else may never occur to us as a choice at all, for we simply do not see the world that way.

The influence of vision on action forces us to expand our understanding of what constitutes a moral judgment. We are thinking too narrowly about moral judgment if we limit it to the results of applying rules in a rationally consistent way. Moral judgment is more than this. We also make moral judgments when we describe what we see: "My wife is a nag"; "My employer is bossy"; "She is always understanding"; "The fetus is innocent human life"; "My students are industrious"; "I always get defensive in his presence." These are moral judgments, not simply descriptive statements, because they evaluate what is going on in the world. As a result, they form the basis on which we make choices and take action. What is peculiar about these judgments is that they have nothing directly to do with rules or logical reasons. They have to do with vision, with the images through which we grasp what we see. Our decisions and choices follow upon what we see going on.

Conscience, Vision and Story

The importance of vision and character for understanding moral judgments of conscience cannot be emphasized enough. Most people most of the time do not make moral choices in the first instance on the basis of impersonal rules, rational abstractions, or logical procedures. Many of our moral decisions do not call for the leisure to sit down and ponder the rational dimensions, general principles and logical procedures that go into every choice. More often than not, the analysis that discovers such dimensions and procedures comes after the fact of the decision. The real world of our moral choices includes imagination, vision, habits, affections, dispositions, and countless non-rational factors that logical generalizations never account for in the immediate moment of making a decision. We make our decisions more out of the beliefs we live by and the habits we have formed than out of the principles we have learned. Linus is a prime example of this in his response to Lucy in this excerpt from one of the "Peanuts" comic strips. As Linus is preparing a snowball to toss, Lucy says:

> "Life is full of Choices.
> You may choose, if you wish,
> not to throw that snowball at me.
> Now, if you choose to throw that snowball at me
> I will pound you right into the ground.
> If you choose not to throw that snowball at me,
> your head will be spared."

> Linus: (Throwing the snowball to the ground)
> "Life is full of choices,
> but you never get any."[18]

160

This illustrates how much character, not rational principles, determines a decision or even whether a decision should be made at all. In this case, Linus' fear of Lucy, his belief that she will do what she says, makes up his mind for him, so to speak. Given what he sees and believes, there is no need to ponder any further.

Properly to understand moral behavior, then, we need to pay attention first to the images shaping the imagination, and the stories giving rise to these images, before we consider moral rules because we live more by stories than we do by rules. All of this tells us that examining deliberate choices and actions is not all there is to examining conscience, and learning moral rules is not the first task in the formation of conscience. We first need to learn *how* to see, and then we need to examine what we see.

Our vision is not something we provide for ourselves by ourselves. Vision is a community achievement. Social scientists tell us that as we grow the vision we acquire is in part the result of internalizing the beliefs and values of the particular communities which make up our environment. Our vision is almost wholly dependent on our relationships, on the worlds in which we live, and on the commitments we have made. As we become members of various communities, we adopt as part of our vision the ways of seeing that belong to those communities. Who we are and what we see become shaped by the causes and loyalties of these communities.

James M. Gustafson, a leading American theologian from the University of Chicago, cites a personal experience that illustrates well how his participation in a religious family and a church community which lived by the religious belief "God is love" shaped his character and vision. He says that the church building of his childhood had across its front a painting of the Gethsemane scene, and above it was printed, "God is love." The juxtaposition of the anguish and suffering of Gethsemane with the affirmation "God is love" made an indelible impression on him. This visual image, together with exposure to preaching on 1 John 4 by his pastor (who also happened to be his father), as well as the experience of human relationships in which the affirmation of God's love was embodied, came together to shape his character and his awareness of being loved by God even in mo-

161

ments of his spiritual suffering of uncertainty and doubt.[19] Gustafson's experience shows how both the historical experience of the community of the Church which gave formal expression to the conviction "God is love," and his lived personal experience of human relationships which affirmed that conviction, entered into the formation of his awareness and helped sustain him even when circumstances might have led him to object to such a conviction.

Yet the world of family and Church are not the only worlds we live in. Religious beliefs and stories are not the only ones that shape our lives. Each of us inhabits many worlds at one and the same time. Each makes demands on our loyalty, and each shapes what we see and value in the world. In addition to family and Church, a few other worlds in which we live are the world of our ethnic community, school, professional world, the world of sports, politics, commerce, advertising, and entertainment, to name a few.

To become aware of the strong impact these worlds have on us, try this little exercise in the formation and examination of conscience. Place yourself in the center of a series of concentric circles.

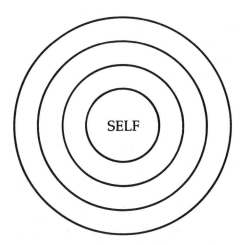

In each circle beginning with the one nearest you, place the name of the world which you think has had the greatest influence on shaping your character and vision. Name some of the concrete particulars of these worlds which have had a significant influence on you. To extend this exercise, arrange the worlds in the order of their greatest influence on your present attitudes toward these moral issues: divorce, homosexuality, pre-marital sex, the arms race, the use of drugs, euthanasia, and a moral issue of your choice. Do the worlds of family and Church take the lead in each instance? We are strongly influenced by many worlds which demand our loyalty and provide us with stories and strong images to shape what we see and value. An exercise like this may not help us become totally conscious of our vision, but it at least helps us see the ways our vision is shaped by participating in communities.

Each world we enter makes demands on our loyalty and is alive with many forms of communicating that loyalty. Rules and regulations try to do it, but stories, images, and rituals do it better. Through these latter means we come to see what life centered around the convictions of these communities is about, and how life is to be lived. The more we participate in the stories, rituals, images, and language of a community which has a great influence on us, the more we begin to take on its way of seeing.

Take the "community" or world of college and professional football, for example. The weekly exposure to the annual Fall ritual of the quest to be "No. 1" becomes the prevailing image that shapes our imaginations each autumn. Soon the image of being "No. 1" becomes the primary image through which we begin to see every form of human interaction. When this happens, then there must be a winner, and everyone is out to be victoriously undefeated. Without this Fall ritual and image, as well as the stories that go with it, the football season would be less exciting. But once we get immersed in this world of sports with its stories and images, it is very hard for us to see what is going on anywhere else in any other way. We may even find ourselves talking about having to "gain yardage" on a deal, or to run "interference" or to "punt," etc. Soon we may begin to approach all forms of human interaction with this image of "No. 1," which tells us someone must win and someone must lose. Aggressive competition, not harmony, is supreme. When everyone is out to be "No. 1," then our lives become filled with competition and conflict, and our styles of interaction become a mixture of aggressively offensive and staunchly defensive behavior.

Another world which shapes our vision and consequently our choices and ways of acting is the world of advertising. Consider how many of our preferences and ways of evaluating what is worthwhile in persons and in life are shaped by the powerful images communicated through the clever world of advertising. Look at the number of commercials on TV and on highway billboards which tell us that enough is not enough: "You need more . . ."; "Get more out of life by . . ." The advertising world's pursuit of "more" communicates a vision about life and how to live it meaningfully. We can soon take this vision of consumerism and use it to interpret the whole of our lives and our relationships. When we begin to look upon all our activities and people with a sense of insufficiency, and know that whatever we have is not enough, the newest, or the most improved, then we have been converted by the images of this world of advertising, and the rest of our lives become shaped by it.

The strong influence of the business world was graphically brought home to me while I was watching the Oregon Shakespearean Festival's production of Arthur Miller's *Death of a Salesman*. This play is a strong indictment of society for its failure to provide its members with a worthy vision of life. The vision which ultimately destroys Willy Loman is born out of his belief in unrestrained individualism and his worship of success. Willy could not make this vision of life work. The competition of the business world, and the pressures of a success-oriented world in which respect is earned by achievement, eventually drive him mad. In a world that looked upon love, acceptance, and respect as something to be earned by achievement, failure was unbearable. The "successful" vision of Willy Loman's world finally led him to suicide. Part of his tragedy is that he had no other story to replace the vision his business world had given him.

These examples of the religious world of James Gustafson and the non-religious worlds of sports, advertising, and business give us a sense of ways our vision is shaped by the multiple worlds in which we live. Each world communicates what is "good" and how life ought to be lived. These examples show clearly that most of what we see does not lie in front of our eyes but behind them in the images that make up our imagination. Images and the imagination, then, are extremely important for the moral life, for personal vision is the result of internalizing images which come to us through our experiences of living in different worlds.

Conscience, Imagination, and Christian Stories

The imagination is a powerful moral resource not to be equated with fantasy or make-believe. Our imagination shapes what we see, feel, think, judge, and act because all thinking relies on images. We are guided and formed by the stories and images that dwell within us even more than we usually think ourselves to be. Our imaginations, shaped by stories and images, involve a kind of felt knowing in which we hold together both what we know about something and how we feel about it. Mary Warnock, in her study *Imagination,* explains this integrating function of the imagination well when she says:

> There is a power in the human mind which is at work in our everyday perception of the world, and is also at work in our thoughts about what is absent; which enables us to see the world, whether present or absent as significant, and also to present this vision to others, for them to share or reject. And this power, though it gives us "thought-imbued" perception (it "keeps the thought alive in the perception"), is not only intellectual. Its impetus comes from the emotions as much as from the reason, from the heart as much as from the head.[20]

The imagination brings together into a meaningful whole the sights, sounds, and other sensations which fill our lives.

Our story-filled imaginations determine what we see and so influence how we respond. Through the stories and images of our imaginations, we reach out and touch the world. Every teacher knows the power of apt examples, and every preacher knows the effect of a story well told. Frequently our students or congregations do not understand a simple point, not because they lack intelligence, but because their frame of vision has them looking in the wrong direction. A good example, or a well-told story, turns their attention to another set of images. Suddenly all is clear: "Oh! I've never seen it like that before!" From the point of view of the imagination, moral conversion is a matter of repatterning the imagination so as to see dimensions of reality that were not available to us before. (Recall the metaphor of "pentimento" taken from Lillian Hellman to illustrate conversion in Chapter One.) When we begin to see differently, we will begin to respond differently. The challenge to pastoral ministry is to feed the imagination with the Christian stories and images through which we can see the world and respond appropriately.

Christian morality is based on the conviction that God in Christ is the final source of moral goodness, the ultimate center of value, the final object of our loyalty. All other "goods" are good only in a relative way to this most basic good. Christian morality believes that the stories and images that come to us in the Christian story portray and describe goodness in the moral life and provide truthful ways of seeing the world.

Undoubtedly, our Christian stories and images will be in competition with others coming to us from the various worlds in which we live. Each world tries to tell us something about what is good and how life ought to be lived. The important question before us, then, is how decisive our Christian believing and beliefs ought to be for shaping our moral awareness. As James Gustafson would have it, "they ought to be the most decisive, most informing, most influencing beliefs and experiences in the lives of people."[21] However, how decisive they actually are will depend on the many ways one has appropriated them in becoming a Christian.

The Church is the one community directly and uniquely responsible for communicating the stories of Christian faith which ought to shape and nurture Christian character and conscience. Herein lies the challenge to the pastoral ministry of preaching, teaching, celebrating, organizing, and individual pastoral care. The importance of the Church in the formation of a Christian conscience is that it hands on particular stories (along with rituals, images, language, convictions, and forms of action) which express a Christian vision. The incorporation of these stories into our own way of seeing, feeling, thinking, judging, and acting can help us engage in the world as a people formed by Christian faith.

The challenge to pastoral ministry is to retell these stories in order to shape and nurture Christian vision. Through its stories of God, Christ, the Spirit, and images of grace, sin, forgiveness, liberation, and its liturgical rituals and spiritual disciplines, the Church can focus our vision on realities we might not otherwise see, and also help us see more deeply into those realities we have begun to take for granted. Because stories shape our interpretation of what is going on, they help us determine in part what is of moral significance to us. They help us see and clarify what we are up against. They help us see what values are at stake, what attitudes are fitting, what principles ought to govern our actions on particular occasions, and what means of action are appropriate.

How might this work in a pastoral setting? There is space in this chapter for only a brief suggestion. The Bible, without a doubt, is the primary source of our stories of faith which ought to shape the Christian conscience. The stories of Jesus, and the stories about Jesus, are the stories par excellence for forming a Christian conscience. This is very good reason, then, for priests and penitents to be sure to include a Scripture reading in any examination of conscience and celebration of Reconciliation. Only through these stories of faith will we be able to experience the conversion which springs from our commitment to God in Christ and transforms the imagination itself. Living as a disciple in our day requires converting our loyalty to God in Christ into a way of life. Living as a disciple necessarily entails forming a Christian imagination. As we hear the stories of Jesus and about Jesus, and as we retell them again and again, our inner eye of love guiding our actions changes.

Through a collage of biblical materials—healing stories, nature miracles, parables, the teachings on the mountain, the passion and infancy narratives—we meet Jesus as the central paradigm of the Christian moral life. He becomes our chief source for the Christian way of looking on the world and responding to it. What might happen to someone who would allow the stories of Jesus to shape his or her imagination? Bruce C.

167

Birch and Larry L. Rasmussen have given a succinct description of what might happen:

> Her general way of seeing life might become characterized by a set of acquired and nurtured moral sensitivities that search out those often invisible to many in society—the poor, the outcast, the ill, and infirm. She might come to possess a basic posture toward life that is more sensitive than most to human suffering and is at the same time unconcerned with her own needs. She might have a "feel" for where people hurt and be able to empathize deeply. She might acquire certain specific dispositions, such as an attitude of initial strong trust in people and a lack of suspicion and fear of strangers, an underlying hopefulness about improvement of the human lot, a deep appreciation for non-human life in the world of nature, and a severe impatience with people's claims to high and enduring achievement. There may be particular intentions present as well, all of them with plausible ties to the reigning example of Jesus in her life: to always seek non-violent resolution to conflict; to champion the causes of the oppressed; to seek the kingdom of God before all else.[22]

When we allow Jesus to be the major image in our imaginations, and the stories of Jesus to shape our imaginations, these are some of the results that may happen in defining what is real for us, in gathering moral priorities, and in disposing us to act in certain ways.

If discipleship means anything, it means the commitment to listen constantly to the Christian story in the depths of our hearts, and to allow our vision and choices to be shaped by what we hear. By allowing our imaginations to be transformed by these stories, we discover truly redemptive responses to life.

Conscience and Decision

From vision comes choice. Even with our emphasis on the priority of vision in the formation of conscience, we still have a place for decision. Our decisions come out of our vision and character. We respond to what we see. The response we make is shaped, too, by the sort of person we have become. In fact, being a good person has a greater influence on our decisions than any system of principles or methods of decision-making. Since we choose on the basis of what we see and who we are, we need some way to check our vision and character. As we said above, the properly informed conscience sees rightly. Do we see what is really there? Or do we see just what we want to see?

A fundamental axiom of Catholic morality is that morality is based on reality. Asking the right questions about the meaning of our human situations is the way to move toward seeing reality rightly. Reality-revealing questions can help us test our vision, character, and our conscience. Daniel C. Maguire offers several which we can use for this test. He asks: What? Who? When? Why? How? What if? What else?[23] We will examine them briefly to see how they help us set our sights on what is real in our human situations.

What is the human situation of this moral reality? *What* may seem too large as a question since it can stretch over all others. However, it does fix our attention on the primary data (physical, psychological, systemic) through which we first meet our world. Good moral judgments are those which fit the situation as it really is. *What* helps us see what is really there. *What* presses us to make distinctions where there are true differences. Unless we see the differences we will not respond to what is really there. Many, if not most, moral disagreements result from the ignorance of what is really the case. Whether war is justified, for example, depends on what war is, what nuclear weapons do. In medical matters, we need to know what chemotherapy does, what death is, what abortions do. In sexual matters, we need to know what masturbation does, what contraceptive pills do, what sexual intercourse is. For everyday morality, we need to know what smoking does, what car pooling does, what over-working and over-eating do.

Next is *who*. We have already explored some of the *who* dimension in our discussion of character. There we saw that character brings important dispositions to bear on our actions. For example, if I am more like Gandhi than Hitler, that will alter the reality of any situation of conflict. Whether I am an authentic conscientious objector or a coward alters the reality of my draft registration. Whether I am a diabetic or not affects the morality of my eating habits. The *who* also includes the other persons involved in the decision. The moral reality of sexual intercourse, for example, is different when my partner is my spouse or my neighbor.

The third and fourth questions are *when* and *where*. Driving 55 mph has different moral meaning when it is done in a school zone at three o'clock than when it is done on Interstate 80. And we all know the difference between yelling "fire" on a rifle range or in a crowded movie theater.

Why and *How* are the next two questions. They also have something to do with character. *Why* is the critical question of motivation that sends us back to clarify our values. What looks like love at the *what* level might truly be manipulation at the *why* level. For example, why do I care for my ailing parents? Is this an expression of love and sincere care on my part, or do I intend to guarantee a substantial cut of the inheritance? Why do I give such large donations to St. Jude's Hospital? To promote the efforts of health care and research carried on there, or to qualify for a sizable tax deduction? "The last temptation is the greatest treason: to do the right deed for the wrong reason," as Thomas à Becket puts it in T.S. Eliot's play *Murder in the Cathedral.*

Answering the *why* question well demands a great deal of personal honesty and integrity. The real enemy is rationalization. We can con ourselves so easily. Wholehearted wanting is the only sound basis for our *why.* Of course, we act for many reasons. We are a mixed bag of motives. We never do anything for only one reason. An examination of conscience helps us become more keenly aware of the real *whys* behind our actions, even if we cannot become conscious of all the motivational forces. The more serious the act, the more critical it becomes to know why we are doing it. A truly healing confession of sins would be able to name the real *whys* and face the false ones.

But good motivation is not all that matters. "The road to hell is paved with good intentions" is a familiar part of Christian folk wisdom,and for good reasons. No matter how noble the motive, the *how* must be taken into account in making a moral decision and in examining conscience. *How* can even tell us much about our *why. How* is a matter of style; it gives expression to our true convictions and real character. Our real *why* sneaks through

170

to show itself in our *how* all too easily. Today we are hearing more and more people assert that while the *why* of saving many American lives in World War II was a good one, the *how* of atomic bombing Nagasaki and Hiroshima did not justify the killing and maiming of thousands of Japanese civilians, or that while the *why* of bringing on emotional calm is a good one, the *how* of taking drugs may not justify the physical and psychological dependency that results.

Overlapping the *how* question are the *what if* and *what else* questions. *What if* probes foreseeable effects. Actions have consequences. The full moral reality of our actions is not limited to the immediate present, but extends into the future as well. Moral responsibility requires that we foresee the impact of our behavior as far as is possible. This is not to say that consequences alone determine whether our actions are right or wrong. This is excessive. The reality-revealing questions point to other factors as well. But because consequences are so often the focal point of moral meaning, foreseeable effects demand our serious attention. The great moral enemy is short-sightedness, the failure to look beyond the immediate good we seek to the evil effects we cause along with it. Our moral universe is not limited to our contemporaries, nor to the immediate moment. Moral responsibility, which is always interpersonal responsibility with a history, has swollen to planetary size and extends through the generations. Discussions surrounding the arms race confirm this. The present tense of our moral action cannot preclude the future. We have learned this lesson all too well in our fight with ecological balance. Action in morality, as in our ecosystem, is interaction. Agency is influence. This is the force of the *what if* question.

We must beware of making decisions based on one or two effects, or of extending consequences only into tomorrow but not the day after. For example, we need reflection on the foreseeable effects of marijuana. Its immediate consequences seem harmless enough, a mild high and no hangover. But what of the possible long range consequences of genetic deformation and brain damage? We also need reflection on the use of prescription drugs to settle tension caused by work. For many people, solving these tensions on the level of biological calm is to ignore the real

171

source of tension which is often interpersonal, not biological, in the first place. As a result of taking the drugs, the effect is not only physical calm but also physical and psychological dependence on the drug, as well as ignoring the needed changes in one's interpersonal relationships. (Incidently, here we see that *why* we take drugs is as serious as the *what if.*) We also need to ask about the foreseeable effects of prolonging a person's dying by the use of machines, of adopting children by single persons, of using pesticides on our lawns, farms, golf courses, and of shoplifting even if it is "nickel-and-dime" stuff.

One thing is for sure when we begin to explore *what if.* We face head-on the stark reality that there is no such thing as a totally private moral act. "It won't affect anyone but me" is an impossibility when we take the relational dimension of our lives seriously, and the consequences of our actions just as seriously. One of the most frequently forgotten dimensions of our examination of conscience and confession of sins is the communal or social dimension of our lives. The *what if* question refuses to let us escape the fact that we belong to others.

Following closely behind the *what if* question is *what else.* What else can be done? What are the viable alternatives? If we think we are forced into an either/or choice, we ought to look again. We generally have more alternatives open to us than we think. What alternatives do we have to abortion for the unwanted pregnancy, to oil as our primary source of energy, to driving alone to work, to working overtime five days a week, to television as our primary source of family entertainment? The point is that when we make moral decisions that inevitably have some good and some bad outcomes, we need to explore alternatives. If there were no alternatives, there would be no moral problems. Too often we make bad moral choices not because we are bad people, but because we are just too unimaginative. We are not able to see the rich potential for good that lies within us and in our situation. Asking *what else* keeps us open and challenges us to be creative and to consult a wide base of moral wisdom and moral vision.

This, then, briefly sketches the reality-revealing questions which help us check our vision in order to see the reality of our human situation for what it truly is. But beyond asking these questions, the mature moral conscience also consults a wide base of moral wisdom and vision to highlight values of our human situation which might otherwise go unnoticed if we were left on our own. Two fundamental sources of moral wisdom and vision for the Catholic Christian to use in the formation and examination of conscience are Scripture and the teachings of the Church. Since our treatment of character and conscience showed the strategic and indispensable role that Scripture and the community play in the formation and examination of conscience, we only need to direct our attention here to the role of the teachings of the Church in the formation of conscience. In the Catholic view, properly informed conscience is inescapably ecclesial. What is the relation, then, of personal moral conscience to the authoritative teaching of the Church?

PERSONAL CONSCIENCE AND AUTHORITATIVE TEACHING OF THE CHURCH

Many Catholics feel that the dignity and freedom of conscience highlighted at the beginning of this chapter have to be compromised when they seem to disagree with the official moral teachings of the pope and bishops. However, this ought not to be the case. We need to explore the proper relation of the teaching authority of the Church to personal conscience.

Since the encyclical letter *Humanae Vitae* of Pope Paul VI in 1968, we have had extensive discussions of the normative character of non-infallible teaching by the pope and bishops (the episcopal magisterium), especially in moral matters. These discussions have shown that while a moral teaching may not be defined as infallible, this does not mean that such a teaching is meaningless, useless, or irrational. It means simply that these teachings, while subject to re-evaluation and the possibility of revision, are still useful for teaching and for highlighting moral values in moral decision-making. By accepting the limitations of the episcopal moral magisterium in specific moral cases, and in formulating moral teaching in the form of particular behavioral norms, we in no way diminish the normative character of the teaching authority of the episcopal magisterium nor the respect due it. The episcopal magisterium remains normative when it has formulated specific moral teachings and behavioral norms for specific moral cases. This means that in the formation of one's conscience, the Catholic must take into account the teaching of the episcopal magisterium. For a Catholic to make a decision of conscience with indifference to, or in spite of, the episcopal magisterium would be forfeiting one's claim to be acting as a loyal Catholic and according to a properly informed conscience. As "normative," the teaching of the episcopal magisterium deserves the presumption of truth on the part of the faithful.

There are good reasons for giving official teaching of the Church on moral matters the presumption in its favor. One reason is that Catholics believe that the Holy Spirit dwells within the whole Church to guide and illumine its actions. Another reason is that the sources of moral wisdom (such as Scripture, the teaching of theologians past and present, scientific information, broad human experience, and the witness of moral lives, to name but a few) are so many and complex that it is hard for any one person to know about all of them, to understand them, or to put them together to make a good decision. Furthermore, the episcopal moral magisterium of the Church approaches moral issues with a concern to protect and improve human dignity. The episcopal magisterium can draw upon worldwide resources to overcome the biases of a particular culture when putting a moral perspective together and taking a moral stand. For reasons like these, an attitude of openness of mind that desires to learn from this teaching, and a readiness of will to assimilate the teaching and make it one's own, are the proper and first responses due the official teaching of the Church. These kinds of responses give the respect to normative teaching that is proportionate to the pastoral office of the episcopal magisterium.

However, although we accept the many advantages that the episcopal magisterium has in taking a moral stand, and although we should give the presumption of truth in its favor, we cannot conclude that the loyal Catholic conscience will, in every instance, conform absolutely with the specific behavioral norms of the episcopal magisterium in moral matters. Official Catholic documents also admit as much. For example, the proper relationship of personal conscience to the teaching authority of the Church is suggested in this statement of the Vatican document on religious freedom: "In the formation of their consciences, the Christian faithful ought carefully to attend to the sacred and certain doctrine of the Church" (*D.H.* #14). The earlier version of this text said that conscience must be formed "according to" the teaching of the Church. This version was rejected as being "overly restrictive." The rendering "according to" would make the precise behavioral prescription found in the Church's teaching the exclusive basis of any moral judgment. However, this would not be in keeping with the long-standing Catholic tradition on conscience. The accepted version of "attend to" admits that no Catholic should simply ignore the moral teaching of the Church, or treat it as irrelevant. To follow one's conscience and to be a loyal Catholic, one must take into account the teaching of the magisterium. This is not to say, however, that the specific behavioral prescriptions of the official teaching of the Church become the exclusive basis of one's conscientious judgment. They are important and indispensable, but if they were the exclusive basis of the judgment of conscience, then we would never have had to explore all the dimensions of the formation of conscience that we have been exploring thus far.

The *Pastoral Constitution on the Church in the Modern World* also had something rather significant to say on the relation of personal conscience to the authority of the Church:

> Let the layman not imagine that his pastors are always such experts that to every problem which arises, however complicated, they can readily give him a concrete solution, or even that such is their mission. Rather, enlightened by Christian wisdom and giving close attention to the teaching authority of the Church, let the layman take on his own distinctive role.

> Often enough the Christian view of things will itself suggest some specific solution in certain circumstances. Yet it happens rather frequently, and legitimately so, that with equal sincerity some of the faithful will disagree with others on a

given matter.... They should always try to enlighten one
another through honest discussion, preserving mutual charity and caring above all for the common good (#43).

These statements bid farewell to the dependency instinct in
all of us. We need to be clear about what these statements do
say and what they do not say. They do not say that we should
never consult before making personal decisions. They do not say
that we should stay completely to ourselves in deciding what to
do. The judgment of conscience properly formed takes seriously
that we are members of a community, and that we are limited in
our personal experience of value and vision of what is good. We
can learn from the community's experience, vision, and reflection. So we need to listen to the community's wisdom and tap
the resources of the community's moral memory in forming our
consciences.

However, these statements do suggest that all of us have
certain competencies and areas of responsibility that we must
learn to respect. As we become more knowledgeable about the
Christian moral demands in these areas, we ought to bring this
wisdom into the service of the entire Church. These statements
recognize that a well-formed conscience willingly faces the limitations of moral experience and the formulation of moral norms
to know that ultimately every moral choice remains a personal
responsibility. The complex and changing character of moral di-
lemmas, and the dignity of the human person, would have it no
other way.

Most recently, the official text of the National Catechetical
Directory, *Sharing the Light of Faith,* gives some guidelines for the
relation of personal conscience to the moral magisterium of the
Church. The Directory recognizes the significant place that the
teaching of the episcopal magisterium ought to have in the formation of the Catholic conscience when it says:

Catholics should always measure their moral judgments by
the magisterium, given by Christ and the Holy Spirit to express Christ's teaching on moral questions and matters of belief and so enlighten personal conscience (#190).

At the same time, however, the Directory goes on to recognize implicitly the limitations of the binding power of this teaching:

> It is the task of catechesis to elicit assent to all that the Church teaches, for the Church is the indispensable guide to the complete richness of what Jesus teaches. *When faced with questions which pertain to dissent from non-infallible teachings of the Church, it is important for catechists to keep in mind that the presumption is always in favor of the magisterium* (#190). (Emphasis added)

With these statements the Directory suggests the kind of respect due the teaching authority of the Church. This respect demands that we give serious attention to the teaching, and that we receive the teaching with an openness that is ready and willing to make the teaching our own. In this way, when we act upon it, we will do so because we are personally convinced of the teaching. That is to say, we would be acting from evaluative knowledge. An appropriate response to the moral teaching of the Church, then, is not unquestioning acceptance, or blind obedience, but a thoughtful attempt to assimilate the teaching.

Approaching the authoritative moral teachings of the Church with an attitude of docility and a readiness to give the presumption of truth in its favor does not exclude the possibility of disagreement between the moral teaching of the episcopal magisterium and personal conscience. After all, the very nature of a "presumption" is that it is conditional. This means we hold to it until we come to clear evidence that overrides the presumption, or confirms it. The presumption of truth must ultimately yield to the truth of the evidence when this is found. Therefore, with sufficient reason and solid evidence, a Catholic can take a stand that disagrees with certain aspects of an authoritative teaching in moral matters. While not disagreeing that the episcopal magisterium can and ought to teach on moral matters, one may have sufficient reason to disagree with the particular formulation of a value, or with whether a particular case fits the application of a given formulation of a value. To dissent in this way is not an act of disloyalty. When done respectfully and thoughtfully, such a dissenting stance can enhance the Church's teaching by making a contribution to a more accurate rendering of a moral position.

History has shown that unless particular teachings become reformulated because contrary opinions raise significant challenge to them, there would be no moral progress, and no communal progress to moral truth. We have already experienced the results of this process of thoughtful disagreement in the very dialogue that brought us the documents of Vatican II. The current official position on religious liberty is an excellent example. If John Courtney Murray had not been a thoughtful yet respectfully dissenting voice on this issue in the Church during the years preceding the Council, we may not have had the position we have today. That we have a different climate in the Church today is due to the fact that there have been conscientious people who have asked challenging questions and have given good reasons for alternate positions to those officially accepted by the Church.

If we can appreciate the importance of taking a critically alert, thoughtful, and respectful approach to official teaching of the Church, then we will realize that disagreement in the Church is indeed a possibility and a necessity. We must have room for legitimate criticism and conscientious decisions different from those of the teaching office of the Church, if we are ever to have growth, development, and a clearer grasp of moral truth in the Church.

The tension between conscience and authority will always be with us. No external authority can ever replace conscience. Yet conscience can never be properly formed without the help of the wisdom of the voice of authority. Because we know how easy it is to deceive ourselves, and because there is normally a presumption in favor of authority, we sometimes take for granted that the authority is automatically right and any contrary opinion is automatically wrong and disloyally disobedient. This need not be so. Both authority and conscience are complementary aspects of the search for what is true and good. Authority may continue to insist on conformity, but conscience will continue to cry out for its own dignity and freedom.

AN EXAMINATION OF CONSCIENCE

I want to end this chapter by outlining a method of examining conscience. This method integrates the themes we have explored by beginning with characteristics of a style of life committed to reconciliation, then moving through the mystery of grace, and on into a person-centered approach to sin and conscience. This method helps integrate the dynamics of the moral life and spiritual life as a single effort to respond to the call of God in our lives. The goal of examining conscience is to come into touch with the deepest orientation of our lives and to determine whether our vision and choices are in line with an orientation toward God, toward life, and toward love. A good examination of conscience is not overly scrupulous, but healthy and healing. It has a positive, forward-looking purpose. The purpose is to discover the direction of the Lord's promptings of love by recognizing the areas in our lives that need to be strengthened and healed.

This method of examining conscience presupposes that we desire nothing more earnestly than to live for God in Christ Jesus. If this is not our starting point, if this is not our hearts' deepest desire, if this is not the fundamental orientation of our lives, then this approach to examining conscience will not make sense. In short, we cannot turn from sin and be healed in any true sense unless we love God above all things. As the new Rite says:

> The follower of Christ who has sinned but who has been moved by the Holy Spirit to come to the sacrament of penance should above all be converted to God with his whole heart. This inner conversion of heart embraces sorrow for sin and the intent to lead a new life (Par. 6).

We want our participation in Reconciliation to be a significant moment in our ongoing conversion. Often we do not experience the sacrament this way. Perhaps one of the reasons we experience little change as a result of our confessing is because there is little preparation that goes into it. If we are interested in exposing only surface sins, their number and kind, and not in

179

uncovering the root cause of our sin, then we will experience little healing, and there will be little change in our lives. By focusing on where the treasure of our hearts lies, we can recognize the root cause of our sins. The process of examining conscience suggested here helps us get to the roots of our sin, and opens us to the healing presence of God in Christ encountered in and through the Sacrament of Reconciliation.

Simply put, conscience, as we have explored it in this chapter, is the sum total of one's present state of moral awareness. The process of examining conscience that comes out of this understanding does not focus first and foremost on actions judged against a set of moral rules. Rather than serving to provide a checklist of possible faults committed, this process of examination probes what is happening in our deeper levels of awareness of being in relation to God present to us everywhere. It seeks to discover the ways our lives have, or have not, manifested a living awareness of being touched by a living God. This examination is concerned with ways we are experiencing the call of God, and with the ways that the attraction of evil and our concurring selfishness lure us away from God. This form of examining conscience is an experience in faith of confronting our lives in Christ and through the Spirit before the Father.

In the second chapter, we saw the importance of the living awareness of the presence of God for a rich celebration of any sacrament. This method of examination gives real "bite" to our living awareness of the presence of God in all things and becomes an important way of practicing the presence of God so necessary for the fruitful celebration of the sacraments.

This method of examination unfolds according to the creative dynamics of four "Let there be's." I will first describe the dynamics of each creative imperative, and then give an example of what attitude is created by each.

Let There Be Gratitude!

Gratitude is the fundamental attitude which gives energy to this method of examination. As we live busily through the day, we can too easily fall into a posture of taking everything for granted, or of seeing everything as being owed to us. We need to take some time to recognize that all we have comes to us as a gift. To recognize that all is gift is to begin to move away from a self-centered view of the world ("I deserve this," "I demand that," 'I am entitled to this") and to become centered on the Giver. When we realize that we live in a world of grace, we look upon our lives as surrounded by gifts to be cherished and shared, not as possessions to be hoarded. When we look upon all the events of our lives as gifts, we come to recognize the many ways we have been graced, or loved by God. We begin our examination of conscience by knowing and feeling the love God has for us by naming our gifts, in other words, by being grateful. The more deeply we establish an attitude of gratitude, then ever more constant, conscious, and loving will be our relationship to God.

A reflection responding to the imperative to be grateful might go something like this:

> I thank you, loving Father, for the many gifts you have given me this day. I thank you for my life, my health, and for the good people you have sent into my life, especially my faithful wife, my children, and the staff in my office. How fortunate I am to be able to live and work with people who care. I thank you for the opportunity I had today to meet a stranger who helped me recognize how fortunate I am to have so many supportive people around me.

Let There Be Awareness of Sin!

When we come face to face with the way God loves us through the ways we are gifted, we can truly see our sinfulness in perspective. We have become so used to thinking of the examination of conscience as a thorough self-scrutiny measured against a list of faults that we can forget the truism of our faith: only God can reveal sin to us. Even the awareness of our sinfulness is a gift of God, a grace. To recognize this is the first step in breaking through our inability to accept God's love. In the light of recognizing our gifts, we become aware of how unloving, insensitive, blind, selfish, or ungrateful we have been in taking these gifts for granted, in hoarding them, or abusing them.

Even without scrutinizing a list of faults, we can become aware of our selfishness and the ways we have allowed love to grow cold in our hearts and in the world of our relationships. We can do this by paying attention to our interior stirrings which come in response to meeting the Word of God in Scripture, or in the living examples of people around us. The Rite directs the penitent to prepare for celebrating the sacrament by "comparing his life with the example and commandments of Christ" (Par. 15). Certainly using any of the Gospel stories of Jesus (like the parables or healing miracles), as well as the teachings of Jesus on love, would be appropriate for this step in the examination of conscience. Appropriate, too, would be a prayerful recollection of our encounter with people who have embodied the example and teaching of Jesus. What stirs within us during these prayerful moments of hearing the call to conversion helps us recognize the quality of our moral lives, as well as those areas which need healing, and those which we are being called to change.

The celebration of Reconciliation begins from the time we come to this awareness of sin. The sacrament begins with our initial response to move away from sin and identify ourselves more completely with Christ in his loyalty to the Father. Since Christ is one with all members of his body, our awareness of sin includes our awareness of our relationship to the Body of Christ. Our desire for conversion includes reconciliation with the community of God's people. The Sacrament of Reconciliation becomes the unfolding in more explicit ways of this desire for conversion and reconciliation.

In coming to awareness of our sin, we usually can recognize one special area of our hearts that is most in need of change. This would be the area of change which expresses our seriousness about loving God in return for the gifts with which we have been graced. This is the area we ought to bring to Reconciliation for conversion and healing. In the Sacrament of Reconciliation, unless there is true mortal sin, we need not worry about listing all our sins. We ought to focus, rather, on the one area most in need of healing. This, then, is what becomes the matter for confession.

A reflection responding to the imperative to be aware of sin might go something like this:

Praying with John 13:1–17

Father, now that I recognize with gratitude the gift of supportive people you have sent into my life, I hear Jesus telling me what the life of such a gifted person ought to be like. In light of the example of Jesus washing his disciples' feet, I can see more clearly that I have not been as encouraging to my younger staff members as I ought to be and want to be, especially with Joe. This is his first year with our firm. He works hard and wants to do well, I know. My envy keeps me from telling him how well he does, and my jealousy compels me to make heavy demands on him so that he will pay attention to me. I am getting older now and am afraid these young men will take over my position and that I will not be included anymore in the plans of the company.

Let There Be Sorrow!

Once we recognize our failure to respond in love, we are ready to express our sorrow. The new Rite regards sorrow, or contrition, as "the most important act of the penitent. . . . The genuineness of penance depends on this heartfelt contrition" (Par. 6a). Our contrition is the sign of our gratitude and the sincerity of our love. We let our expression of sorrow come from our hearts. We can then express this sorrow in our own words and in our own ways. This sorrow must not be looked upon as shame, or as depression due to sin. Above all, sorrow is an expression of trusting faith that God is the merciful Father ready to welcome us back and throw a party for us. God does not forgive us because we are repentant. Rather, we are able to be repentant precisely because God is always welcoming, always forgiving. Our expression of sorrow is an expresion of gratitude that God loves us still, even in our sin. Expressing sorrow moves us toward communion, not only with God but also with the people of God. Looking at sorrow this way makes our confession an expression of faith through our sin, and not merely a confession of sin itself.

A reflection responding to the imperative to be sorry might go something like this:

> Father, I am grateful to have Joe working with me. I am sorry that I have not encouraged him in his work only to have more attention brought to me. I am sorry for being so envious, jealous, hard-hearted, and self-centered. Heal me of these sins, and help me to be different in the future.

Let There Be Love!

The expression of sorrow before a loving, accepting God frees us to face the future with renewed vision and sensitivity to the ways we are being called to respond to the gifts we have been given. Hope is what carries us into the future. We show our sorrow and express our hope for conversion with a specific resolution that will be our first step in that direction. This particular action will help break the sinful pattern and strengthen our resolve to be instruments of healing and peace. This specific resolution can become the penance that we will do to signify, seal, and deepen our commitment to reconciliation. Rather than looking upon our penance as a punishment for sin, we should see it as a grateful response of praise in love for the healing that is coming to us in and through this examination and confession of sins.

A reflection that responds to the imperative to be loving might go something like this:

> Father, I want to be a more hospitable person toward Joe. Tomorrow I am going to tell him what a great job he has been doing on our most difficult project, and I am going to let the supervisor of our department know that Joe's ideas are the ones that have been implemented on this project, not mine. With the strength of your Spirit living in me, may I be able to be loving in these ways.

With an examination of conscience like this, we are now ready to enter into the Sacrament of Reconciliation, making it the act of worship in praise and thanksgiving it is supposed to

184

be. A good examination arouses not only sentiments of sorrow but also those first stirrings of praise and thanksgiving for the ways God has been working in our lives. The reform of our lives, like the forgiveness of our sins, does not start in the reconciliation room, nor does it stop there. The process of conversion begins long before we confess, and continues long afterward. With an examination of conscience like the one just described, we have the ingredients for a rich experience of healing and reconciliation in and through the Sacrament of Reconciliation. We can go now to celebrate the forgiveness already begun, and to deepen the reform of our lives and the reconciliation already in progress.

FOURTH MOVEMENT: APPROPRIATING THE CHRISTIAN STORY

How does the above presentation on conscience affect your understanding of conscience? In what ways has this chapter affirmed you? In what ways have you been challenged? Complete the following sentences:

I realized that I . . .
I relearned that I . . .
I was surprised that I . . .
I wonder if . . .
I wonder why . . .
I wonder when . . .

FIFTH MOVEMENT: CHOOSING A FAITH RESPONSE

How might you go about forming your conscience now? How might you examine your conscience in the future? Complete the following sentences:

Next time, I want to . . .
I need to think more about . . .
I hope that I . . .

Suggestions for Further Reading

John Carmody   *Re-Examining Conscience*

Craig Dykstra   *Vision and Character*

Nicholas Lohkamp   *Living the Good News*

C. Ellis Nelson, ed.   *Conscience: Theological and
                            Psychological Perspectives*

6

Reconciliation
Through the Ages

FIRST MOVEMENT: PRESENT PRACTICE

Remember your first confession? What was it like? How is your experience of the Sacrament of Reconciliation any different now?

SECOND MOVEMENT: CRITICAL REFLECTION

How many different ways have you experienced the Sacrament of Reconciliation? How do you account for the differences and similarities? What is the most important part of the Sacrament of Reconciliation for you? What makes this part so important to you?

THIRD MOVEMENT: THE CHRISTIAN STORY AND VISION

The Sacrament of Reconciliation as we know it has assumed various forms in the course of history. The shape which Reconciliation, or Penance, has today was not always with us. Although Penance has always signified the forgiveness of Christ, the requirements surrounding the practice of penance and the manner of celebration have changed significantly over the centuries. Perhaps no other sacrament has undergone such radical and frequent revision. The historical changes of this sacrament demonstrate that it is a living part of the development of the Church renewing itself through the ages. National traditions, local customs, and the strength of faith, along with the creativity and ingenuity of the community responding to the changing needs of the times, have shaped and reshaped this sacrament through the centuries.

If the Church is going to continue renewing itself, we can expect that this sacrament is not yet finished changing. We will always need to be ready, then, for the possibility of further modifications in the future and realize that what we have now does not represent the last days of a fixed form. Perhaps our current experience of the dramatic decline in the practice of Penance may be a signal that we are entering a new period in this sacrament's history. The direction the Church is taking at this time is also expressed in the recent revision of the Rite of Penance. Before we can understand these revisions, however, we need to see where we have been. The purpose of this chapter is to trace the lifeline of the Sacrament of Reconciliation and to keep an eye on those features which have made their mark on the shape of our present Rite.

THE BIBLICAL PERIOD

We do not find the Sacrament of Reconciliation as we know it in the Bible. Yet repentance and the forgiveness of sins are central to the biblical witness and are at the heart of the teaching of Jesus. Penitential liturgies in the Bible provide the roots to the gradual development of the sacramental rites of reconciliation. So our historical survey needs to begin with these biblical roots.

The Old Testament

God's compassion for repentant sinners, and forgiveness of them, is a pervasive theme in the Bible. From the perspective of the covenant in the Old Testament, communion with God is life. If that communion is ruptured or broken through human fault, divine forgiveness would be the only way to restore it. Just as communion with God is a gift of grace, so restoration of that communion after sin is a gift of grace. This restoration cannot be achieved by mere human effort. And so Israel trusted in the love and fidelity of God, knowing that it is more consistent with the character of God to forgive than to punish. Israel acknowledged her sin and appealed to the kindness of God through penitential practices: there were fasting, weeping, mourning, and the wearing of sackcloth, the penitential garb (Jl 1—2); there were prayers for mercy (Lam 5; Pss 51, 60, 74, 79); sacrifices of expiation were offered (Lev 1—7); the Day of Atonement (Yom Kippur) was celebrated as the most solemn ritual of reconciliation (Lev 16); and intercessions of a community leader were sought (Ex 32:30; Jer 14).

While rituals of reconciliation abound, rituals by themselves are not enough. Conversion is necessary. Rituals of repentance without conversion of heart are a sham. The prophets knew this and so often spoke against superficial ritualism (Jer 36; Am 5; Hos 1—6; Is 1:11—17). The prophetic call to conversion specified the conditions for returning to God: acknowledgment of one's sins, purification of one's heart, and change of one's conduct. This prophetic teaching on conversion is most clearly expressed in Psalm 51, the famous, "*Miserere*":

Verse 1 begins the prayer with an expression of trust in the love and fidelity of God: "Be merciful to me, O God, because of your constant love."

Verses 3 and 4 are a confession of sin: "I recognize my faults; I am always conscious of my sins. I have sinned against you—only against you—and done what you consider evil."

Verse 10 prays for the grace of a change of heart: "Create a pure heart in me, O God, and put a new and loyal spirit in me."

Verses 16 and 17 express an orientation toward a renewed and fervent life: "You do not want sacrifices, or I would offer them; you are not pleased with burnt offerings. My sacrifice is a humble spirit, O God; you will not reject a humble and repentant heart."

In summary, the Old Testament perspective on reconciliation tells us that God is the one who takes the initiative in restoring harmony. God loves us first. We are to remove the barriers that sin raises between us and God. Rituals of reconciliation alone are not enough. Interior conversion of heart that gives rise to a change in our conduct is also necessary.

The New Testament

The New Testament, too, approaches reconciliation from the point of view of the convenant which is Jesus the Christ through whom God the Father manifests that merciful love reconciling the world. The life-death-resurrection of Jesus the Christ is the reconciling event par excellence. The main effect of this reconciling event is to restore us to communion with the Father. This notion finds its clearest expression in St. Paul, in Romans 5:10–11, Colossians 1:20–21, Ephesians 2:16, and especially in 2 Corinthians 5:18–20:

> All this has been done by God, who has reconciled us to himself through Christ and has given us the ministry of reconciliation. I mean that God, in Christ, was reconciling the world to himself, not counting our transgressions against us, and that he has entrusted the message of reconciliation to us. This makes us ambassadors for Christ, God as it were appealing through us. We implore you, in Christ's name: be reconciled to God!

For Paul, the Father has reconciled us, and the world, through Christ—particularly through the death of Christ. The Old Testament expiatory sacrifices of atonement lie behind this Pauline interpretation. Christ's blood is not shed to appease an angry God, but his blood is poured out to rededicate us to God by cleansing us from sin and so to give us "access" (Rom 5:2) to the Father.

The key to this interpretation of reconciliation is that God has taken the initiative in this act of reconciliation in Christ.

Reconciliation is something that God does for us. It comes as a pure gift and is a permanent condition. Against this background of the Christ-event as the ritual of reconciliation par excellence, there is never a time in our lives when reconcilation is not available. It is a permanent condition, not a temporary reprieve. Through the life-death-resurrection of Jesus, we have been made one with God. Our peace with God is restored. This complete act of reconciliation only awaits our appropriation through a renewal of our hearts which changes our lives.

From within the covenant perspective of the Bible, we know that none of us is related to God as a private, solitary person. We are all related to God insofar as we are members of God's people. Just as this always makes sin a communal rupturing or breaking of life-giving and loving relationships, so too it makes reconciliation a communal happening. The Church participates in the covenant of Christ by living obediently according to the law of love. The inseparability of the love of God and love of neighbor commandment tells us that reconciliation with God is inseparable from reconciliation with others. The Church participates in the reconciliation of Christ and makes it visible and tangible through the ages by its ministry of reconciliation. We participate in this ministry by meeting the daily challenges to mutual forgiveness.

Part of the mission of the Church is to extend the reconciling presence of Christ to the world. The Church is to be a reconciling community in which everyone recognizes the need to establish peace through mutual forgiveness. The reconciling activity of Christ that is present in the whole Church becomes focused in a special way in the Sacrament of Reconciliation.

Although the New Testament offers no evidence of Reconciliation in the sacramental form as we have come to know it, it does take conversion and forgiveness seriously. The New Testament writers saw Jesus' mission to be one of forgiveness and reconciliation from the very beginning. His name, Jesus, means "God saves" (cf Mt 1:21). The Gospel of Mark has Jesus begin his public ministry with the call to conversion (Mk 1:15). During his public ministry, Jesus announces forgiveness to those who show sorrow for their sins (Lk 5:18–26; 7:36–50). He visits with sinners (Lk 19:1–9) and speaks in parables about the Father's love for those who stray (Lk 15). When asked how many times we are to forgive one another he says, in effect, "every time" (Mt 18:22), and he poured out his blood "for the forgiveness of sins" (Mt 26:28).

When Jesus makes his call to conversion, or when he forgives sins, he does not make any allusion to penitential liturgies. What counts for him is the change of heart that will issue in a new way of life. Yet as early as the apostolic communities we do have evidence of some forms of penitential practices which shape the Church's ministry of proclaiming forgiveness. The reconciliation of the sinner was apparently accomplished in at least two different ways. The first way is marked by fraternal correction, prayer, and confession to one another. For example, in Matthew 8:15–20 Jesus addresses the disciples on the subject of community discipline and mutual correction, and he advocates fraternal correction to effect reconciliation. The community and its official representatives are not to attempt reconciliation until the divisiveness is so great that it cannot be dealt with privately. Galatians 6:1–2 also advocates gentle fraternal correction to encourage one another against sin. 1 John 5:16 encourages prayer to strengthen another against sin; James 5:16 does the same and, like Matthew 5:23–24, encourages confession to one another.

The second way of reconciliation is for especially serious and public sins. We find evidence of this way in the Corinthian Church (1 Cor 5:1–5; 2 Cor 2:5–11) where the sin is understood to be social, and the sinner seems implicitly willing to submit to the judgment of the community. One phase of this process of reconciliation involves separating the sinner from the community in order to arouse an awareness of sin; the second phase is the reconciliation which comes with the community's extending its love to the offender who shows signs of repentance and conversion.

While these texts may show us that the New Testament communities were realistic about sin and forgiveness, they do not suggest a ritual of reconciliation like that which we know today. There is no text in the New Testament which does. Most Catholics, however, would be prone to associate the institution of the Sacrament of Reconciliation with the text from John's

Gospel where Jesus appears in the midst of the disciples on Easter Sunday night and says:

> Receive the Holy Spirit. If you forgive people's sins, they are forgiven; if you do not forgive them, they are not forgiven (Jn 20:23).

Many have tried to read this text, along with the ones from the Gospel of Matthew which attribute the power to bind and loose first to Peter (16:19) and then to the other disciples (18:18), as saying that Jesus commissioned the apostles to forgive sins through the Sacrament of Reconciliation, and that the apostles were empowered to pass on this authority by ordaining successors.

Modern biblical scholarship would not be so quick to conclude the institution of the Sacrament of Reconciliation from these texts. In fact biblical scholars today are telling us that it does not seem possible to see in the Gospels an institution of the Sacrament of Reconciliation as being directly affirmed. For example, with regard to the text in John referred to above, Raymond E. Brown writes this:

> ... we doubt that there is sufficient evidence to confine the power of forgiving and holding of sin, granted in John xx 23, to a specific exercise of power in the Christian community, whether that be admission to Baptism or forgiveness in Penance. These are but partial manifestations of a much larger power, namely, the power to isolate, repel, and negate evil and sin, a power given to Jesus in his mission by the Father and given in turn by Jesus through the Spirit to those whom he commissions. It is an effective, not merely a declaratory, power against sin, a power that touches new and old followers of Christ, a power that challenges those who refuse to believe. John does not tell us how or by whom this power was exercised in the community for whom he wrote, but the very fact that he mentions it shows that it was exercised. (In Matthew's community the power over sin, expressed in the binding/loosing saying, must have been exercised in formal decisions about what was sinful and/or in excommunication.) In the course of time this power has had many differ-

ent manifestations, as the various Christian communities legitimately specified both the manner and agency of its exercise. Perhaps John's failure to specify may serve as a Christian guideline: exegetically, one can call upon John xx 23 for assurance that the power of forgiveness has been granted; but one cannot call upon this text as proof that the way in which a particular community exercises this power is not true to Scripture.[1]

What we can conclude from the New Testament evidence is that the tenors of certain texts do not invalidate developments in the Sacrament of Reconciliation, even though they do not explicitly affirm the institution of the sacrament. Matthew's teaching on binding and loosing preserves the connection between the saving work of Christ and the responsibility of the Church to forgive and heal its members. The Gospel of John more explicitly connects the ministry of forgiveness in the Church with the presence of the Spirit in the community. But none of the texts specify the particular shape that the ministry of reconciliation must take in sacramental form to manifest the reconciling action of God in Christ and through the Spirit. However, the texts do testify to the forgiving and reconciling action of God in and through Jesus the Christ and the ministry of reconciliation in the Church. Through the Church, as an ongoing witness to Christ, God continues to forgive and reconcile. The particular shape Reconciliation takes in the community is subject to the creativity and ingenuity of each era meeting the needs of its times.

EARLY CHRISTIAN PENANCE

The early Christian communities which gave us the first forms of a rite of penance were small in numbers and were made up of members who were baptized as adults, for the most part. The situation of adult baptism produced its own form of celebrating the reconciliation of sinners. The rites of penance emerged out of the need to have some form of readmitting post-baptismal sinners to the community.

We have little data regarding penitential practice during the first three centuries. Among the earliest evidence hinting that penance for baptized sinners is possible is in the *First Letter of Clement* (c. 96). This letter stresses the role of the community's prayer and intercession on behalf of those who need repentance. Another early document of significance is the *Shepherd of Hermas* (c. 140). The unknown author of this letter steers between a rigorist position that has no room for a second chance at reconciliation after baptism, and a free-wheeling laxity. The significance of this document is that it recognizes reconciliation is available to the baptized sinner, but only once. This once-in-a-lifetime rule remained in effect until the sixth century.

These earliest references to post-baptismal reconciliation do not describe a formal ritual of readmission to the community. We do not have any evidence for that until Tertullian in the early third century. The shape of the penitential discipline which he describes is threefold. After confessing one's sins to the bishop, the penitent would be assigned acts of penance to show true conversion. Only after the penance was completed would the penitent be readmitted to the community of faith. This is the shape which the penitential discipline was to assume as "canonical penance" in the fourth century along with the once-in-a-lifetime character of penance. Tertullian regarded penance as a "second plank after shipwreck," Baptism being the first. Penance is like another Baptism since through it the sinner regains full remission of sins and full incorporation into the community. The analogy with Baptism explains why Reconciliation was regarded as unrepeatable.

Tertullian is also important in the history of penance for the influence he exercised on introducing a clear distinction among sins which were classified not by an analysis of the act itself, but by the way in which the sin was to be expiated. The full rite of reconciliation which he described in his writings was required only for grave sins. Lesser sins were expiated by private acts of mortification, such as prayers, fasts, almsgiving, and fraternal correction. We have no uniform list of grave sins and lesser sins from this era. As a Catholic, during which time he wrote *De Paenitentia* (c. 203), he acknowledged the full forgiveness of all sins.

After his conversion to Montanism (a group which preached strict moral conduct in preparation for the imminent second coming), during which time he wrote *De Pudicitia* (c. 220), Tertullian denied this Catholic practice and claimed that the Church had no power to forgive sins. Such sins could still be forgiven by God, but the Church should not forgive such sins lest it encourage others to sin. From this point of view, the bishop's pardon, or the community's prayerful intercession for the sinner, did not extend to those guilty of mortal sin. Though he may still have agreed with the Catholics on the part that the Church played in the procedure of Penance, and as to which sins were mortal (idolatry, murder, and adultery occupying a primary but not exclusive place among capital sins), he did not agree with Catholics that the bishop's pardon extends to those guilty of mortal sin. However, the force of the Catholic practice prevailed against the Montanist principle of irremissible sins so that ecclesiastical forgiveness for sins prevailed.

Shortly after the time of Tertullian, the question of penance became pressing again in the wake of the religious persecutions in the Roman empire. Could those who renounced their faith under the pressure of persecution be readmitted to the Church? A group led by Novatian in Rome argued that such apostasy was unforgivable. At the other extreme were those granting swift reconciliation by invoking the "martyr's privilege," the right of heroic persons who suffered for the faith to reconcile lapsed Christians. What was the Church's policy to be?

The Council of Carthage in 251 sanctioned the attitude common to Sts. Cyprian and Pope Cornelius which vigorously affirmed the possibility of forgiveness, but no less forcefully insisted on an adequate penance being done before reconciliation could be granted. The views of Cyprian and Cornelius won the day to mark an important step in establishing episcopal and conciliar control over the discipline of penance and in giving shape to "canonical penance."

CANONICAL PENANCE

We have no sharp dividing line in history between the doctrine and practice of the early Christian penance and the "canonical" penance of the fourth to sixth centuries. After the Peace of Constantine (312), the whole of the penitential system was eventually brought more directly under the regulation of conciliar decisions, papal decretals, and episcopal synods. The directives coming from these official sources acquired canonical force. The term "canonical penance" derives from the form and requirements of the penitential procedures coming under the regulation of these canons. Canonical penance was also called "ecclesiastical" or "public" penance. The term "public" is often the more confusing title. To call this discipline "public" is *not* to suggest that there existed simultaneously a private sacramental practice as an alternative discipline. *Nor* does "public" suggest the practice of "public confession" where sinners announced their sins aloud before the public gathering. "Public" suggests the liturgical character of the whole process in which the sinner was clearly evident to the community as a penitent, and the community itself was visibly involved in the ministry of reconciliation.[2]

The general procedure of canonical penance had three major parts: (1) enrolling in the order of penitents; (2) doing acts of penance; (3) being reconciled with the Church-community by the bishop. We will consider what was at stake in each.

1. *Enrolling in the Order of Penitents*

Sinners, moved by sorrow for sin, would confess their sins to the bishop and ask what had to be done to be reconciled to the community. This confession of sins was not done aloud before a public gathering. In fact, as early as 249 Pope Leo I condemned the practice of making a public declaration of sins an abuse of the penitential practice. This same attitude toward public declarations of sins was retained in the era of canonical penance. The confession of sins was made in secret to the bishop when the sinner first asked to enroll in the order of penitents.

The entry into the order of penitents was a public act which took place in the presence of the assembled faithful. The assembly would in turn make its confession of praise to God's mercy for bringing the sinner to repentance. The public character of this first phase of canonical penance was for the sake of making an appeal for prayers from the faithful. The faithful were then to watch over the penitents in a fashion similar to the way catechumens were watched over by their baptismal sponsors.

The liturgical rite of enrolling in the order of penitents was led by the bishop who would impose his hands on the penitent, dress the penitent in the penitential garb of sackcloth and ashes, and then dismiss the penitent from the church as a sign of being cut off from the community of the faithful and especially from the Eucharistic table. This final act did not mean that penitents could not return to church during the time of doing penance. It did mean that they would occupy a special place in the rear of the church, where they would prostrate themselves and beg the prayers of the community gathering for Eucharist. Penitents would also be assigned special rites, like bearing the dead to church and to burial, or kneeling throughout a feast day. But penitents were not allowed to receive the Eucharist.

2. *Doing Acts of Penance*

The bishop judged the length of time the penance was to be done as well as the nature of the penance. A penance commonly extended for several years, or in some cases for a lifetime. For example, sins of murder, adultery, and apostasy would receive a lifelong penance. However, an apostate who had not sacrificed to gods would receive a penance of only several years.[3]

During the time of doing penance, the penitent was expected to live a life of mortification, fasting, prayer, and almsgiving. During the period of doing penance, and in some cases even after reconciliation, certain prohibitions of a more severe type were imposed. For example, a penitent, even after being reconciled, could not be part of the military service, or hold public office, or be ordained a cleric, and, if married, could not have sexual intecourse with one's spouse. "Once a penitent, always a penitent" was the rule. Once one entered the order of penitents, one's life would never be the same again. To become a penitent was to begin a new life. The purpose of doing penance was clearly for rehabilitation.

Given the severity and length of canonical penances, and since this could be administered only once in a lifetime, bishops would not permit certain persons who could not abide by such a discipline to enter the order of penitents. For example, young people who might possibly sin again as well as young married persons who could not abstain from sexual relations for the rest of their lives were excluded.

3. *Being Reconciled with the Community*

At the close of the period of doing penance, the penitent was received back into full communion with the Church in a public ceremony through the liturgical gesture of the laying on of hands by the bishops accompanied by a prayer. Priests were permitted to be ministers of reconciliation only in cases of necessity, such as in danger of death. The rite of reconciliation was completed by admitting the penitent to full Eucharistic fellowship. Receiving the Eucharist was the culmination of the rite of reconciliation. From the fifth century, this rite of reconciliation took place on Holy Thursday.

Evaluation

This richly symbolic, yet rigorous system did not last. In fact, it became obsolete even before it reached the height of its development in the fifth century. From the fifth century onward, participation in canonical penance became more and more rare. The practice of disregarding opportunities for reconciliation early in life and deferring confession and reconciliation until near death became common. For this reason, deathbed reconciliation with Viaticum occupied a prominent place in the pastoral ministry of reconciliation rather than the solemn imposition of hands by the bishop. By the sixth century, the system of canonical penance ceased to play a part in the life of the Christian, and Penance was generally looked on as one part of preparing for death.

That the system of canonical penance did not become a permanent pattern in the Church is no surprise. The severity of the penitential requirements, the length of penances, and their lifetime effects, together with the limitation of being a once in a lifetime practice, were reasons enough to discourage its use. Though these serious disadvantages of canonical penance warrant its decline, the loss of some of its positive features has left the Church poorer as a result. Our approach to the new Rite of

Penance can aim to recover some of these features. What might these be?

The most obvious advantage of canonical penance is the clear acknowledgement of the corporate involvment in sin and reconciliation. Sin was seen as damaging the fabric of the whole community, and so reconciliation was the work of the whole community. Canonical penance is thoroughly a communal action throughout. The community of faith is the minister of reconciliation in the canonical system. This is not to denigrate the role of the ordained minister in reconciliation. Rather, it underlines the shared responsibility of the ministry of reconciliation. Because the whole community shares in the responsibility of calling the penitent back to faith and communion through its prayers, example, and fraternal support and correction, the bishop's role in the reconciliation stands out as an expression of the ministry of the entire community.

A second advantage of the canonical system was its witness to reconciliation as a process, and not as a magic moment. Reconciliation is not effected in a moment, but requires time, hard work, and the cooperation of the entire community. In this process, the confession of sins becomes meaningful only insofar as it is part of the process of conversion. What was most important in this ancient system was all that followed the confession of sins to manifest and deepen true sorrow and genuine conversion on the part of the penitent, and genuine participation in the process of reconciliation on the part of the whole community. In the work of reconciliation the community calls out new commitment from its sinful members, asking them to walk in a way that bespeaks the Christian vision and Gospel way of life. The penitents as well call out new commitment from the larger community by challenging them to examine their priorities, and assess their vision and the way they walk in their commitment as Christians.

A third feature which we ought not to lose from this ancient system is its witness to other means of effecting reconciliation. The fact that few people entered the order of penitents on their own, that some bishops discouraged others from so entering, and that becoming a penitent could be done only once in a lifetime suggests that the Church witnesses to other viable and effective means of reconciliation. Canonical penance helps us see the sacramental Rite of Reconciliation within the larger framework of conversion and means of reconciliation which include Baptism, prayer, fasting, works of mercy, and the Eucharist.

These strengths of the canonical discipline of penance challenge our current penitential practice. Do we see the Rite of Reconciliation as a significant moment in the long process of conversion, or do we think that Reconciliation stands alone? Our recent practice has led us to collapse the process of conversion into a few moments in the confessional box. When we lose the sense that reconciliation takes time, we easily fall into the trap of thinking that conversion and reconciliation happen in a magic moment of the sacramental ritual itself. Furthermore, how well do we situate our sacramental Rite of Reconciliation within the context of other sacraments of reconciliation, especially Baptism and Eucharist? Do our penitential celebrations renew the Church community's commitment to walk the way of Christ as well as enable personal conversion to that way? Do our penitential practices effectively demand change in our lives as well as motivate others to a life of service and a style of life that bespeaks the Christian vision? Do our penitential practices equate personal reform with active witness to the Gospel in our times? At least the new Rite asks for this in the Introduction where we read:

> Thus the people of God becomes in the world a sign of conversion to God. All this the Church expresses in its life and celebrates in the liturgy when the faithful confess that they are sinners and ask pardon of God and of their brothers and sisters (Par. 4).

MONASTIC SYSTEM OF PENANCE

Canonical penance had reached the height of its development in the fifth century in the Mediterranean countries. By this time, however, it was already becoming obsolete. By the end of the sixth century, the rite of canonical penance collapsed under the weight of its rigorist demands. The shape of Penance that remained took the extreme form of deathbed reconciliation. This practice only encouraged looking upon Penance as one part of preparing for death. Without any efforts to modify the canonical system in order to lessen its harshness, canonical penance became practically inaccessible to the great majority of sinners, and ceased to play any significant role in the ongoing, daily life of the faithful, even though it remained officially in force.

Meanwhile, another penitential discipline was developing in the Celtic and Anglo-Saxon Church, where they had never heard of canonical penance. This was the monastic system of the so-called "tariff" penance. The system of "tariffing" was taken over from Celtic secular law where a penalty was given to satisfy a crime. In the Church, the tariff penance was the practice of assigning penances to persons who privately confessed their sins.

The monastic system of penance was introduced to the Continent by monks who became missionaries. Since the monastic practice of frequent confession of one's sins was a direct violation of the officially approved practice of only one repentance after Baptism, the Third Council of Toledo in 589 condemned the practice of repeated confessions as detestable. But within sixty years the practice became more common and acceptable. A synod of French bishops gathered at Chalon-Sur-Saone between 647–652 found this practice to be a "medicine for the soul" and good for all.

Gradually the tide turned in favor of the monastic system across the Continent. As the practice grew, a penitential literature grew up with it as an aid to confessors for dealing with all sorts of people and all sorts of moral and spiritual maladies. These manuals were called "penitentials"—collections of proportionately measured penances for many offenses. Some of these books were arranged methodically according to the capital, or deadly, sins, and became the standard manuals for anyone in charge of the care of souls. From these monastic penitentials of the Celtic and Anglo-Saxon Church, we can understand what this system of penance was like and what attitudes informed it.

As the beginning of the *Penitential of Cummean* (c. 650) has it, penances are the "health-giving medicine of souls."[4] Healing was the primary metaphor which directed this practice of penance in its early stages. Later attitudes of judgment and penalty in administering penances, as well as the notion of a penance as a "tariff," represented a deterioration of the monastic system.

The healing metaphor for penances aptly fits the principle of contraries which is frequently found in the penitentials. Cummean states the principle this way: "Contraries are cured by contraries; for he who freely commits what is forbidden ought freely to restrain himself from what is otherwise permissible."[5] This principle has roots in the Fathers of the Church who were fond of medical analogies when it came to the care of souls. Its use in the penitentials gives us a clear indication of how the penitentials interpreted the purpose of penance. For example, the *Penitential of Finnian* (c. 525–550), the earliest document thought to be a complete penitential book, employs this principle like this:

> If a cleric is wrathful or envious or backbiting, gloomy or greedy, great and capital sins are these; and they slay the soul and cast it down to the depth of hell. But there is this penance for them, until they are plucked forth and eradicated from our hearts: through the help of the Lord and through our own zeal and activity let us seek the mercy of the Lord and victory in these things; and we shall continue in weeping and tears day and night so long as these things are turned over in our heart. But by contraries, as we said, let us make haste to cure contraries and to cleanse away the faults from our hearts and introduce virtues in their places. Patience must arise for wrathfulness; kindliness, or the love of God and of one's neighbor, for envy; for detraction, restraint of heart and tongue; for dejection, spiritual joy; for greed, liberality. . . .[6]

Similarly, the *Penitential of Columban* (c. 600) says this:

> The talkative person is to be sentenced to silence, the disturber to gentleness, the gluttonous to fasting, the sleepy fellow to watchfulness, the proud to imprisonment, the deserter to expulsion; everyone shall suffer suitable penalties according to what he deserves, that the righteous may live righteously.[7]

The principle of contraries regards sins as diseases of the soul, and so penances are prescribed to counter the disease and to promote healing. In this way, penance is looked upon as a medicinal remedy that can restore the sinner to moral health and social acceptance. McNeill and Gamer summarize this conception of penance well when they write:

> The penitentials offer to the sinner the means of rehabilitation. He is given guidance to the way of recovering harmonious relations with the Church, society, and God. Freed in the process of penance from social censure, he recovers the lost personal values of which his offenses have deprived him. He can once more function as a normal person. Beyond the theological considerations, we see in the detailed prescriptions the objective of an inward moral change, the setting up of a process of character reconstruction which involves the correction of special personal defects and the reintegration of personality.[8]

Generally, the penances tried to fit the sin to its contrary, at least in intensity if not in kind. However, the penances were not uniform in all penitentials. This created great diversity, and it occasioned increasing opposition to them as they spread over the Continent.

The penances of the penitentials reflect, by and large, the monastic context out of which they came. They generally mirror the monastic ascetical practices of prayer and various spiritual disciplines, such as praying the psalms, keeping vigils, assuming penitential or prayer postures like kneeling with arms outstretched, flagellations, fasting, almsgiving, living in seclusion, and making pilgrimages. Here are a few samples from various penitentials:

From the *Penitential of Finnian* (c. 525–550):

> If anyone has started a quarrel and plotted in his heart to strike or kill his neighbor, if the offender is a cleric, he shall do penance for half a year with an allowance of bread and water and for a whole year abstain from wine and meats, and thus he will be reconciled to the altar.

But if he is a layman, he shall do penance for a week, since he is a man of this world and his guilt is lighter in this world and his reward less in the world to come.[9]

From the *Penitential of Cummean* (c. 650), which is organized according to the capital sins, we find under "anger" the following:

One who curses his brother in anger shall both make satisfaction to him whom he has cursed and live secluded for seven days on bread and water.[10]

We find this penance for stealing in the *Penitential of Columban* (c. 600):

If any layman commits theft, that is, steals his neighbor's ox or horse or sheep or any animal, if he does it once or twice he shall first make restitution to his neighbor for the damage which he has done, and he shall do penance for the three forty-day periods on bread and water. But if he has been accustomed to commit theft often and is not able to make restitution, he shall do penance for a year and the three forty-day periods and shall promise in no circumstances to do it thenceforth; and so he shall take communion in the Easter of the following year, that is, after two years, having moreover previously given alms to the poor from the product of his labor and a feast to the priest who administers his penance; and thus he shall be absolved from the guilt of his evil course.[11]

In order to avoid impossible situations in the case of those not able to fulfill the penance, a system of commutations, or substitute penances called *arrea*, was established. Here is an example from an eighth century *Irish Table of Commutations:*

Now, as there is a difference between laybrothers and clerics, between nuns and laysisters, so there is a difference between their work and penance. There is also between the *arrea* which it is right for them to perform.

First, the *arrea* of former laybrothers and laysisters: sleeping in waters, sleeping on nettles, sleeping on nutshells, sleeping

205

with a dead body in a grave; for there is hardly a laybrother or laysister that has not had a share in manslaughter. These now are the *arrea* that are right for clerics and nuns, except those of them that have slain a man, unless (something) be done to increase the reward, viz. they sleep in cold churches or in secret chambers, performing vigil and praying without ceasing, viz. without sitting, without lying, without sleeping, as though they were at the mouth of hell, save that a little weariness may take place in a sitting posture only between two prayers.[12]

The system of commutations led to great abuse. For example, some penances could be substituted by paying a fine. This would benefit the rich but not the poor. Another commutation would be to read a set number of psalms in place of a harsher penance. This would benefit those who could read but not the illiterate. Further abuses came when some penances could be performed by one person for someone else. Those who did not wish to do penance could pay another person a certain fee in order to have the penance done in one's place. The system of commutations not only led to relaxing the penitential discipline, but it also brought opposition to the penitentials and helped prepare the way for the abuses in the indulgence system which was to come later.

The historical interpretations of the way this monastic system worked and the impact it had on the development of the Sacrament of Reconciliation in the Church are mixed. There are some points, however, about which there seems to be general agreement. The monastic system was "private." This means that it was wholly dissociated from church assemblies and communal worship. Unlike the canonical penance, the monastic system did not include a public liturgy of entering into the order of penitents, and the bishop was not the ordinary minister of reconciliation. The monastic system also eliminated the penitential prohibitions that would mark the penitent for life, and it eliminated the once in a lifetime restriction so characteristic of the canonical penance. Another great distinguishing feature of the monastic system was that it permitted and encouraged the sinner to have recourse to penance as often as one desired. However, like the canonical system, the monastic system prohibited receiving the Eucharist until after the acts of penance were completed.

Historical interpretations of monastic penance disagree on precisely what constituted the procedure and the constitutive parts of this system of penance. According to the common assumption of many historians, the monastic system included a rite of reconciliation with some form of absolution after the penance was completed and before the penitent received Eucharist. However, a recent study by James Dallen challenges that assumption and argues quite convincingly that the monastic system lacked a ritual expression of reconciliation.[13] Dallen contends that the monastic system involved only two phases: confession and doing penance. Dallen shows that without including a ritual expression of reconciliation, the monastic system radically individualized the communal and liturgical process that was one of the great strengths of canonical penance. Reconciliation in the monastic system came through the penitent's own efforts in doing the penance which satisfied for sin and earned a person the right to receive Eucharist. With the absence of a ritual of reconciliation, this system tended to encourage an "earn your own salvation" attitude and orientation in life, and it rendered the process of reconciliation void of any awareness of a shared commitment to walking the Christian life together in community.

How might we account for the absence of a rite of reconciliation in this monastic system? Reasons seem to lie in the very monastic foundations of this practice. The Celtic Church was more a monastic than an episcopal church. From the sixth century, the leaders of the Celtic churches were abbots and learned monks who were not necessarily bishops. The Celtic culture by this time was almost completely embraced within monasticism.[14] Monastic practice favored a monk's having an "anmchara" (a soul friend) or, as we would say today, "a spiritual director" with whom he could share his commitments and failings in living the Christian life, and this practice influenced the new approach to Penance.

The Celtic Church prized having a soul friend. "Anyone without a soul friend is like a body without a head" is believed to have been a popular adage.[15] Some soul friends were unordained men, and some were women. But a common expectation of the monastic church was that everyone ought to have this special person in one's life to whom one could manifest one's conscience and seek spiritual guidance. Therefore, confession to laymen and laywomen in this system was not unusual. The soul friend was essentially a guide, and the role was not regarded in specifically sacramental terms, as we might think of it. In this unique context, the Irish Christian could manifest his or her conscience to the soul friend who would in turn prescribe ascetical practices for the purpose of spiritual growth. In this relationship there was no ecclesial judgment involved regarding the person's relationship to the Christian community. Therefore, there was no need for an official ecclesial judgment on behalf of the community through an ecclesial officer, whether bishop or priest, in the form of absolution to reconcile the penitent with the community.

Celtic monasticism knew only this private forum of spiritual direction, which would include something similar to a religious community's practice of a Chapter of Faults, followed by prescribing private acts of ascetical practices for the purpose of spiritual growth. It did not know of a communal liturgical rite expressing reconciliation. As lay people associated with the monasteries began turning to the monks for advice and spiritual counsel, the monks naturally used with them the very forms to which they had grown accustomed for themselves in the monastery. Those who served as the primary ministers of this form of penance did so without the authority of an officially commissioned ecclesial office. One did not have to be a priest or bishop to be a confessor. If personal holiness was what was needed, and not being a commissioned ecclesial officer, then private confessions could be made at any time to anyone noted for holiness. The ingenious wedding of the practice of spiritual direction with the Sacrament of Reconciliation inaugurated a new era in the development of this sacrament.

Evaluation

While we cannot say that the monastic system of penance as it was practiced between the sixth and ninth centuries is the beginning of our modern practice of "private confession," we can say that the monastic system occasioned the development of our modern practice of penance. Before considering the more immediate origins of our modern practice of private confession, we need to consider the strengths as well as the weaknesses of the monastic system since it had such a wide ranging impact on the future development of the Sacrament of Reconciliation.

One of the great strengths of this system is that it made repeated and frequent confession more practical. Another strength is that the original context for private confession was spiritual guidance. In the context of spiritual direction, the model of penance was a medical model of the cure of souls. Penance was primarily for healing and spiritual growth, not for judgment, guilt, and expiation. The task of the monastic confessor was not to judge and impose a sentence of penalties, but to be a compassionate discerner of what heals and helps the rehabilitation of the penitent's commitment to walk in a way that bespeaks a commitment to the Gospel. Our modern penitential practice could be well served by retrieving this monastic spirit of compassionate discernment. As this monastic spirit waned, penances degenerated from being steps toward healing to becoming acts of expiation for sin, "tariffs," or punishments of judgment. Our modern practice needs to retrieve the orientation toward healing, not punishment.

The monastic system also had some weaknesses which have left their mark on the future development of Penance. The most significant of these centers around the absence of a ritualized moment of reconciliation. This absence left this penitential practice with a markedly a-liturgical and private character. Furthermore, it contributed to locating the communal context, once so prominent in canonical penance, in the confessor and penitent alone. Without a strong community context, this practice of penance contributed to an individualistic understanding of sin and reconciliation from which we are still trying to recover. It also left the individual penitents on their own to be converted and to overcome sin, and served to encourage the thought that we earn our own salvation. Without a ritual of reconciliation, the ecclesial community no longer participated with the penitent in the work of reconciliation. Lost was the experience of the community's ministry of reconciliation through which prayerful intercession, good example, and fraternal correction were part of the community's involvement in the penitent's efforts to be converted. Lost, too, was the penitent's call to the community to assess its priorities and commitment to walk in a way that bespeaks an active witness to the Gospel.

Furthermore, the tendency to give little attention to the ministry of the reconciling community made it difficult for later theologians to explain the relation between contrition and absolution, between what the penitent does and what the Church does. Also, the role of the priest in the process of reconciliation became obscure without the context of the ministry of the reconciling community. Questions like "Why confess to a priest?" and "What does the priest really bring to the process of reconciliation?" and "Which is more important, contrition or absolution?" became issues subsequent theology had to face, and issues which are still with us today.

Another weakness of the monastic system is evident in the development of the penitentials. The use of the penitentials implied that the gravity of sin and repentance from sin could be measured. The experience of our moral tradition tells us that when we begin to put the emphasis on measurement, then legalism, minimalism, and scrupulosity in the moral and spiritual life are soon to follow. The penitentials also provided a catalogue of sins which contributed toward an emphasis in confession on actions apart from underlying attitudes. The quantifying mentality shaped by the tariff system helped form habits of self-examination and styles of confession which put a high priority on recalling the exact number and kinds of sin as well as the circumstances which changed their nature. This became reinforced by the teachings of the Council of Trent as we shall soon see. Such an approach to confession too easily obscures the healing potential of identifying the underlying attitudes that are the root cause of sin.

In no way should isolating these weaknesses of the monastic system of penance detract from the genuine penitential spirit in which many Christians used this form of penance to turn to God with greater commitment. Nor should it detract from the pastoral sensitivity that prompted a different generation of

Christians to respond to the need for some penitential practice in more practical ways than canonical penance provided. The development of the monastic system of penance showed the flexibility of the Church for shaping in practical ways its commitment to walk in the way of the call of the Gospel to conversion and reconciliation.

ORIGINS OF OUR MODERN PRACTICE

As the monastic system became the common practice, bishops and councils of bishops tried to regulate it by Church law. The Mediterranean Church of the ninth century must have recognized the revolutionary character of the monastic system over the official canonical penance. The Carolingian reform councils of the early ninth century tried to restore the system of canonical penance and outlaw the penitentials. But the monastic practice was too well established. The efforts of the Carolingian reform councils to end it and to reintroduce canonical penance did not succeed in abolishing private penance.

However, they must have had the effect of adding a ritual of reconciliation to the monastic system. Poschmann's study, for example, indicates that by the end of the ninth century a ritual of reconciliation was added immediately after the confession and before doing the acts of penance or receiving the Eucharist.[16] The study of James Dallen finds a possibility for this development by pointing to the Romano-Germanic Pontifical (c. 950) as the earliest evidence recording immediate reconciliation after confession and before doing acts of penance or receiving the Eucharist.[17] In any case, by the eleventh century we find well established a system of private penance which includes a rite of reconciliation after confession as well as frequent confession to a priest. Not until this ritual of reconciliation is introduced and well established in the practice of private penance can we claim the beginnings of our modern practice of penance. The procedure of contrition-confession-absolution-acts of penance-Eucharist has survived to our day.

With the repeatable character of the practice of penance now in place, progressive steps toward leniency began to occur.

211

Gradually, confessors made less use of the penitential books in judging appropriate acts of penance. In fact, by the twelfth century the penitential books were no longer being used, and the severe penances prescribed in them gradually disappeared in practice. With the decline in the importance of the acts of penance, the accent began to shift to the confession of sins. The humiliation and shame inherent in confessing one's sins began to be regarded as the penitential work of significance. The significance given to making a detailed confession of sins contributed to calling the whole rite by the name of only one part, namely, "confession."

Fourth Lateran Council

By 1215 the practice of repeated, private confession, which had begun as an unofficial practice, and which had been denounced by the Council of Toledo in 589, and again by the Carolingian reform councils of the ninth century, became the official, required discipline of the Church. The Fourth Lateran Council of 1215 decreed that all Catholics who committed mortal sins had to confess those sins to their pastor within a year. This disciplinary rule has survived to our day in the form of one of the Precepts of the Church. The recent National Catechetical Directory, *Sharing the Light of Faith* (1979), lists among the expectations for Catholics the following:

> To lead a sacramental life; to receive Holy Communion frequently and the Sacrament of Reconciliation regularly—minimally, to receive the Sacrament of Reconciliation at least once a year (annual confession is obligatory only if serious sin is involved); minimally also, to receive Holy Communion at least once a year, between the first Sunday of Lent and Trinity Sunday.[18]

Note that the Lateran Council's restriction of confessing to one's pastor has been removed in this rendering. According to the Introduction to the new Rite of Penance, "The precept which obliges each of the faithful to confess at least once a year to a priest all the grave sins which he has not individually confessed before also remains in force" (Par. 34). Notice in this rendering that "a priest" replaces "one's pastor" of the Lateran decree to extend the range of those to whom one may confess.

The significance of the decree of Lateran IV regarding the history of the development of this sacrament is that we find here the highest teaching and legislative body of the Church ratifying the disappearance of the canonical system of public penance and validating the system that had its roots in Irish monasticism. This is the decision that was later confirmed by Trent and is still with us today.

The Scholastic Period

By the end of the twelfth century, then, the external procedure of this sacrament had attained the format we know today. Though the format was settled, the speculative questions about the inner make-up of the sacrament were not. Two related issues regarding this sacrament that received attention during the Scholastic period were the mutual relationship of the acts of the penitent (sorrow, confession, and acts of penance) to the action of Christ in the Church through the priest (absolution), and the relationship of these to the forgiveness of sins.[19]

The debate first raged between two extremes, the contritionists and absolutionists. Mediating positions developed later in the Scholastic period. On the side of the contritionists were Peter Abelard and Peter Lombard. Abelard (d. 1142), the pioneer of the Scholastic method, maintained that sincere sorrow motivated by the love of God was the cause of forgiveness. Absolution was primarily a prayer on behalf of the sinner petitioning God for mercy (e.g., "May Almighty God have mercy on you and forgive you your sins"). He regarded the absolution as a judicial act only in those instances of excommunication where absolution marked readmission to the Church for one who has already been reconciled with God through sincere sorrow.

Peter Lombard (d. 1160) promoted this view by incorporating it in his *Sentences,* the major theological text book of the Middle Ages. Lombard is the one who gave us the list of the seven sacraments, and he places Penance in the fourth place. Lombard taught that sins are forgiven from the moment one begins to regret one's sins and turns back to God in love. Sincere sorrow, not absolution, is the sign and cause of forgiveness. The priest does not grant forgiveness but declares what is in fact already the case. The acts of penance are an outward expression of interior sorrow, and together with absolution help remit some of the punishment due to sin.

This contritionist approach of Abelard and Lombard was opposed by the absolutionist approach of Hugh (d. 1141) and Richard (d. 1173) of the School of Saint-Victor. For these Victorines, sorrow opened one's heart to the forgiveness which ultimately comes through the absolution of the priest. Hugh and Richard argued that the priest effectively forgives sins by virtue of the power entrusted to him by God through Christ who gave the apostles the power of the keys to bind and loose. The School of Saint-Victor interpreted the power of the keys not in terms of admitting people to the Church after excommunication, but as the power to admit or exclude people from divine forgiveness.

When this interpretation of absolution grew, especially through the theological efforts of John Duns Scotus a century later, confession to a lay person which had grown up in the monastic system was no longer seen as effective for forgiving sins. The absolutionist position linked the power to forgive sins unequivocally with the power of the keys and priestly ordination. Those experienced in the life of the Spirit and who have a special gift for healing the brokenness of sin and promoting the conversion of heart were distinctly barred from sacramental or ecclesial reconciliation. Even though their ministry of guiding others through the process of conversion may be very effective, it could not be valid as sacramental or ecclesial reconciliation.

Subsequent theological reflection in the Scholastic period tried to reconcile these two extreme positions by making further distinctions. By the thirteenth century, Aristotelian categories were being used in theological reflection to provide a means for some fresh distinctions. St. Thomas (d. 1274) used Aristotle's categories of matter and form to great effect in his approach to the sacraments. These categories became a way of uniting into an organic whole the acts of the penitent with absolution. The personal factors of sorrow, confession, and the acts of penance are the matter of the sacrament. The ecclesial action of absolution is the form of the sacrament.

Matter and form do not produce their effect separately, but

only when taken together. In this way, Thomas was able to establish that the efficient cause of the forgiveness of sin is the personal acts of the penitent and the absolution of the priest working together. In this approach of Thomas, both the acts of the penitent and the absolution of the priest are integral to the sacrament. This had wide-ranging implications for the practice of this sacrament and in the development of the penitent's spiritual life.

In the practice of the sacrament, the penitent has an integral place in contributing indispensable features of the full sacrament, namely, true conversion of heart, which is expressed externally in the confession, and the acts of penance. Absolution could not be effective without contrition and conversion. This means that the priest should not absolve where no signs of sorrow are evident. Furthermore, the sacrament begins at the very moment conversion begins and the penitent turns back to God in sincere sorrow. The sacrament reaches its high point in the rite itself, and continues to extend as far as the process of conversion extends. So, the sacrament in its fullest sense is not restricted to the ritual moment but is intimately woven into the daily life of the penitent. In this way, the sacrament participates in the ongoing spiritual development of the penitent. This Thomistic approach assumes an integration of what happens in the daily life of the penitent with the sacramental moment.

(Such an approach to the sacrament lies behind efforts at renewing our practice of Penance today, and in shaping a spirituality of reconciliation which integrates the sacramental expression of forgiveness into the penitent's daily life. Implications of this approach for a spirituality of reconciliation are evident in the first chapter. The chapter on our renewed sacramental theology explored other implications, and the next chapter will sketch some of the implications of this approach in our ways of celebrating the new Rite.)

As helpful and sensible as it may seem to us, however, this approach of St. Thomas was opposed by John Duns Scotus (d. 1308). Scotus tended toward the emphasis of the School of Saint-Victor by maintaining that the acts of the penitent are necessary as a way of disposing the penitent for the sacrament, but are not essential parts of the sacramental reality. The only sacramental reality for Scotus is the absolution of the priest. Basic to the teaching of Scotus is the understanding that sincere sorrow motivated by love of God (perfect contrition) is one way to forgiveness. But no one can know for sure whether one's sorrow is perfect and sufficient for forgiveness. Sacramental absolution, however, leaves no doubt that forgiveness is granted. In the sacrament, God and the Church are operating so that not as much needs to be demanded of the penitent. The sacrament, in a sense, makes up for what is lacking in the penitent's sorrow and is the surer way to forgiveness.

Much of our catechetical training on the sacrament has followed this approach of Scotus rather than that of Thomas. The approach of Scotus led to separating the personal life of the penitent from the sacramental ritual which Thomas tried to keep integrated. Whereas Thomas required the personal response of conversion as being integral to the sacrament, Scotus regarded the acts of the penitent as non-essentials. Scotus put a great emphasis on the action of the Church, namely, absolution. Under the influence of Scotus, the sacrament became liable to charges of magic, since little involvement of the penitent was necessary. The sacrament (meaning "absolution") became the means of turning imperfect contrition into perfect contrition which brought the forgiveness of sins.

Gradually, the granting of absolution dominated our understanding of the sacrament. Our language reflected this, and so did our practice. We would use the passive expression "receive the sacrament" and mean "be given absolution." In some instances, the practice of Penance became reduced to "Give me absolution, Father, for I'm sorry in general." Such a mentality saw absolution as the only factor necessary for a valid sacrament. This made confession to a priest a must, since only the priest could grant absolution which guarantees forgiveness. In this sense, some people would hold the position that without priests there would be no forgiveness. These are all evidences of the powerful influence Scotus had on our teaching and practice.

As a result of making absolution the only important element in the sacrament to effect forgiveness, minimalist attitudes grew up toward contrition, confession, and doing acts of penance. The routine repetition of the same lists of sins, together with the mechanical recitation of formula prayers as a penance on a frequent basis, led to the condition in the lives of many Catholics where this sacrament had no noticeable effect on anyone's life. The sacrament gradually became separated from the rest of the person's moral and spiritual life until it fell out of the person's life altogether. This reflects much of the situation we are facing today, and signals some of the reasons we need to renew the sacrament in the lives of the Catholic people.

The Council of Trent

In session fourteen of the Council of Trent (1551), nine doctrinal chapters and fifteen canons were drawn up on the Sacrament of Penance.[20] Regarding the external structure of the rite, Trent did not change what had been established by Lateran IV, but ratified it. Regarding the inner meaning of the sacrament, Trent was primarily concerned with responding to the reformers' denial of the sacramental nature of Penance and its capacity to forgive sins through the ministry of the Church. Trent left unresolved the theological problem of the relationship between the acts of the penitent and the action of the Church in the forgiveness of sins. The complex discussion of the reformers and Trent do not concern us here. We are concerned with the tone and direction which Trent set for the catechesis and practice of this sacrament until Vatican II, primarily by its use of the metaphor of judgment.

Insistence on the courtroom analogy and the notion of the sacrament as a judicial act has had some wide-ranging implications coloring the responsibilities of the priest as a judge who was to know the case thoroughly by requiring a detailed confession of sins. Then the priest was to judge the disposition of the penitent, impart a fitting penance as a penalty for sin, and finally pronounce a judicial sentence in the form of absolution.

Charles Curran has shown that interpreting the judgment of absolution exclusively in terms of the courtroom analogy distorts the real meaning of the sacrament. Curran finds in Trent's judgment metaphor a richer biblical and theological meaning than has often been mined. The biblical and theological meaning

217

respects the properly judicial character of absolution as a public proclamation of pardon. But it also includes the proclamation of the mercy of God in Christ, the ecclesial role of making this mercy present to the penitent, and the worship aspect of giving thanks for the gift of forgiveness.[21]

On the controverted issue of the role of personal sorrow, the Council of Trent recognized the already existing distinction of imperfect and perfect contrition. It acknowledged that perfect contrition could bring the forgiveness of sin without sacramental confession, but maintained that perfect contrition included within itself the desire for the sacrament which God has given us for the purpose of forgiving sins. So, in the end, even perfect contrition led to the individual confession of sins according to Trent.

The Council further insisted on an "integral confession" as being essential to the forgiveness of sins in the sacrament. By "integral confession" the Council meant that the number of times a mortal sin was committed had to be confessed along with the circumstances which might change the nature of the sin. Trent's teaching that an integral confession of mortal sins is required by divine law had once been thought a stumbling block against general absolution as valid sacramental forgiveness. However, after a careful study of this question, Carl Peter of the Catholic University of America concluded that no real block is there.[22] One of the key points of his study is that Trent recognized integral confession to be a serious value in the process of conversion which requires some form of public manifestation of mortal sin to the authorized leader of the community. As Carl Peter says,

> Trent recognized clear and unambiguous confession of sin as a value. In a day when the social consequences of sin are emphasized, there is less tendency to see repentance as exercised in the depths of one's heart independently of any visible connection with God's People and its leaders. What the Council in question equivalently asserted is that God expects as a remedy for sin conduct corresponding to its social nature, therefore ecclesial and hierarchical. He established integral confession as a value and called it to man's attention.[23]

218

However, Trent did not present integral confession as an absolute value. There are exceptions to the obligation of integrity. The value of integral confession co-exists with other values which at times may take precedence. The Church had traditionally recognized this in cases of urgent necessity, such as instances of near death, or other moral and physical impossibilities in the way of making an integral confession. Trent recognized that the value of integral confession always exists in the midst of other values. But Trent did not decide what all those other values might be, nor did it establish a fixed hierarchy of values which could be used to determine whether to waive or delay the requirement of integral confession at any particular time. Carl Peter concludes his study by suggesting that the teaching of Trent does not exclude "a ceremony involving only general confession and communal absolution coupled with the obligation of confessing specifically within a definite period of time.[24] The new Rite of Penance allows precisely this possibility. While stating that individual, integral confession is the normal way to be reconciled through the sacrament, the new Rite does not prevent those in grave sin from participating in general absolution (see Par. 31). However, the instruction on general absolution is followed by this requirement:

> Those who receive pardon for grave sins by a common absolution should go to individual confession before they receive this kind of absolution again, unless they are impeded by a just reason. They are strictly bound, unless this is morally impossible, to go to confession within a year (Par. 34).

Venial sins, however, are not included in this requirement for integral confession. Venial sins can be forgiven by means other than sacramental confession. We have seen this as a long-standing tradition throughout the history of Penance. However, the Council recommended confessing venial sins as an aid in spiritual growth. Out of this has grown the practice of "devotional confession" which is the regular confession of sins, even though one is not guilty of mortal sin.

The frequent confession of even venial sins has been a recommended practice since Trent. In 1943, Pius XII encouraged frequent confession of venial sin in his encyclical letter *Mystici Corporis:*

> It is true . . . that venial sins may be expiated in many ways which are highly to be recommended. But to hasten daily progress along the path of virtue We wish the pious practice of frequent confession to be earnestly advocated. Not without the inspiration of the Holy Spirit was this practice introduced into the Church. By it genuine self-knowledge is increased, Christian humility grows, bad habits are corrected, spiritual neglect and tepidity are conquered, the conscience is purified, the will strengthened, a salutary self-control is attained and grace is inceased in virtue of the sacrament itself.[25]

Karl Rahner presumes reasons such as these summarized by Pius XII for the usefulness of frequent confession and goes on to explore the proper function and distinctive character of devotional confession in one's spiritual life. John Dedek has summarized Rahner's reflections on the special identity and function of devotional confession this way:

> . . . the special characteristic of devotional confession, which gives it its own identity and special function among all the other ascetical practices, is that it directly effects the sacramental pardon of venial sins. This differs from the pardon effected through other sacraments or extra-sacramentally because it manifests in a clear and dramatic way that all repentance and forgiveness is the free action of God in man, that God's grace touches man personally and historically, and that the repentant sinner is reconciled with the Church which also has been harmed by his sin.[26]

Therefore, what devotional confession does, that other ways of forgiving venial sins does not do clearly enough, is manifest that forgiveness comes from God in and through a personally and historically tangible way to effect reconciliation with God and the whole People of God at one and the same time.

From this, the value of frequent confession becomes clear.

But exactly how frequently one ought to confess cannot be pre-determined in any mathematical way. So the question "How often should I go?" cannot be answered with a mathematical precision (like every week, every month, four times a year, etc.) by reference to the documents of Trent or any other Council. The once a year regulation of Lateran IV referred to mortal sins, not to devotional confession of venial sins. Yet the pastoral practice and wisdom of the Church has encouraged the frequent and careful celebration of this sacrament for venial sins as well. As the Introduction has it,

> This is not a mere ritual repetition or psychological exercise, but a serious striving to perfect the grace of baptism so that, as we bear in our body the death of Jesus Christ, his life may be seen in us ever more clearly (Par. 7b).

The purpose of such frequent celebrations of sacramental reconciliation is "to conform more closely to Christ and to follow the voice of the Spirit more attentively" (Par. 7b).

We can also say that frequent sacramental celebrations of reconciliation are necessary in order to hear, see, and feel that we are loved, forgiven, and accepted by God and the community. As human persons who know through sense experience, we need more than telling ourselves that we are loved and accepted. We need to hear it, feel it, and see it in very tangible ways. The Sacrament of Reconciliation can be one of the moments to communicate that love where we can be "hugged by God," as it were.

In addition to these general ways which indicate when sacramental reconciliation is necessary for us, some useful pastoral norms have come down to us since Trent on the practice of frequent confession. One of these is that we are encouraged to confess during significant liturgical times of the year, such as Advent and Lent. Confession has also been encouraged for those times which mark a significant change in a person's life, such as confirmation, marriage, ordination, and a second career. Other occasions in which confession is encouraged are those times specifically aimed at deepening our commitment to God, such as a retreat. Those times which mark a significant change in the normal routine of our lives are also good, such as the beginning of school or the end of vacation.

In the end, specifying a set number of times for frequent confession is not easy. The sacrament can be too easily dulled either by forcing a person to confess with unnecessary frequency, or by delaying too long. The rhythm we choose to adopt ought to be one that expresses a healthy honesty regarding our commitment to spiritual growth and to ongoing conversion. At any rate, frequent confessions are opportunities to see Reconciliation as an act of recognizing one's own sinfulness and, at the same time, as giving praise and thanks to God for the gift of the forgiving mercy of God in Christ and through the Spirit in the Church. The goal of devotional confession is to enter more deeply into the life of conversion which is integral to the Christian life. When this focus on frequent confession can be kept clear, Trent's recommendation of confessing even venial sins carries great weight as a means of growth in living the Christian life.

Out of the metaphor of judgment which shaped Trent's teaching on Penance, the acts of penance often became a kind of penalty or punishment for sinning. The acts of penance were to serve not only as a deterrent to future sin, but also as a way of being punished now so as to avert extended punishment after death. Doing a penance for the purpose of taking the first step in the direction of living a reconciled life and healing one's pre-disposition to sin needs to be retrieved from the earlier history of the sacrament. This may help correct the largely judicial framework for approaching the acts of penance in particular, and the whole sacrament in general. An overly juridical approach to sin, forgiveness, and the sacramental ritual easily turned the whole experience into a kind of courtroom drama that promoted an attitude of fear and condemnation, rather than one of gratitude, healing, and hope which we are trying to promote today.

From Trent to Vatican II

Between the time of Trent and the Second Vatican Council, any further changes pertaining to the sacrament were mostly canonical aimed at protecting the penitent. For example, one note-worthy change was the introduction of the confessional box in the sixteenth century, seemingly by St. Charles Borromeo. Listening to confessions from behind a screen protected the anonymity of the penitents, and helped prevent any compromising solicitation in the privacy of the confessional setting.

The theological debates on the Sacrament of Penance which enlivened the Middle Ages have since lost their energy. Impetus for a change in the Rite has been stimulated by recognizing some of the limitations in our practice of Penance, as well as by some further developments in theology responding to the spirit of a new age. One serious limitation that has been with us since the Scholastic period and Trent is an absent, or underdeveloped, sense of the communitarian aspects of Reconciliation. The Sacrament of Reconciliation, as we have come to know it, has been not only private, but privatized. We have felt this not only in our individualistic approach to sin and the consequences of sin, but also in our approach to doing penance and being reconciled. Furthermore, the legislated pattern of the sacrament that came out of Trent which insisted on listing sins with number, kind, and circumstances often focused on a series of discrete acts while missing the more comprehensive issues of conversion and spiritual growth. The monastic practice of situating the confession of sins within the context of ongoing spiritual direction made it easier to focus on the roots of one's sinfulness and see individual acts as expressive of a more pervasive disorientation. The courtroom drama of the confessional box, along with the anonymity of the penitent, imposed a strained and artificial context on the confessional conversation.

Furthermore, the impetus of the biblical renewal in theology, as well as the influence of personalist philosophies on theological reflection and catechesis, has moved us beyond the legal metaphors that controlled much of our catechesis on morality and the sacrament since Trent. Biblical and personalist metaphors, like conversion, covenant, reconciliation, interpersonal encounter, and personal responsibility, have given us a new way of thinking about morality, as we saw in our earlier chapters on sin and conscience. In the next chapter we will see how they have shaped our approach to celebrating the new Rite of Penance.

One thing that clearly emerges from tracing the lifeline of the Sacrament of Reconciliation is the Church's ability to adjust its sacramental practices to the needs of the people and to changing historical circumstances. We do not want to say that the shape which Penance took in any era was an inauthentic expression of the Gospel call to conversion and the commission to be forgiving. Each shape of Penance responded to the spiritual needs of the people within the limits of a specific cultural context. Each era and each shape of Penance reflects an authentic, though limited, expression of the Gospel commission to undergo conversion and to be forgiving. The same can be said of our era and the shape in which Reconciliation comes to us in the new Rite of Penance. Change has occurred in our practice of Penance, though change has occurred slowly. Still more change can come in the future. We are not yet in the last days of a fixed form for this sacrament.

I want to close this historical sketch of the development of this sacrament by taking a summary look at its lifeline. The accompanying chart summarizes in a schematic way the main features of the lifeline under the four primary requisites for this sacrament.

FOURTH MOVEMENT: APPROPRIATING THE CHRISTIAN STORY

How has this history of the Sacrament of Reconciliation affected your understanding of this sacrament? How has this chapter affirmed you? How have you been challenged? Complete the following sentences:

I realized that I . . .
I relearned that I . . .
I was surprised that I . . .
I wonder if . . .
I wonder why . . .
I wonder when . . .

HISTORICAL SHAPE OF FOUR SUBSTANTIVE ELEMENTS
OF SACRAMENTAL RECONCILIATION

	CONTRITION	CONFESSION	ACTS OF PENANCE	RECONCILIATION
Period of Canonical Penance (4th–6th centuries)	*CONTRITION* — The first movements of conversion in coming to awareness of sin with heartfelt sorrow.	*CONFESSION* — Enrolling in the order of penitents through a public liturgical ceremony. (This confession of sins is not a public pronouncement.)	*ACTS OF PENANCE* — Acts of penance were generally severe, lasted a long time, and had consequences marking one's whole life. Aim is to rehabilitate the sinner.	*RECONCILIATION* — Reconciliation with the community occurs in a public liturgical rite led by bishop with prayers and imposition of hands, followed by receiving Eucharist.
Monastic System (7th–9th centuries)	*CONTRITION* — The first movements of conversion in heartfelt sorrow.	*CONFESSION* — Disclosure of conscience to a spiritual guide (not necessarily a cleric) seeking spiritual growth and renewal. Done in private without a communal context.	*ACTS OF PENANCE* — Ascetical practices assumed for purposes of remedies for sin and means of spiritual discipline and growth.	*RECONCILIATION* — There is *no* evidence of a rite of reconciliation existing in monastic system. Returning to Eucharist presumes reconciliation
Origins of Present System (10th century)	*CONTRITION* — First movements of conversion in coming to an awareness of sin with heartfelt sorrow and desire to change.	*CONFESSION* — Private disclosure to a priest. Respecting the integral confession of mortal sins.	*RECONCILIATION* — Prayer of absolution and imposition of hands follow upon the penitent's prayer of sorrow.	*ACTS OF PENANCE* — The acts of penance are done after the rite of reconciliation is complete. The penance is the concrete expression of conversion and first step in direction of healing.

FIFTH MOVEMENT: CHOOSING A FAITH RESPONSE

How might you look upon each of the parts of the sacrament now? What attitudes do you need to change with regard to the sacrament? Complete the following sentences:

Next time, I want to . . .
I need to think more about . . .
I hope that I . . .

Suggestions for Further Reading

Monika K. Hellwig	*Sign of Reconciliation and Conversion: The Sacrament of Penance for Our Time*
Joseph Martos	*Doors to the Sacred*
Bernard Poschmann	*Penance and the Anointing of the Sick*
Karl Rahner	*Theological Investigations, Vol. XV, Penance in the Early Church*

Celebrating the Rites
of Reconciliation

FIRST MOVEMENT: PRESENT ACTION

How are you presently celebrating the Sacrament of Reconciliation? How do you prepare for it? What do you do after the sacramental celebration?

SECOND MOVEMENT: CRITICAL REFLECTION

Why do you go to confession? What are your hopes in celebrating this sacrament? What do you want the celebration of this sacrament to be for you? What place does it have in your spiritual life?

THIRD MOVEMENT: THE CHRISTIAN STORY AND VISION

Anyone planning a celebration of the Sacrament of Reconciliation needs to know that the experience of reconciliation lies at the heart of this sacramental encounter. In the third chapter, we reviewed some of the fundamental principles of sacramental theology. We saw there that "personal presence" is a key to attractive and effective sacramental celebrations. Before giving a brief commentary on ways of celebrating sacramental reconciliation according to the revised Rite, we need to ask a prior question: What do we need in order to facilitate personal presence and to create a humanly attractive and expressive sacramental celebration? We need hospitality. We need hospitality in priests as well as in penitents. For this reason, we need to prepare for celebrating sacramental reconciliation by preparing ourselves to be persons of hospitality.

The first half of this chapter will present some pastoral guidelines for priests and penitents to prepare for celebrating Reconciliation. Of course, expecting every effort of preparing for Reconciliation to be this way would be idealistic. These pastoral guidelines are presented here as goals toward which we ought to strive. These guidelines are presented primarily with the Rite for Reconciliation of Individual Penitents in mind. However, many of these suggestions will pertain to the rites for several penitents as well. The hope in presenting these guidelines in this fashion is that we will do everything possible to facilitate attractive and effective sacramental celebrations of reconciliation.

PREPARING FOR THE RITES

In the chapter on sacraments, we saw that hospitality best expresses the kind of love we would hope to find in Christian communities in order to enable good liturgical celebrations to happen. There we saw that hospitality in liturgy is paying attention to one another, to what is going on around us, and to what is going on inside ourselves as a result of what is happening around us. By paying attention we open ourselves to God, to others, and to ourselves. This kind of paying attention is necessary in the Sacrament of Reconciliation as well.

Henri Nouwen has explored dimensions of hospitality to great effect for growth in the spiritual life. Two dimensions apply especially to the Sacrament of Reconciliation. One is receptivity (which agrees with "paying attention"). The other is confrontation. Both are necessary and must remain in careful balance. As Nouwen puts it:

> Receptivity without confrontation leads to a bland neutrality that serves nobody. Confrontation without receptivity leads to an oppressive aggression which hurts everybody. This balance between receptivity and confrontation is found at different points, depending upon our individual position in life. But in every life situation, we not only have to receive but also to confront.[1]

To create an effective celebration of Reconciliation, we need both sides of hospitality. We will explore the implications of "receptivity" and "confrontation" for the priest as well as the penitent.

Hospitality as Receptivity
1. *For the Priest*
The first instruction given to the priest in the Rite of Reconciliation of Individual Penitents is this: "When the penitent comes to confess his sins, the priest welcomes him warmly and greets him with kindness" (#41). This first step in the Rite calls for an attitude and expression of hospitality. How might this happen? What might hospitality as "receptivity" look like? What does it mean for the priest to be hospitable?

Of the priest, hospitality asks, "Will the penitent meet a person or a functionary?" We all know stories of priests who did not enter into the sacrament in any personal way, but often stood above it in some judgmental way, or went through it in some mechanical way. From the moment the priest pulled back the slide and the penitent began, "Bless me Father . . ." to the closing "Go in peace and pray for me," we have known a very stylized ritual where everyone's lines were well rehearsed, and all the rubrics were faithfully followed. Informality, humor, spontaneity, and personal transparency were often out of the question. Of course there were exceptions—but, and here's the rub, not always. The new Rite, however, calls for what was once an exception to become the norm. The new Rite encourages the priest and the penitent to relax and be natural. It calls for the warmth and personableness of an interpersonal rapport to prevail from beginning to end. The whole Rite recognizes, in keeping with the sacramental theology which underlies it, that an encounter with the saving forgiveness of God which brings pardon and peace takes flesh in the human interaction between the priest and the penitent.

Since the Council of Trent's Decrees on the Sacrament of Penance (1551), we have looked on the priest in this sacrament as a judge. Now from the perspective of a renewed sacramental theology and the importance of hospitality for sacramental celebrations, we can write a new "job description" for the priest. The priest in this sacrament is the host of the reconciling community welcoming the penitent home again. As the host of reconciliation, the priest eases the process by leading the penitent from the experience of being a sinner isolated from the community to being accepted and incorporated into the community.

As the host facilitating reconciliation, the priest is more than a private individual in this sacrament. He is both the instrument through which God communicates forgiveness and the representative of the whole community of faith granting pardon and peace. We confess to a priest because he is the one designated to act on behalf of the community. He needs to communicate this welcoming tone of acceptance and to create a hospitable environment of peace at the very beginning of the celebration. For example, the priest can do much to set the tone and put the penitent at ease by receiving the penitent with a smile, a handshake, and a few kind words. In the face-to-face meeting in the reconciliation room, a little "small talk" with the penitent can be appropriate for setting the penitent at ease and establishing an atmosphere of comfort and welcome. At least, a warm, welcoming greeting is in order. It may go something like this: "Welcome. We (meaning the Christian community of the local parish whom the priest represents) are glad to have you. And I am happy to be invited to pray with you to come to know the forgiveness of sins and the gifts of pardon and peace."

Warm and welcoming words are crucial as a greeting, not only in the well-lighted reconciliation room, but even more especially in the dark confessional box where there is no chance to communicate through physical touch, by an affirming facial expression, or with a reassuring nod. The tone of voice, the cadence of one's speech, and the words chosen have to do all the work. But whether in the reconciliation room or in the confessional box, the primary responsibility of the priest, as the instrument of God's forgiveness and representative of the community's pardon and peace, is to show in clear signs that the penitent is loved, accepted, and forgiven. Through the signs of a compassionate ministry, the penitents can feel the personal love of God and of the community who cherish sinners even in their deepest misery.

As the ritual continues, so must the expressions of hospitality. In the course of the celebration, hospitality means that the priest maintains eye contact with the penitent (which is different from staring), nods with understanding, and sits in a relaxed posture (though not a slumped one) while communicating verbally as well as non-verbally with relaxed, reassuring facial expressions. Hospitality also uses humor appropriately to lighten the atmosphere which may become too somberly serious, or to put something in perspective when it becomes too somberly absolute.

Hospitality is also sensitive enough to know when to reach out and touch the penitent by taking hold of the penitent's hands during a time of prayer, for example, or at least by using the gesture of the imposition of hands during the prayer of absolution. Hospitality also knows when to be more reserved. Through these expressions of hospitality, the priest can image a loving God and a reconciling community ready and willing to welcome the penitent home again.

Hospitality is also reverent. This means that throughout the celebration the priest allows the penitents to express themselves in their own ways. The hospitable priest does not interrupt a penitent's manner of praying or confessing by insisting on a particular style (which usually turns out to be a style which makes the priest comfortable). Hospitality invites penitents to be themselves in their confessing and in their praying. Hospitality allows the penitents to say as much as they are able to say, and in the manner in which they are able.

Hospitality also respects silence, and says no more than is

necessary. We know from our everyday experiences of hospitality that hosts who feel they have to talk all the time and keep
their guests constantly entertained make hospitality oppressive
rather than recreative and liberating. The same applies to Reconciliation, where the priest should lean toward saying too little
rather than too much.

Priests can communicate a healing understanding more by
sensitive listening than by talking, or assuming the role of pastoral counselor, marriage counselor, sex therapist, or even spiritual director. This last point needs to be stressed because of the
almost universal and deeply entrenched tendency of minister-
ing-type persons who become priests to want to inculcate truth,
instruct, advise, set people straight, and solve problems. This
tendency rears its head so quickly that priests as confessors often do not listen well and, as a result, do not facilitate forgiveness well. Although telling is a central task of the Church as it
proclaims the good news, paying attention comes first.

Hospitality in the Sacrament of Reconciliation listens more
than it talks. The new Rite of Reconciliation of Individual Penitents, especially when celebrated in the face-to-face situation of
the reconciliation room, easily promotes the tendency to do pastoral counseling (and often by an incompetent counselor). The
danger of psychologizing within the sacrament is great. This is
especially true today with our climate of personalism and the increasing interest in psychology among the Catholic clergy which
has caused us to face a fundamental question concerning the integrity of this sacrament: "Is sacramental reconciliation primarily an act of worship, or is it first and foremost a forum for
pastoral counseling and spiritual direction?" Since this issue has
been a point of debate and confusion since the renewal of this
sacrament, it deserves some specific attention.

To state the integrity of sacramental reconciliation as clearly
as possible, and to make the contrast between sacramental reconciliation and pastoral counseling and spiritual direction as
starkly as possible, I would say this: the Sacrament of Reconciliation is primarily an act of worship in and through which the
penitent turns to God in praise and thanksgiving for the forgiveness of sins. The primary role of the priest is to be the host inviting the penitent more deeply into the reconciling activity of God

in Christ and through the Spirit in the community of God's people, the Church. The priest must attend to his business of making the essential signs of this reconciling activity clear, especially the signs of forgiveness, acceptance, and affirmation. He does this by being a hospitable host expressing human care and welcome as an instrument of God's forgiving love and as the representative of the whole community of God's people. Through human signs of reconciliation, the priest helps the penitent feel loved, accepted, and healed in the presence of the community and by God.

Pastoral counseling and spiritual direction are best done elsewhere, and perhaps by another person, unless the priest himself is well skilled in these forms of helping relationships. Pastoral counseling and spiritual direction can easily come into conflict with the task of facilitating reconciliation. But they should not be mixed up. The objectives are different: Reconciliation is for forgiveness; counseling is for therapy; direction is for cultivating one's personal relationship with God. This is not to say that a good host of reconciliation would not make use of some elements and skills common to pastoral counseling and spiritual direction. The skills of establishing rapport, empathy, and active listening are certainly ones which have a place in the Sacrament of Reconciliation. But the emphasis must be on the priest as the host of reconciliation who uses effective helping skills for reconciling. The priest ought not to be a counselor who uses the Sacrament of Reconciliation as the forum for doing counseling.

Admittedly, no pure instances exist which express the clean distinction between sacramental reconciliation and pastoral counseling or spiritual direction as clearly as I have here. Certainly the distinction is easier to maintain in communal rather than individual Reconciliation. Still, I have put the case starkly for the sake of clarity. Above all, priests as confessors ought to try to avoid fostering a counseling relationship in the sacramental forum. The primary reason is that such a practice diverts the focus of the sacrament, and compromises its integrity.

Anyone who has been a confessor in the Sacrament of Reconciliation knows that undoubtedly some instances of sacramental reconciliation for some penitents in certain situations might call for a pastoral counseling or spiritual direction response from the priest. Good pastoral practice would be alert to such instances and be ready to accommodate them. However, such accommodation within the sacramental forum is not the rule, but the exceptional practice. The rule is that pastoral counseling and spiritual direction are usually out of place in the sacramental forum. Changing the focus of the sacramental encounter from reconciliation to counseling therapy or spiritual direction can harm the identity and integrity of the sacrament in the long run. No wonder some people who had been regular penitents, but now are in therapy, say, "Why do I need your Sacrament of Reconciliation anymore, now that I have my professional therapist?" The "one-stop shopping" mentality that wants to use the sacramental moment to satisfy multiple personal needs (such as counseling, spiritual direction, and reconciliation) will eventually compromise the sacrament's integrity. If a penitent is in need of counseling, a counselor should be sought. If the priest discerns that the penitent is in need of counseling, then a referral is in order. If spiritual direction is what the penitent seeks, then a spiritual director ought to be found and a relationship for spiritual direction established.

Louis Monden made some astute observations about the integrity of Reconciliation in the days prior to the implementation of the revised Rite. His observations are still worthwhile and deserve repeating.

> The address of the priest is an intra-sacramental event, and not, in the first instance, an occasion for moral or psychological counseling. What absolution will accomplish in the sinner is anticipated liturgically in the priest's address. It is therefore a sign of the concrete appeal of a merciful God, creating a new life, but also inviting, urging, demanding; of a God who is to meet, in Christ and in the Church, this concrete sinner in his concrete sinfulness.

> The priest may use this religiously very intimate moment to give practical advice, to propose certain things, to help develop insight into the problem created by the situation. The function of spiritual direction and moral counseling may be exercised on the occasion of confession.

Yet this function has nothing to do with confession as such, even though historically it has often been associated with it. Furthermore, the priest will not, in most instances, have gathered enough information from the penitent to give safe psychological guidance without endangering the religious character of confession through a long conversation mainly profane in content. A directive given with the best intention, but based on inadequate information, may have exactly the opposite effect, and the penitent, who mistakenly includes it in the sacred content of the sacrament, will often be afraid of disobeying it, lest he should refuse to do what the sacrament itself demands. Thus innumerable conflicts of conscience originate in the platitudes uttered too hastily for complex situations by a well-meaning confessor. Aversion to a conversation forced on him in confession, anxiety about a too human curiosity trying to pry into his intimate affairs, put a damper on many a Christian's enthusiasm for the sacrament of penance and make him unwilling to use it.

Modern man wants to receive this sacrament again in its religious integrity, and we must satisfy his need. This makes it desirable that *confession* and eventual *spiritual direction* should be carefully kept *apart* wherever possible, and that psychological counseling should take place outside the confessional.[2]

Monden's observations also ought to make priests cautious about being too ready to offer advice without having really known fully the person being advised, or understanding the wounds needing to be healed. Generally speaking, considering the little the priest really knows about the penitent on the basis of the brief sacramental encounter, advice-giving in such situations can too easily be more harmful than helpful. Michael Cavanaugh's estimation of advice-giving in a helping relationship pertains to the ministry of sacramental reconciliation as well:

Giving advice is generally not only unhelpful but destructive because it communicates to the person: "You're right; you're not capable of making your own decisions." It also deprives the individual of the very *process* that is necessary to become a reasonably autonomous decision-maker and shifts the burden of responsibility to the helper. A good general principle is: "The times we are most convinced that giving advice is legitimate and helpful are likely to be the times when giving advice will do the most harm."[3]

One of the tasks of the priest in the Sacrament of Reconciliation is to provide a safe space where penitents can manifest their consciences freely enough to come to a more profound understanding of themselves and of what their lives mean. For this reason, the priest may call to the attention of the penitent some of the values, consequences, and perspectives which the penitent might otherwise miss. But the healing of Reconciliation comes more through kindness and gentle mercy than from advice. Only when priests are able to listen with the heart to the hearts of the penitents will they *together* be able to make a realistic assessment of the roots of sin and focus on new patterns of behavior that will bring about the changes that truly heal. Hospitality does not set out to change people by telling them what to do. Hospitality creates the free space where change can take place in those who want it. The highest form of hospitality is paying attention with the heart. Listening with the heart is the experience that says to the penitents, "You are lovable. You are forgiven. Welcome home! Let's walk together again!"

Hospitality also means making good preparations before entering into the celebration of the sacrament. If he is to be as attentive as the interpersonal framework of the sacrament demands, the priest must take care to prepare himself. This means being properly rested (taking a short nap before the scheduled time for the sacrament helps), psychologically oriented (setting aside one's own agenda in order to be emotionally free and attentive), and spiritually disposed.

A further word on being spiritually disposed to celebrate Reconciliation is in order. To be properly disposed spiritually, the priest needs to take a few moments of prayer immediately prior to the sacramental moment. Before entering the reconciliation room, the priest needs to open his heart to the Spirit, to ask for the gift of the Spirit to be the light and strength of what he is about to do, and to center himself so that he can receive penitents with an interior peace and a welcoming space in himself.

236

Furthermore, genuine discernment of what God might be doing in the penitent's life and what the penitent might do in response (such as through a "behavioral penance") can happen only if the priest (along with the penitent) is first a person of prayer. Discernment is a gift. But our tradition clearly affirms that a regular regimen of prayer is a common condition for opening oneself to this gift. The kind of prayer appropriate for being a discerning person, as well as for being a "prayerful" person, is not the matter of repeating formula prayers. Often this way of praying has little to do with personal experience and the concrete circumstances which give rise to the need for discernment in the first place. Also, repeating formula prayers gives the illusion of being prayerful when one's heart is really far from being open to God. Prayer for discernment is a contemplative-like "listening prayer" that takes a long loving look into one's own life and experiences to discover God's presence there. Listening prayer of this nature pays attention and notices what is happening in one's experiences and how one feels about what is happening. By paying attention to our experiences and feelings we can begin to hear what God is saying to us. This is the kind of prayer that leads to an openness of mind and heart that makes discernment of God's presence and call possible.

Moreover, entering the sacramental celebration as a praying and prayerful person is a prerequisite not only for genuine discernment, but also for making the sacramental moment a true experience of worship and a genuine expression of liturgical prayer. The greater the priest's commitment to personal prayer, the greater will be the potential for making Reconciliation a prayerful expression of praise and thanksgiving.

Good preparations also involve providing a hospitable environment which is welcoming. This means that the reconciliation room needs to be a warm, friendly, inviting place. The priest exercises hospitality by seeing that the room is not cluttered with papers and books, that the lights work, and that the furniture is comfortable. No junk stuff, please. Beauty is very healing. Entering a pleasant room can fill a person with confidence, allay fears, and reduce anxiety long before any words are spoken.

In addition to providing a welcoming room, the priest himself ought to appear in a hospitable way. This means he should not be disheveled in personal appearance, nor offensive in body and breath odors. The physical appearance of the reconciliation room, as well as the personal appearance of the priest, has a lot to do with enhancing or obstructing the reconciling encounter with the Lord. Remember the principle for good liturgy: good signs increase and nourish faith; poor signs weaken and destroy faith. The person of the priest and the environment of the room are tremendously powerful signs.

A final aspect of hospitable preparation that needs attention is the time when the sacrament is scheduled. The Rite addresses the time factor very squarely in Paragraph #13:

> The reconciliation of penitents may be celebrated at any time on any day, but it is desirable that the faithful know the day and time at which the priest is available for this ministry. They should be encouraged to approach the sacrament of penance at times when Mass is not being celebrated especially during the scheduled periods.

The pastoral responsibility of the priest is that "he should always be ready and willing to hear the confessions of the faithful when they make a reasonable request of him" (#10b). As for scheduled periods, the trend of Saturday afternoons, or immediately before Mass, may have to be revised if new understandings of this Rite encourage a revival. The practice of "confession before Mass" easily reinforces the one-stop shopping syndrome toward matters religious, continues the attitude of confession before each Communion, or suggests that sacramental reconciliation is useless except for the gravest of offenses which would require sacramental reconciliation before Communion anyway.

The full celebration of the revised Rite requires a little more time than we have been accustomed to give in the traditional confession box approach. Scheduling should respect the need for more time. Perhaps the best times for scheduling the sacrament are the times which the members of the community designate upon consultation with them, and after proper catechesis on this sacrament, and after good experiences of the new Rite. The important goal of scheduling is not to discourage or inconvenience the community. Whatever time is finally chosen, by all means the Sacrament of Reconciliation should not conflict with the Eucharistic liturgy as the instructions of Paragraph #13 quoted above designate. To celebrate Reconciliation and Eucharist at the same time is an abuse of both sacraments, and a most inhospitable gesture.

2. *For the Penitent*

Hospitality as receptivity also belongs to the penitent. Practically, what does this mean?

First of all, the hospitable penitent comes to the sacrament with a proper disposition. A proper disposition begins with sorrow, or contrition. About the importance of contrition, the Introduction says this:

> The most important act of the penitent is contrition, which is "heartfelt sorrow and aversion for the sin committed along with the intention of sinning no more." "We can only approach the Kingdom of Christ by *metanoia*. This is a profound change of the whole person by which one begins to consider, judge, and arrange his life according to the holiness and love of God, manifest in his Son in the last days and given to us in abundance" (see Hebrews 1:2; Colossians 1:19 and *passim*). The genuineness of penance depends on this heartfelt contrition. For conversion should affect a person from within so that it may progressively enlighten him and render him continually more like Christ (#6a).

The penitent can come to a proper disposition by taking some quiet time for prayer before beginning the sacramental celebration. In prayer, the penitent can not only renew faith in God and confidence in God's merciful love, but also face the roots of sin with honesty and ask for the strength of the Spirit to live more lovingly. Also in prayer the penitent can discern the ways of God's acting in his or her life, as well as the ways he or she might be able to respond to God through gratitude and conversion. Particular actions can then be suggested as the behavioral penance which the penitent would be willing to assume as an expression of conversion, and as a commitment to a life of reconciliation. With such prayerful preparation and a proper disposition, the penitent can help make the celebration of the sacrament a genuine expression of worship and a Spirit-filled experience of liturgical prayer.

Just as the priest needs to have a clear image of what his role is (namely, to be the hospitable host of the reconciling God in Christ and through the Spirit in the Church), so too does the penitent need a clear image of his or her role. The penitent is to be just that—a repentant sinner coming home again, coming to the sacrament to deepen his or her awareness of being a sinner who is still loved by God and welcomed by the community. Such a penitent not only admits to sins of the past, but even more is open to the present action of the Spirit and to the future possibilities of a better life in union with God in Christ and through the Spirit and in union with the Church.

The penitent who understands his or her "job" in this way will use the sacrament primarily as an act of worship encountering the forgiving God in community. Such a penitent will not use the sacrament primarily as a time to do "problem-solving," nor even to "talk things out" in the way one would do with a therapist. Problem-solving and talking things out in a therapeutic way are needs which may be better met in another forum and with a skilled counselor. The penitent's "job" is to express one's awareness of one's own sinfulness which comes out of the awareness of being loved by God, and to deepen one's commitment to a life of reconciliation in the community.

In the sacramental celebration itself, the hospitable penitent pays attention to the priest, just as the hospitable priest pays attention to the penitent, and not only to his words but to his whole person. The priest often communicates much more about the love and acceptance of the Christian community and of God through his person and personal style than he does through his words. The penitent who enters into the sacramental encounter with a receptive attitude that pays attention to the priest in every dimension enhances the experience of reconciliation.

Furthermore, just as the penitent likes to encounter a person in the priest rather than a functionary, so too the priest likes to meet a person in the penitent. This means that the hospitable penitent shares in contributing to the interpersonal rapport and the welcoming tone of a hospitable environment for this sacrament by being as spontaneous, natural, and transparent as one is able to be. This can happen not only in responding to simple greetings, but also in times of prayer, in using Scripture, and in the confession of sins itself. By responding to greetings and invitations to prayer, or even taking the initiative to request a moment of quiet, or prayerfully reading a passage from Scripture, or sharing prayer with the priest, the penitent acts hospitably. Letting the priest know one's needs for prayer and taking the initiative in prayer are very hospitable gestures which the penitent should not be afraid to use.

The penitent can further extend hospitality by being personal and transparent in the manner of self-disclosure in making his or her confession of sins. Confessing in a less stylized but more natural and conversational way can stimulate the dynamics of a genuine experience of Reconciliation. The more natural, personal style releases more easily the healing potential of the interpersonal environment advocated by the new Rite. Even while hospitality asks the penitent to be natural and personal, the new Rite allows the penitent to reserve the right to remain faceless by confessing from behind a screen, or to remain nameless even when in the face-to-face situation of the reconciliation room. In either instance, the penitent can still enhance the interpersonal and hospitable environment of the sacrament by volunteering some background information about oneself when such information would help illumine the more complete context of what is being confessed. This means that the penitent might share something of his or her married status, occupation, primary responsibilities, major conflicts, or whatever else might help establish a clearer focus and proper context for the confession of sins.

Thus far we have explored only one dimension of hospitality, namely, paying attention or receptivity. The other side, confrontation, is also important. What might hospitality as confrontation look like?

Hospitality as Confrontation

If we were to limit hospitality just to receptivity, we could too easily reduce those extending hospitality to neutral "nobodies" and the receptive place to an empty space. Henri Nouwen

241

gives a helpful description of the need for confrontation as the other side of hospitality:

> Real receptivity asks for confrontation because space can only be a welcoming space when there are clear boundaries, and boundaries are limits between which we define our own position. Flexible limits, but limits nonetheless. Confrontation results from the articulate presence, the presence within boundaries, of the host to the guest by which he offers himself as a point of orientation and a frame of reference. We are not hospitable when we leave our house to strangers and let them use it in any way they want. An empty house is not a hospitable house. In fact, it quickly becomes a ghost house, making the stranger feel uncomfortable. Instead of losing fears, the guest becomes anxious, suspicious of any noise coming from the attic and cellar. When we want to be really hospitable we not only have to receive strangers but also to confront them by an unambiguous presence, not hiding ourselves behind neutrality but showing our ideas, opinions and life style clearly and distinctly. No real dialogue is possible between somebody and a nobody. We can enter into communication with the other only when our own life choices, attitudes and viewpoints offer the boundaries that challenge strangers to become aware of their own position and to explore it critically.[4]

This description of the indispensable place for confrontation in hospitality gives some direction to its place in the Sacrament of Reconciliation.

While the Christian moral life is open to diverse expressions, these have limits. We cannot do whatever we want and still remain faithful to the Gospel and our Christian identity. The Gospel along with the living tradition of the Christian people and the teaching of the Church establishes the framework for living the Christian life and provides a point of reference for establishing and maintaining our Christian identity. Without this framework and these points of reference, no real dialogue with penitents is possible since we would have no boundaries within which to explore our lives critically. In the Sacrament of

Reconciliation, we face our life styles, our limits, and the boundaries for living the Christian life. Hospitable confrontation, like hospitable receptivity, pertains to the priest and to the penitent alike.

1. *For the Priest*

The priest can express hospitable confrontation first by proclaiming the Word of God. Scripture, above all, sets the limits between which we define ourselves and within which we test our lives. A word, a phrase, an image from a Scriptural text used in the celebration can give rise to a feeling (consolation, sorrow, fear, anger) or insight which calls the penitent to a fresh understanding of oneself and to conversion. The words and images we hear in the Scriptural reading, as well as the feelings we have at these times, can strike us in a new way to help us realize the sort of persons we are becoming and the way we are being called to live a life in the Spirit. Such a moment is an instance of hospitable confrontation.

Another instance is the moment of the priest's dialogue with the penitent. This moment can be a witnessing to the Gospel's call to conversion. To be so, this dialogue must not intimidate by probing with unnecessary questions, by blaming, accusing, or condemning. Such action is manipulative and abusive, not healing and liberating. Hospitable confrontation that witnesses to the call to conversion begins with the priest receiving the penitent with reverence, with an attitude of real love. It continues with his listening deeply to the penitent's heart and to his own.

The priest who lives his own life attuned to the Spirit through a regular discipline of listening prayer need not hesitate to trust what he senses deeply within himself. Our spiritual heritage tells us that a prayerfully attuned heart is an entrusted instrument of God's voice. While always exercising prudence and sensitive delicacy, the priest can express to the penitent what he senses deeply within himself while listening to the penitent. Words that come from a heart attuned to God can be words of confrontation without being words of harshness. If they are words born out of love, they can reveal to the penitent the

Lord's call which he or she may not be recognizing, or which he or she has been resisting for so long because of the change which listening to the Lord might entail.

The priest continues to allow the voice of the Lord to confront the penitent by helping him or her specify a behavioral penance which will carry out the Word of God stirring in the penitent's heart. Assigning a penance becomes a way of confronting the penitent with the call to growth and with a means of growth.

Hospitable confrontation also occurs in those moments of gently educating conscience. Hospitality does not hide behind neutrality. As Henri Nouwen put it, "An empty house is not a hospitable house." Hospitality involves taking a stand. The priest exercises hospitable confrontation by speaking for the Church and explaining the teaching of the Church on matters relevant to the penitent. To be truly hospitable, the priest needs to be able to do this in a language easily understood by penitents, and with clear reasons for the teaching which aid the formation of conscience. This is generally done more effectively by clarifying the values that are being expressed in the teaching of the Church, rather than simply stating rules of the Church without their connection to values. For example, the obligation to participate in the Eucharist is communicated more effectively by speaking about the values of prayer and communal expressions of faith rather than simply saying, "As a Catholic, you are obliged to go to Mass on Sunday and holy days of obligation."

Furthermore, whenever a priest finds it necessary to educate conscience in the sacramental forum, he must be careful not to confuse moral teachings of the Church, along with the moral imperatives and moral norms of these teachings, with his pastoral judgment. Since this is such a delicate matter in the sacramental forum, a further word needs to be said about it. Moral imperatives and moral norms (like do not steal, do not lie, do not commit adultery, give to others their due, be just, be honest, etc.) express the good that ought to be in order to promote the well-being of persons and our environment.

Pastoral judgments, however, while not completely dissociated from these moral norms, are not necessarily equal to them. A pastoral judgment recognizes the difference between the good that ought to be and the good that cannot be as yet. This is because penitents are often caught by inhibiting factors impeding their knowledge and freedom. While such impediments diminish responsibility for immoral actions, they do not render the actions morally acceptable. Good pastoral practice helps the penitent discern actions which are wrongdoing and morally evil from sins for which the penitent is culpable.

A pastoral position meets the person where the person is. It deals with the person's perceptions and strengths, seeking to discern the person's capacity to respond to moral imperatives and to appropriate the values which moral norms express. A pastoral judgment does not dictate what must be done regardless of the person's strengths or the situation. A pastoral procedure within the realm of hospitable confrontation may attempt to expand a person's perspective and maximize a person's strengths, but the procedure of pastoral care always recognizes the limits of these attempts.

The priest needs to be able to appeal to the moral teachings of the Church in educating conscience in order to express the good to which we ought to aspire. In this way, the priest exercises hospitable confrontation by serving as a source of criticism for any individual and cultural judgments, while at the same time challenging the penitent to move toward working for a better humanity. However, the pastoral use of these moral teachings will look to what is a possible achievement for the penitent in light of the normative moral judgment at stake. In doing this, the priest avoids confusing the pastoral judgment with a moral one, and so avoids mistaking a pastoral compromise for a moral position. In this way we can withstand the temptation to turn pastoral judgments into moral policy, and avoid concluding that a moral position is erroneous simply because it cannot be fulfilled in this particular pastoral situation.

Hospitable confrontation also occurs at the moment of assigning an appropriate penance or in helping the penitent arrive at a personal choice of a penance. True conversion is expressed in acts of penance which actually express the desire to change and the willingness to restore the harmony disrupted by sin (cf. #6c). Acts of penance which express hospitable confrontation are ones which first express a healing remedy for the root cause

245

of sin so as to restore the harmony disrupted by sin, and also point the penitent in the direction a reconciled life ought to take. Penances of this nature help "underline the fact that sin and its forgiveness have a social aspect" (#18). Hospitable confrontation through assigning acts of penance should also be sure not only that the penance corresponds to the seriousness and kind of sin, but also that it is suited to the personal condition and ability of the penitent (#6c). Good pastoral practice never tries to impose what the penitent cannot sincerely internalize and express as his or her own.

2. *For the Penitent*

The penitent, too, participates in the confrontational side of hospitality. Prayer, especially praying with Scripture, can be a significant moment of confrontation. In prayer with the Word of God the penitent faces squarely the call to conversion, the call to live as one chosen by God to be a disciple of Christ in the world today. Images in the Bible, the teachings of the prophets, the words and deeds of Jesus can all be challenging to the penitent's vision and choices for a way of life. By praying with Scripture, the penitent can come to a fresh awareness of the sort of person he or she has become, and to a fresh awareness of the sort of person he or she is being called to be. Penitents who learn to use Scripture in this way can bring Scriptural texts of personal importance to them into the sacramental celebration to share with the priest at the appropriate time. This helps to personalize the celebration and make one's confession of sins truly a response to the Word of God.

The examination of conscience is another moment of hospitable confrontation on the part of the penitent. The examination of conscience is a moment in the process of conversion which the penitent wants to celebrate in sacramental reconciliation. The examination of conscience actually begins when the penitent starts to "see" things differently. Someone or something enters the life of the penitent, and, in subtle or not so subtle ways, challenges him or her to look at the self all over again. The penitent begins to see his or her life differently and is moved to do something about what he or she sees. Maybe for the first time the penitent begins to feel "uncomfortable" about the selfishness which had been taken for granted for so long. The feeling of "I don't like what I see" is the feeling of guilt which is healthy because it moves the penitent to action. Whereas the penitent was once content with the way he or she had been, now the penitent wants to do something about being that way. This is the power of the Spirit acting, this is a moment of grace energizing the penitent to move further on the way to conversion.

In the examination of conscience, the penitent faces the underlying convictions that have given rise to a particular way of looking upon life and its responsibilities. In the examination, the penitent also faces those actions which have contributed to the growth and destruction of life-giving relationships in his or her life. At the end of the chapter on conscience, I suggested a simple formula for examining conscience that is consistent with the theologies of grace and sin which underlie the new approach to the Sacrament of Reconciliation. Appendix III of the Rite of Penance suggests other examinations of conscience which can also be used by the penitent for this confrontational side of hospitality.

Finally, the penitent can help determine an appropriate behavioral penance which addresses the root of sin and opens an avenue for healing. Coming to one's own penance is a way of converting the examination of conscience from private reflection to life-giving action in the community. Then in the dialogue with the priest in the sacramental celebration, the penitent can let the priest know what needs to be changed and suggest an appropriate way to effect that change. Arriving at and suggesting one's own behavioral penance would be a most hospitable gesture on the part of the penitent.

This concludes some of the pastoral guidelines for priest and penitent to prepare for celebrating the Sacrament of Reconciliation. Hospitality is the key to good preparation and good celebration. Now that we have looked at what is necessary to prepare for this sacrament, we can continue with some pastoral guidelines for celebrating the various rites of the revised Rite of Penance.

CELEBRATING THE RITES

In the atmosphere of hospitality and through the expressions of hospitality described above, we celebrate the rites of Reconciliation. The new Rite has three forms (or rites) for sacramental reconciliation: Form 1—Rite for Reconciliation of Individual Penitents; Form 2—Rite for Reconciliation of Several Penitents with Individual Confession and Absolution; Form 3—Rite for Reconciliation of Several Penitents with General Confession and Absolution. We will consider the structure of each form along with some comments to enhance the celebration of each rite.

Everything that follows should be understood and qualified by the potential for adaptation which the Introduction to the Rite allows:

> It is for priests, and especially parish priests: a) in reconciling individuals or the community, to adapt the rite to the concrete circumstances of the penitents. The essential structure and the entire form of absolution must be kept, but if necessary they may omit some parts for pastoral reasons or enlarge upon them, may select the texts of readings or prayers, and may choose a place more suitable for the celebration according to the regulations of the episcopal conference, so that the entire celebration may be rich and fruitful . . . (#40).

This openness to adaptation does not mean that the ritual need not be taken seriously. The openness which allows the priest to add or subtract does not mean that we should violate the integrity of the ritual by ignoring its essential structure when making additions. Nor does it mean we should so limit the options that we minimalize the signs of this sacramental worship. Adaptations of whatever shape should always aim to enhance the richness and fruitfulness of the celebration in light of the particular circumstances of the penitent. The suggestions made below for each form come from my experience, style, and preferences in celebrating Reconciliation. These suggestions seem to have enhanced the richness of the celebration and aided the fruitfulness of the experience for many people. While the structural features that constitute the integrity of the sacrament are not presented here as "suggestions" which can be omitted at will, the comments for implementing each structural feature of the rite are suggestions and can be improved and amended, and need to be adapted to each person's style and to the circumstances in which the sacrament is being celebrated.

FORM 1:
RITE FOR RECONCILIATION
OF INDIVIDUAL PENITENTS

The structure of this rite is as follows:

Reception of the Penitent
    Greeting
    Sign of the Cross
    Invitation to trust in God

Reading of the Word of God

Confession of Sins and Acceptance of Satisfaction

Prayer of the Penitent and Absolution

Proclamation of Praise of God and Dismissal

We will now take each step of this rite and make some comments on the pastoral implementation of each step.

Step # 1: Reception of the Penitent
The way the priest receives the penitent will set the tone for the entire celebration. First steps are hard. They need to be done with care. To make this "rite of welcome" work, the priest needs to be at ease with his "personal presence" and hospitality.

These traits are noted and encouraged in the very first rubric of this rite: "When the penitent comes to confess his sins, the priest welcomes him warmly and greets him with kindness" (#41). This rubric encourages a measure of informality and allows the priest to speak in his personal language rather than in a stereotyped formula. A handshake may also be exchanged along with the personal greeting as a tangible sign of warmth, understanding, support, and welcome. Other non-verbal expressions like a smile and eye contact also promote a feeling of warmth and acceptance. Above all, the priest should not be afraid to be personal, and neither should the penitent. For example, if the priest knows the name of the penitent, he may use the name in greeting the penitent, "Good afternoon, Mary." Or the penitent may volunteer his or her name to the priest: "Father, we have never had a chance to meet personally. My name is Fred." The priest might reply, "Thank you for introducing yourself to me, Fred. My name is Fr. Rich." In instances where the priest does not know the name of the penitent, and the penitent does not volunteer it, the priest ought to respect the desire to remain nameless and not press the penitent to disclose his or her name.

The formal beginning of the rite comes with the penitent's sign of the cross, which the priest can make also. The sign of the cross is our most explicit way of beginning a liturgical celebration and calling everyone to prayer. Unfortunately, familiarity and frequency of signing ourselves has made this gesture a near thoughtless routine lacking dignity and meaning. We can all afford to be more careful with this gesture of prayer, and with all our liturgical gestures.

The priest then urges the penitent to have confidence in God. He can do this either by using one of the six formulas given in the ritual (#42), or he can use his own words. In either case, the penitent responds with "Amen."

This "rite of welcome," as I like to call it, can set a personal, relaxed, and prayerful mood for the entire celebration, if it is done well. Being able to create such a mood can strengthen everyone's confidence in using this new ritual as well as enhance our attitude toward this sacrament as an act of worship, praise, and thanksgiving, rather than clouding this sacrament with debilitating guilt, fear, and obligation. If we can approach this sacrament as a prayerful act of worship, we might be able to break through preoccupations with "getting it done" while not really experiencing an encounter with the saving power of Christ in and through the Church.

Step #2: Reading the Word of God

All the revised rites of the sacraments include a reading from Scripture. And like every other sacrament, Reconciliation is to be a response to the Word of God. In Reconciliation, the Scripture reading is optional since some pastoral circumstances will not be particularly appropriate for using the reading. The ritual provides a wide selection of readings that may be used. It also allows the priest and the penitent to select any other biblical texts which will enhance the call to conversion and express the work of reconciliation begun by God in Christ and through the Spirit.

Before beginning the reading, some brief words of introduction and/or an invitation to silent prayer before hearing the Word of God would be helpful. This is especially necessary for the many penitents who might still find using a Scriptural reading in this sacrament awkward and upsetting. The introduction or invitation to silent prayer can serve not only to put the penitent at ease with the use of Scripture, but also as a transition into this step of the rite to encourage a prayerful, receptive attitude. The ritual offers such an invitation in these words: "Let us listen to the Lord as he speaks to us."

The reading of the Word can be enhanced if the penitent chooses the text to be read. In this way, the penitent personalizes the celebration and makes it an expression of a personal response of faith and trust in God. Whether the priest or penitent does the actual reading is a matter of choice. But forcing a hesitant penitent to choose a text, or to do the reading, is not hospitable pastoral practice.

A brief response appropriately follows the reading. This can come in a variety of ways. A few moments of silence may be possible for some. For others, a moment of shared prayer or simple reflection on the text is good. For example, a simple way to share prayer on a text is for each to express his or her response to the following: "What I hear the Lord saying to me in this reading is . . ." Comments on the text by the priest and penitent can also serve as a way to make a smooth transition into the personal confession of sins.

Step #3: Confession of Sins and Acceptance of Satisfaction
a. The Penitent's Confession

Making a confession of sins after hearing the Word of God enhances the sign value of our confession as being a response to the Word of God calling us to conversion.

There is a great diversity in the styles of confessing. Some may begin with a general formula for beginning the confession, but this is not absolutely necessary. Some penitents follow a very rigid form of confessing with formula prayers to begin, followed by a listing of the number and kinds of sins. Other penitents are more conversational in their approach and use no recognizable formula.

The priest needs to be respectful of the personal styles of each penitent. Those penitents who are set in their ways with a rigid, mechanical way of confessing can be gently encouraged to be less formal and more natural or personal in their manner of confessing. Hospitality does not force these people to change, and above all does not ridicule them for following a very rigid style. The goal in establishing, or teaching, a style of confessing is to have the confession flow from a prayerful encounter with the Lord, rather than from a close scrutiny of laws and obligations which lead to listing isolated pieces of legal transgressions. The matter of confession should disclose the root causes of sin and the underlying attitudes and trends in one's life, which express one's characteristic way of responding to God's invitation to love in all the relationships that make up one's life.

b. The Response of the Priest

After the penitent confesses in whatever style he or she is able, the priest can then respond in a way that lets the penitent know that he or she has been heard, understood, and accepted. The response of the priest, however, is not inspired by the need to do psychological counseling or spiritual direction, or the need to derive a complete listing of sins. (Remember, integral confession requires only that mortal sins be confessed as to the number of times and the circumstances which may have changed their nature.) Rather, the response of the priest is inspired by the desire to enable the penitent to express as authentically as possible his or her personal awareness of sin. Therefore, the response of the priest is hospitably respectful and understanding, and does not moralize or embarrass, harangue, or shame the penitent. Even questioning the penitent, if done at all, aims to promote understanding, healing, and support, and not to satisfy the priest's curiosity. If questioning is necessary, it is done prudently and sparingly, and is well-timed (i.e., it is not interruptive). Above all, questioning does not become an interrogation. Two good pastoral norms regulate the use of questions in the sacramental forum: "Don't be nosey" and "Less is more."

When the rubrics say that the priest may give "suitable counsel" to the penitent, they are not opening the door for converting the reconciliation room into a psychologist's office. We have already said enough about keeping reconciliation and counseling separated. The "counsel" which is appropriate for the priest in the Sacrament of Reconciliation is counsel which, as the rubrics say, reminds the penitent "that through the sacrament of penance the Christian dies and rises with Christ and is thus renewed in the paschal mystery" (#44). This does not need to be done all the time lest it become reduced to shallow piety. It certainly does not need to be done in a preachy way and with pious ferverinos. Simple responses that let the penitent know he or she has been heard, and that encourage the penitent to bring one's desire for forgiveness to the Lord, are sufficient.

c. Acceptance of Satisfaction

After hearing the confession, the priest can help the penitent accept an appropriate penance. The basic attitude we ought to take toward acts of penance is expressed in the Introduction to the Rite this way:

> True conversion is completed by acts of penance or satisfaction for the sins committed, by amendment of conduct, and

also by the reparation of injury. The kind and extent of the satisfaction should be suited to the personal condition of each penitent so that each one may restore the order which he disturbed and through the corresponding remedy be cured of the sickness from which he suffered. Therefore, it is necessary that the act of penance really be a remedy for sin and a help to renewal of life. Thus the penitent, "forgetting the things which are behind him" (Philippians 3:13), again becomes part of the mystery of salvation and turns himself toward the future (#6c).

This is a very positive attitude toward penance. Hopefully, it can be a reference point for correcting many false popular notions of what penance is for and what penance ought to be.

Doing penance, above all, is for growth in love. As agents of growth, acts of penance are ways to practice mortification. That is to say, acts of penance are a kind of dying to self, giving up of selfish ways in order to give birth to a new way of life promoting life and love in the community. In doing penance, we share in Christ's dying and rising and work to bring about genuine reconciliation in the world. The satisfaction, or reparation, element of penance does not mean making up to God for our sins by punishing ourselves, or "making it hurt." What a strange sort of God we would be praising who enjoyed our inflicting pain on ourselves! This is not the God of the Bible. But in the minds of many, "temporal punishment due to sin" evokes such an image of God and an image of penance as "punishment" on themselves.

Reparation, at its roots, is repairing or correcting sinful life-patterns. The temporal punishment due to sin is the continuing pattern of sin and the prolonging of those habitual ways of thinking and acting which sin creates in us. This temporal punishment of sinful attitudes and selfish life style must be removed from our lives. Doing acts of penance helps us do this. This is done most effectively when the penances we do are determined on the basis of the major responsibilities that make up our lives, and when the penances focus specifically on the areas that need healing and strengthening in our lives. Only then will penances be a remedy for sin. In this light, doing penance becomes the particular way of taking the first step in the direction of living a converted life.

The attitude toward penance found in the new Rite expresses well the spirit behind the practice of doing penance in the early Church without asking us to repeat in some archaic fashion precisely what the early Church did. For example, the period of canonical penance looked upon doing penance as part of the process of rehabilitation and reconciliation. The monastic system of the Celtic church looked upon penances as a kind of remedy for sin, or healing medicine for the soul, and applied the "principle of contraries" to enable the penitent to take steps to undo sinful patterns of life. Keeping within such a rich tradition, the new Rite encourages the creative use of behavioral penances imitating the early practice of prayer, fasting (self-denial), and almsgiving (works of mercy).

Creative penances can replace the routine use of reciting formula prayers (three Our Fathers and three Hail Marys) for everything. Furthermore, the creative use of behavioral penances may well restore the true significance of penance as a definite expression of conversion and the willingness to restore the harmony disrupted by sin (#6c). Giving alms for sins of greed, fasting for sins of lack of self-control, and doing acts of devotion for being lax with one's religious responsibilities could help the penitent continue the process of conversion and express it by a renewed life. Such penances also enhance the social dimensions of sin and reconciliation which have been sorely lacking for too long.

In arriving at appropriate penances, the priest need not feel solely responsible. The penitent, who knows his or her own situation better than the priest does, is in a better position to determine the appropriate penance that would promote reconciliation. For this reason, the penitent need not be afraid to take the initiative in suggesting his or her own penance, and the priest need not hesitate to ask the penitent to suggest one. By suggesting one's own penance, the penitent might make a deeper personal commitment to carrying it out. The penitent might come to an awareness of what such a penance might be while making an examination of conscience, or in dialogue with the priest. Whether the penitent or priest arrives at the penance is not the

255

major issue. Of greater significance is the nature of the penance. Some features we can strive to obtain in our penances are that the penance be *specific* (e.g., "be kind" is too vague), be *possible* for the penitent to do (this means it respects the penitent's condition, age, sex, and disposition), be *pertinent* to the roots of the sin confessed (e.g., fasting is appropriate for sins rooted in a lack of self-control), and be *limited* in time (e.g., once this coming week fast from television).

Step #4: Prayer of the Penitent and Absolution

This step represents two distinct moments: first, the penitent expresses personal sorrow before God and the Church; second, the priest expresses the pardon and absolution of God in and through the Church. These moments happen sequentially. In this way, the penitent is not expressing an act of contrition at the same time the priest is praying the prayer of absolution.

a. The Prayer of the Penitent

While the penitent can and is expressing sorrow in a number of ways, such as coming to the sacramental rite itself, assuming the penitential posture of kneeling, or even making a confession of sins, the rite makes it clear that there is also a distinct moment for the penitent to express personal sorrow. The ritual provides a number of possible expressions of sorrow, and also allows the penitent to use his or her own words for this. Some of the given options are brief excerpts from Scripture. Those serve as examples of the kinds of expressions of sorrow penitents can use, and open the riches of Scripture, especially the psalms, as ways of expressing sorrow.

b. The Prayer of Absolution

The priest responds to the penitent's contrition by using the gesture of the imposition of hands while praying out loud the prayer of absolution. The imposition of hands is a clear, visible sign of the Church invoking the healing, life-giving Spirit. This gesture signifies in the sacrament that the forgiveness of sins is the work of the Spirit through the community of the Church.

The prayer of absolution expresses the meaning of Reconciliation as an action that begins with God and happens for us in Christ and through the Spirit in the community of God's people.

The priest may wish to pray his own private prayer for the penitent either before or after the prayer of absolution. In either case, the priest's private prayer is not to be confused with, nor be a substitute for, the prayer of the Church expressed in the absolution prayer.

Step #5: Proclamation of Praise of God and Dismissal
The conclusion of the celebration is brief and simple. The ritual provides a single expression of praise and thanksgiving as follows:

> *Priest:* Give thanks to the Lord, for he is good.
> *Penitent:* His mercy endures for ever.

This expression puts in a brief form the expression of praise, sums up the entire celebration and brings it to a close. The priest then dismisses the penitent with: "The Lord has freed you from your sins. Go in peace." The priest can personalize the dismissal by using his own words which bring that closing touch of warmth and joy: "Welcome back to the community, Joe. We are happy to have you with us." A farewell handshake of peace, or a hug (if appropriate), can be a final gesture of homecoming and sending forth.

FORM 2:
RITE FOR RECONCILIATION OF SEVERAL PENITENTS WITH INDIVIDUAL CONFESSION AND ABSOLUTION

One criticism often made of the individual rite (Form 1) is that it lacks clear signs of being a community's worship and of expressing the communal nature of sin and reconciliation. Form 2 tries to reinstate the communitarian dimension of sin and reconciliation that seems to have been lost in Form 1. The format of Form 2 tries to achieve the goals of reforming this sacrament in the first place—namely, to give expression to the social and ecclesial dimensions of sin and reconciliation.

257

Form 2 is quickly becoming the most familiar form for many penitents and the normal experience of sacramental reconciliation in the vast majority of cases. This form tries to preserve the best of both worlds by including in one rite the individual confession of sins, as well as the communal celebration of reconciliation with God and the community of God's people, the Church. But combining the strengths of two forms into one does not always make for a fruitful and effective celebration of this sacrament. Form 2 is quite clearly a mixed rite. Inserting private confession into a communal celebration involving large numbers of people does not guarantee that the individual penitent is being inserted into the community and oriented toward communal reconciliation. Furthermore, it can too easily make the individual confession a formalistic element that must be done, and done quickly.

The structure of Form 2 is as follows:

Introductory Rites
> Song
> Greeting
> Introduction
> Opening Prayer

Celebration of the Word of God
> First Reading
> Responsorial Psalm
> Second Reading
> Gospel Acclamations
> Gospel
> Homily
> Examination of Conscience

Rite of Reconciliation
> General Confession of Sins
> Litany or Song
> Lord's Prayer
> Individual Confession and Absolution
> Proclamation of Praise for God's Mercy
> Concluding Prayer of Thanksgiving

Concluding Rite
  Blessing
  Dismissal

This structure may appear alarmingly complex, but is really quite simple. Adequate preparation helps it to flow smoothly.

Celebrating this rite, like the first one, allows many adaptations and provides many options. If we are going to make proper adaptations and effective use of the options while respecting the integrity of the rite, we need to do some careful planning. Because of the variety of Scriptural texts and prayers given in the ritual, choices need to be carefully made in advance. Selecting readings, prayers, and music that carry a consistent message for the celebration is essential. Appointing adequate readers, cantors, and musicians and having enough priests will be necessary if we want to respect the different ministries celebrating this rite. As in other liturgical prayer, so too here we want to make every effort to keep the various ministries distinct. We want to avoid, for example, having the reader also serve as cantor.

This form of celebrating the sacrament usually demands a number of priests to minister as confessors. To insure having enough priests available, liturgical planning teams from neighboring parishes may want to coordinate their services so that they are not conflicting with each other on the same day. In this way, all the priests of these parishes can be free to assist one another and insure that an adequate number of confessors will be present to accommodate the number of people who wish to make an individual confession.

Good liturgical practice has the priests assisting in this rite present for the entire celebration. This means that the priests serving as confessors do not appear just for the individual confessions and then leave. Entering from the wings and leaving quickly before the dismissal is not only an expression of poor hospitality, but it also destroys the sign of the communal commitment to reconciliation.

Finally, all other materials necessary to create the environment and carry out the celebration need to be gathered beforehand. This would include such items as candles, books, cross, water, incense, visual aides, music, tapes, etc. Checking all mechanical devices (like tape recorders, slide projectors, and lights) beforehand to ensure their proper functioning can prove to be a valuable step in preparation. With these sorts of preparations we are ready to celebrate the rite.

Step 1: Introductory Rites

The opening song can take a variety of forms, just as it might at the Eucharistic liturgy. The opening song generally serves as an entrance song to accompany the procession of liturgical ministers. If there is no formal entrance, this song may be shorter and serve more as a mood setter for quieting the assembly and establishing a prayerful disposition. Listening to a tape of gentle instrumental music often has this effect.

The introduction that comes after the greeting, like the one proper to the beginning of the Eucharistic liturgy, can serve as a "call to prayer." Using the introduction as the time to give explanations of the order of worship can too easily break the mood. Any explanations that need to be given are best kept brief and simple. Usually explanations of the order of worship and other sorts of announcements can be done effectively before the opening song and entrance procession. If the celebrant senses that the spirit of the worship service has been hindered by the introduction, he may want to try to recover the prayerful disposition of the assembly by making use of silence before the opening prayer, and then making a reverent, well-paced expression of the opening prayer.

Step 2: Celebration of the Word of God

The celebration of the Word of God is very flexible. It may have several readings or only one. If only one reading is used, it is the Gospel text. A psalm sung or recited, or even a silent pause, makes for a good response to the reading. Because the celebration of the Word can be wearingly long and overly wordy, great care needs to be given to planning this segment of the celebration. The flexibility envisioned by the ritual means that the celebration of God's Word can take many creative forms. The use of drama, film, slides, and other art forms is possible here as long as they are done in the context of God's Word and enhance that Word, rather than distract or overwhelm its message.

Paragraph 26 of the Introduction says that the homily may be replaced by an examination of conscience. This opens the possibility for creative integration of the Gospel, homiletic reflections, and an examination of conscience. Such integration can streamline the celebration of God's Word, reduce its wordiness, and keep God's Word sharply focused. I have included a sample of how this might be done in the service provided in the Appendix.

Step 3: Rite of Reconciliation
a. General Confession of Sins

The general confession of sins is to be accompanied by a penitential posture, such as kneeling or bowing. The general formula of this confession which begins "I confess to almighty God . . ." is one most people already know by heart, and it works well here.

This general confession of sins is followed by a brief litany or song, and then by the common recitation of the Lord's Prayer (the most ancient prayer of reconciliation). This is followed by the concluding prayer of the priest. The ritual gives two options for this part. (The ritual takes for granted that a litany will be preferred over the use of a song at this point.) Additional examples of litanies are also provided in the ritual. The litany needs to be prepared in advance since there are so many intercessions from which to choose.

b. Individual Confession and Absolution

For the effective implementation of this segment, a large enough number of priests is needed to accommodate the number of people who will be making an individual confession. Also, appropriate places need to be established as confessional stations which respect the privacy of each priest with his penitents.

In making the individual confession at this point, the complete rite for individual reconciliation as described above is not followed. Since the initial greeting, the Scriptural reading, and the prayer of the penitent have already been expressed communally, these are now omitted. All that is necessary is the confession, the designation of a penance, and the absolution.

Please note: this rite does not permit a *single* public act of the presiding priest alone, or all assisting priests joining together, praying the prayer of absolution for all those who had confessed privately. Such a practice was common in the years of "experimentation" immediately following the Second Vatican Council, and prior to the implementation of this revised Rite of Penance. The new Rite demands that each priest absolve the individual penitent who confesses to him. The repetition of the individual absolution in a communal rite, however, has been criticized for weakening the ecclesial significance of reconciliation. Yet, the practice of individual absolution for each penitent is the acceptable form. This form tries to keep unified and personalized the confession and absolution of each penitent.

Lest the whole value of the communal celebration be jeopardized by these individual confessions, the confession of the penitent needs to be clear and succinct. Reminding the penitents of this before the service begins can be a worthwhile instruction to give. Generally, instructing the penitents to focus on that one area in their lives which is most in need of healing through Reconciliation helps keep these individual confessions clear and succinct.

The priest receives these individual confessions and responds appropriately to let the penitent know he or she has been heard. But lengthy dialogues with the penitent at this point are inappropriate in these communal services. Following the designation of a penance, the priest prays the prayer of absolution while using the gesture of the imposition of hands over the penitent. (In some instances, the penitents may be asked to participate in a common, communal gesture of penance which serves to enhance the meaning of recommitting oneself to others in the process of reconciliation in the community. The sample communal service which I have included in the Appendix uses such a gesture of a common penance for this purpose.)

The period of time when individual confessions are being made deserves some special attention. How many times people have commented to me that their overall response to the service depended on what happened during this time of waiting for the individual confessions to conclude. If the time is too long and empty, the spirit of prayer gets broken, people become bored, and the service falls flat. Rather than leaving this time empty, and leaving people to their own devices to use the time well, planners of this service can arrange for ways to sustain the spirit of prayer. Some helpful ways of doing this are to have quiet music playing either on tape or by the musicians. This music can be interspersed with selected readings from Scripture, or accompanied by slides, or other visual aides to promote a spirit of prayer.

c. Proclamation of Praise for God's Mercy

When the individual confessions are completed, all the priests stand in front of the assembly and near the presiding priest. This helps extend the sign of the public and ecclesial nature of this celebration and avoids creating an anticlimax which might be created if the priests were to take a place among the assembly. The presiding priest then invites everyone to give thanks and praise by means of a hymn, a psalm, or a litany. Usually a hymn of praise works best. The ritual suggests using the *"Magnificat"* or one of several psalms. If a litany of petitions had been used above at the point of the general confession of sins, then another litany here would be out of place.

After the proclamation of praise, the presiding priest prays a closing prayer of thanksgiving followed by a blessing. The ritual provides a number of options for each. After the dismissal, a recessional hymn may be used, or it may be eliminated so as not to conflict in an anticlimactic way with the hymn of praise just completed.

If my experience is typical, this rite as just described works best with small groups where the proportion of priests to penitents is such as to cause no great delays with the individual confessions. This rite has often been awkward with large assemblies, and when there are insufficient priests to accommodate all those who wish to make an individual confession in a reasonable amount of time. In cases like these, pastoral prudence may demand concluding the common service at the point of the invitation to individual confessions and not reassembling the people for the concluding prayers of praise and thanksgiving.

FORM 3:
RITE FOR RECONCILIATION OF SEVERAL PENITENTS WITH GENERAL CONFESSION AND ABSOLUTION

Form 3 is a fully developed, legitimate rite of sacramental reconciliation. Of the three forms, this is the one most poorly understood and most often abused. It deserves a lengthier introduction in order to clarify its purpose and the conditions which surround its proper use.

Even though the Church now has this fully developed rite for general absolution, this form is not to be used regularly. Individual Reconciliation with absolution continues to remain the ordinary form of sacramental reconciliation. According to the prescribed discipline of general absolution, this rite does not stand on equal ground with individual Reconciliation so that a penitent has two complementary styles of Reconciliation from which to choose on any occasion. Paragraph 31 from the Introduction to the new Rite which describes the conditions for using Form 3 makes this clear. This paragraph is worth repeating in full:

> Individual, integral confession and absolution remain the only ordinary way for the faithful to reconcile themselves with God and the Church, unless physical or moral impossibility excuses from this kind of confession.

> Particular, occasional circumstances may render it lawful and even necessary to give general absolution to a number of penitents without their previous individual confession.

> In addition to cases involving danger of death, it is lawful to give sacramental absolution to several of the faithful at the same time, after they have made only a generic confession but have been suitably called to repentance, if there is grave need, namely when, in view of the number of penitents, sufficient confessors are not available to hear individual confessions within a suitable period of time, so that the penitents

264

would, through no fault of their own, have to go without sacramental grace or holy communion for a long time. This may happen especially in mission territories but in other places as well and also in groups of persons when the need is established.

General absolution is not lawful, when confessors are available, for the sole reason of the large number of penitents, as may be on the occasion of some major feast or pilgrimage.

Canon lawyer Frederick R. McManus has commented at length on this paragraph to provide an interpretation which helps us see the conditions for the lawful use of general absolution. His commentary is as follows:

A careful study of the wording reveals what is common enough in church law, namely, that generous exceptions are often overlooked in a superficial reading of prohibitions or restrictions:

(a) The availability of ministers of the sacrament is a relative matter. Sometimes confessors are considered "unavailable" because of circumstances—small parish communities in remote areas, for example—which deny freedom of choice or anonymity to penitents.

Reasonable attempts should be made to provide confessors; these attempts may fail without any deliberate effort to subvert the ordinary practice of individual reconciliation.

(b) Another criterion for "availability" of ministers of reconciliation is the expectation, explicit in the ritual, that they are able to celebrate the individual rite "properly" (rite), that is, according to the revised ritual and its rather great expectations. To put it differently, the fact that hurried, routine, mechanical confessions and absolutions are possible does not satisfy: it would instead justify the rite of general reconciliation.

The new ritual calls for a generous opportunity for the individual penitent to be received warmly and to hear God's word before the actual exchange of confession and counsel; it calls for a deliberate prayer of the penitent and act of reconciliation by the minister, completed by expression of praise to God and dismissal. Even in simplified form (no. 21), individual confessions are more demanding than before. If they are not possible in a proper fashion, there may be reason for the rite of general reconciliation.

(c) The so-called hardship on the penitents is also broadly stated. First, it is not exclusively the deprivation of eucharistic communion (that is, as affecting those in grave sin) that is at issue. It is the extended deprivation or postponement of the sacrament of reconciliation: if we appreciate, in traditional terms, the value of sacramental grace or "confessions of devotion," we should consider delay a matter of concern and reason for general absolution.

(d) For those unfamiliar with the interpretations of canonists and moralists, the reference to "lengthy" postponement of reconciliation may mean a matter of months. This is reasonable enough, but in similar cases long delay in receiving sacramental absolution is understood most generously, even to the point of rendering the regulation almost meaningless. In such similar cases a delay of only a day or even less is considered to be a hardship on the penitents.

(e) Finally, a careful reading makes it clear that, once the conditions are satisfied (and the decision is made in communion with the diocesan bishop . . .), then all who are assembled for the rite may freely seek general absolution without individual confession. The rite is not restricted in any way to the special needs of those in grave sin or to the especially devout who will experience hardship in not celebrating the sacrament.[5]

McManus then summarizes the occasions when this rite may be used with this principle:

The rite may be celebrated when there are members of the faithful who would otherwise expect to confess their sins individually but, because of the numbers of penitents and the fewness of confessors, are deprived of the opportunity.[6]

Paragraph #32 of the Introduction states that the judgment about whether the conditions for the lawful use of this rite are met or not is reserved to the local bishop of the diocese in question. This will necessarily mean there will be unevenness in the use of this rite across the country and throughout the world. Some dioceses will permit its use, others will not. The priest has the responsibility to know the local custom and to inform his bishop of his intention to use this rite in those instances where general permission has not been granted. As Paragraph #32 says:

> Over and above the cases determined by the diocesan bishop, if any other serious need arises for giving sacramental absolution to several persons together, the priest must have recourse to the local Ordinary beforehand, when this is possible, if he is to give absolution lawfully. Otherwise, he should inform the Ordinary as soon as possible of the need and of the absolution which he gave.

Paragraph #33 describes the dispositions expected of the penitent for this rite. They are the same ones expected of the penitent for any rite of sacramental reconciliation:

> Each one should be sorry for his sins and resolve to avoid committing them again. He should intend to repair any scandal and harm he may have caused and likewise resolve to confess in due time each one of the grave sins which he cannot confess at present.

The priest has the responsibility to call these dispositions to the attention of anyone about to participate in general absolution.

Paragraph #34 affirms that grave sins are pardoned in general absolution but specifies the requirement to confess these grave sins in individual confession before receiving general absolution again:

> Those who receive pardon for grave sins by a common absolution should go to individual confession before they receive this kind of absolution again, unless they are impeded by a just reason. They are strictly bound, unless this is morally

impossible, to go to confession within a year. The precept which obliges each of the faithful to confess at least once a year to a priest all the grave sins which he has not individually confessed before also remains in force.

This paragraph clearly shows that a practice of general absolution is not to replace individual Reconciliation by reaffirming the norm of annual confession of grave sins derived from the Fourth Lateran Council (1215). But it is also open to possible exceptions to this rule. McManus comments on this paragraph to provide some necessary clarifications of what is entailed by it:

But the new inhibition is qualified. The faithful may receive general absolution a second time or even repeatedly without the individual confession of grave sins if "they are impeded by a just reason" from being reconciled individually. The "just reason" is or may be precisely the reason or reasons which justified general absolution in the first place, as these are explained at length in nos. 31–32 of the Introduction. People should be aware of the rule but equally aware that exceptions may be many—and that, in any case, it is not applicable to those who have sought general absolution without being conscious of grave sin.

Similarly, the same avoidance of fear or scrupulosity among the faithful should move priests to explain—with greater clarity than in the past—the precept of annual confession. Serious catechetical abuses have taken place in the past: many older penitents confuse the precept of annual confession of grave sins with the precept of paschal communion; perhaps even more think the precept obliges even when there is no question of grave sins to be confessed.

It is in this context that no. 34 must be understood. It seeks to clarify one point only: the norm of annual confession of grave sins refers exclusively to individual confession—as had been understood for centuries. The participation of a penitent in the rite of general absolution does not free him or her from the ordinary precept of annual individual confession of previously unconfessed grave sins.

In this case the saving clause is phrased differently: penitents are bound to annual individual confession "unless this is morally impossible." *A fortiori* the rule is not applicable to those who are physically impeded: those in isolated areas, those who are prevented by confinement to home or imprisonment from having access to a minister of the sacrament, etc. The moral impossibility which is equally excusing may be understood generously, expansively. Again, the problem is to walk the delicate line between allowance for human weakness (which might permit large numbers of the distressed, anxious, and disaffected to be satisfied with general absolution only) and the genuine danger of subverting the practice of individual reconciliation.[7]

With this as our introduction, we are ready to comment on the structure of this rite. The structure of the rite is this:

Introductory Rites
 Song
 Greeting
 Introduction
 Opening Prayer

Celebration of the Word of God
 First Reading
 Responsorial Psalm
 Second Reading
 Gospel Acclamations
 Gospel
 Homily

General Confession
 Sign of Peace
 General Confession of Sins
 Litany or Song
 Lord's Prayer

General Absolution

269

Proclamation of Praise and Conclusion
   Song or Hymn
   Blessing
   Dismissal

Note that *Steps 1 and 2,* the Introductory Rites and the Celebration of the Word, are done here as they would be in Form 2. Therefore, all the flexibility and creative possibilities for these steps in Form 2 would be available here. The sample service in the Appendix takes advantage of this flexibility to illustrate what is possible.

In Form 3, however, after the homily or as part of the homily, the priest is to give a more elaborate instruction that would prepare the penitents for the exceptional nature of general absolution. In this instruction, three points are to be made. First, the priest is to explain the proper disposition (see Par. 35) each penitent should have to receive general absolution. Second, the instruction is to make explicit that the proper disposition for general absolution includes the resolve to confess individually at a later time all serious sins which cannot now be confessed. Third, the priest is to designate the penance which applies to the whole group receiving general absolution. Since the penance in this case is something that is thought to be suitable to everyone in the group, and not everyone may be able to do what is proposed, the rubrics suggest that each individual may add something he or she desires to complete the penance. This rubric allows for a reasonable substitution of a designated penance, a practice we saw introduced in the era of the monastic system of penance.

Step 3: General Confession
   The general confession of sin in this rite replaces the individual confession of sins in Form 2. All who are seeking sacramental reconciliation are asked at this point to make some sign (such as bowing one's head, or kneeling) to indicate one's sorrow. Along with making this sign, each penitent is to give a verbal expression of sorrow in the form of the general confession using the formula, "I confess to almighty God. . . ." This is fol-

lowed by a litany or appropriate song as in Form 2, and then the Lord's Prayer.

Step 4: General Absolution

The priest then prays the prayer of absolution while extending his hands over the whole group. The ritual offers two forms for this absolution prayer. The priest must decide which to use.

Step 5: Proclamation of Praise and Conclusion

This rite closes in the same manner as Form 2, and comes with the same flexibility of options for a litany or song of praise and closing blessing.

The instructions on the discipline for general absolution express a noticeable fear that widespread use of this form would destroy the individual celebration of Reconciliation. The restrictions on the use of this form, and the priority given to the individual rite, seem to suggest that these two styles of Reconciliation cannot exist side by side on equal footing. The emphasis which the instructions in the Introduction give to the individual rite are consistent with the Catholic tradition which takes the incarnation seriously.

One way of understanding the priority which the individual rite has over general absolution is from an incarnational perspective. With sacraments, this means that the sacramental encounters with redeeming grace need to be personalized in such a way that the mystery of salvation can be felt individually and experienced as something happening "for me" by the Spirit in and through the community of God's people, the Church. The one-to-one interaction that would enhance this sacramental encounter seems to be preserved in all the revised sacramental rites after the Council. For example, in Baptism we say while pouring the water, "Mary, I baptize you . . ."; in Eucharist we say while giving the bread and the cup, "Ann, the body of Christ . . ."; in Marriage we say, "John, do you take Marsha . . ." The danger of a steady diet of general absolution is that we can easily lose this personalized encounter with redeeming grace.

271

CONCLUSION

The new Rite of Penance by itself, in whatever form it is celebrated, is not going to solve the "quiet revolution" of the penitential malaise in the Catholic Church today. For sure, the new Rite must be accompanied by a catechetical and pastoral effort that makes reconciliation come alive in the community. Even these efforts must be matched by the interior renewal of heart, upon which all sacramental renewal depends. Such an interior renewal will support, and be supported by, renewed efforts to live consciously a style of life committed to reconciliation. The Sacrament of Reconciliation will then become more clearly a privileged moment in a life committed to reconciliation. But the sacramental ritual can never replace the need to be an agent of reconciliation in everyday life. Just as reconciliation does not begin with the sacramental moment, neither does it end there. The new Rite recognizes this when it ends its explanation of the Rite for Reconciliation of Individual Penitents with this sentence:

> The penitent continues his conversion and expresses it by a life renewed according to the Gospel and more and more steeped in the love of God, for "love covers over a multitude of sins" (1 Peter 4:8) (Par. 20).

The Sacrament of Reconciliation presupposes a commitment to reconciliation in life (cf. Chapter One) and deepens the action of reconciliation already going on. The Introduction concludes its explanation of reconciliation in the Church with these words, which also form a fitting conclusion to this book:

> In order that this sacrament of healing may truly achieve its purpose among Christ's faithful, it must take root in their whole lives and move them to more fervent service of God and neighbor.

> The celebration of this sacrament is thus always an act in which the Church proclaims its faith, gives thanks to God for the freedom with which Christ has made us free, and offers its life as a spiritual sacrifice in praise of God's glory, as it hastens to meet the Lord Jesus (Par. 7).

FOURTH MOVEMENT: APPROPRIATING THE CHRISTIAN STORY

How has the above commentary affected your understanding of the way to celebrate this sacrament? How have you been affirmed? How have you been challenged? Complete the following sentences:

I realized that I . . .
I relearned that I . . .
I was surprised that I . . .
I wonder if. . .
I wonder why . . .
I wonder when . . .

FIFTH MOVEMENT: CHOOSING A FAITH RESPONSE

How might you look upon each of the rites and their parts now? What feelings and attitudes do you have toward the sacrament now? Complete the following sentences:

Next time, I want to . . .
I need to think more about . . .
I hope that I . . .

Suggestions for Further Reading

Joseph M. Champlin   *Together in Peace*

Ralph Keifer and   *The Rite of Penance:*
Frederick R. McManus   *Commentaries, Vol. 1:*
                            Understanding the Document

Appendix:
Rites of Reconciliation

This Appendix includes examples of each of the forms for Reconciliation. The first is a sample dialogue which serves to illustrate how the parts of Form 1 might flow.

Rite for Reconciliation of Individual Penitents
RECEPTION OF THE PENITENT

Greeting:
Priest: *(Standing and extending his hand)* Good afternoon, Joe. Welcome! We are happy to have you with us, and I am honored to be with you in this celebration of God's mercy.

Penitent: *(Accepting the priest's hand)* Thank you, Fr. Rich.

Sign of the Cross:
Priest: We begin our prayer together today in the way we begin all our prayers.

Priest and **Penitent:** *(Making the sign of the cross together)* In the name of the Father, and of the Son, and of the Holy Spirit. Amen.

Invitation to Trust:

Priest: Joe, may the Lord be in your heart and help you to confess your sins in true sorrow.

READING THE WORD OF GOD

Priest: *(Taking the Bible)* Would you like to begin with a short reading from the Bible?

Penitent: Yes, that would be good.

Priest: Is there any particular passage which you have used in your prayer of preparation that you would like to use here?

Penitent: Yes. There is a passage from one of the prophets which has struck me. I found it to be very consoling as well as quite challenging. It is Hosea 11:1–4.

Priest: Since this passage has special significance to you, would you care to read it for us?

Penitent: *(Taking the Bible from the priest)* Sure.

Priest: Before we listen to this word, let us take a brief moment of quiet prayer and ask the Spirit to open our hearts to this word. *(Pauses for about the length of time it would take to say the Lord's Prayer silently.)* Okay, Joe, please read your text.

Penitent: *(Reads the text.)*

Priest: *(Taking the Bible from the penitent)* Joe, what did you hear the Word of God saying to you in this reading?

Penitent: When I first came upon this passage I was consoled by knowing that God loves me just like that. It all sounds so gentle, caring, and very tender. Coming to this awareness was challenging to me, too, because I wish I could love like that as a father.

Priest: Yes, Joe. These words about God's love for us are consoling and challenging at the same time. With confidence in that offer of love being made to you now, you may confess your sins. Be trusting in God's mercy and confident that God will not abandon you either. What is it that you want to confess today?

CONFESSION OF SINS AND ACCEPTANCE OF SATISFACTION

Penitent: *(Pausing for a moment)* Well, Father, you know I'm a married man with a lovely wife and three darling children. I work as a carpenter and love working with my hands. But it seems the past month has been all work with very little time for my family. I have been getting more and more irritable with the children asking for attention. My work is too important to me now to be always interrupted. In this past month, I have been too tired to give them any attention or time. I really regret how cold I have been to them and how I yelled at them this week. I feel terrible about slapping Joey. He really was being a good boy, but he just happened to be the nearest one around when I finally lost my cool. I regret the hurt I have caused my children, especially Joey. And not just the physical hurt, but even more I regret the fear I see them have in me now. They seem to have a sense that I don't love them. I guess they aren't experiencing me the way I experienced God in that reading we just heard. That's why I said the reading was so challenging.

Priest: I hear your regret, Joe. And I hear you wanting to be more like the loving Father you know God to be with you. You seem to be telling me that love has grown cold in your life because you have become so caught up in your own achievements.

Penitent: Yes, my preoccupation with my work is taking its toll on the life and love in our family. How can I make things different?

Priest: I am not sure, Joe. We will have to explore that together. What seems to be lying at the roots of your behavior?

Penitent: Well, I think it is my attitude toward my work. I give it priority over everything else. And it is my busyness. I just haven't left any space in my life for anything else, or anyone else.

Priest: If healing and reconciliation are going to take place in your family, then, it sounds as though you will need to examine your priorities and create some space in your life. What can you do to show your children you love them and that your work doesn't have to come first all the time?

Penitent: *(Pausing to think)* I need to give them some time and attention for one thing. And it is time we did something playful together.

Priest: What might that be? And when could you do it?

Penitent: Maybe I can take them to the beach this weekend and help them to get up that kite they have been assembling.

Priest: Sounds like a good idea to me. That would even make a good penance for you, Joe. For your penance, then, go fly a kite with your kids this weekend. How does that sound to you?

Penitent: It's not the kind of penance I've known in the past, but it certainly makes sense. It surely sounds like what I need. I'll do it, Father.

Priest: Good. Now let's take a moment to pray together, Joe. You pray your prayer of contrition in the way you would be most comfortable, and then I will pray for you in my own name, and then in the name of the Church by praying the prayer of absolution while imposing my hands on you.

PRAYER OF THE PENITENT AND ABSOLUTION

Penitent: *(Praying out loud)* Dear Father, I want to thank you for my family and especially for my little Joey. I want to thank you for my being able to make this confession today. I am sorry that I have allowed love to grow cold in our home, and that I have so frightened my children. Help me to be better and not to take my work so seriously that I have no time or energy to be playful, or attentive to my family's needs. Forgive me, and help me, I pray, in Jesus' name. Amen.

Priest: Lord, I want to thank you for the beauty you have revealed to me in Joe. Grant him his heart's desire to be loving in the way you are loving. Bless him this day with confidence and new life.

(Standing to impose hands on Joe's head, then praying:)

Joe, God, the Father of mercies, through the death and resurrection of his Son has reconciled the world to himself and sent the Holy Spirit among us for the forgiveness of sins; through the ministry of the Church may God give you pardon and peace, and I absolve you from your sins in the name of the Father, and of the Son, and of the Holy Spirit.

Penitent: Amen.

PROCLAMATION OF PRAISE OF GOD AND DISMISSAL

Priest: Give thanks to the Lord, Joe, for he is good.

Penitent: Yes, his mercy endures for ever.

Priest: The Lord has freed you from your sins. Go in peace.

Penitent: Thanks, Father. *(Both shake hands.)*

Rite for Reconciliation of Several Penitents with Individual Confession and Absolution

Remote Preparations

This service is based on the Beatitudes. It integrates into the "Celebration of the Word of God" the reading of the Gospel, the homily, and the examination of conscience. Since the assembly responds with a communal prayer after each reflection, a program with these communal prayers will need to be prepared in advance.

This service needs the following ministers: a celebrant, assisting priests in sufficient number to accommodate the number of penitents present, music ministers (cantor and organist), a technician to operate the tape recorder.

Music for congregational singing will come from the hymnal, *We Celebrate with Song*. The songs the music ministers need to prepare are "We Are the Light of the World" and "Now Thank We All Our God." Tapes of the following music should be made: "Lay Your Hands" from Carey Landry's album, *Abba Father*; quiet music, such as Albioni's "Adagio for Strings and Organ"; Bach's "Air" from Suite No. 3 in D Minor; Handel's "Pastoral Symphony" from "Messiah," Part I; Vivaldi's "Spring" (Largo) from Four Seasons, Op. 8, Concerto No. 1.

A tape recorder with adequate amplification for the size of the room being used should be available. The person operating the tape recorder needs to be instructed on when to play recorded music and how to fade music out before turning off the recorder. The technician should have a copy of this service with parts clearly marked where recorded music is to begin and end.

A large glass bowl (like a punch bowl) filled with water and a sufficient supply of hand towels needs to be obtained for the common reconciliation action after individual confessions.

Preliminary Preparations
The Church is to be illumined with soft lighting. The atmosphere should be calming and welcoming, not dark and frightening. Before the entrance procession the lights can be brightened.

While the people are gathering, quiet music plays in the background until five minutes before the service begins. At this point, any music practice that needs to be done should be done,

279

and any instructions which will help the service move smoothly ought to be given.

The program with the order of worship and the prayers for the assembly can be distributed as the people enter the Church.

The assisting priests are to be instructed to share the reading of the Beatitudes. Each priest can speak his Beatitude from his place in the sanctuary. The Beatitudes are to be distributed as evenly as possible among the assisting priests.

INTRODUCTORY RITES

Opening Song: "We are the Light of the World," verses 1–2.

Greeting:
Celebrant: Grace, mercy, and peace be with you from God our Father and Christ Jesus our Savior.

All: And also with you.

Opening Prayer:
Celebrant: *We pray now for true conversion, first in silence.*
Almighty and merciful God,
you bring us together in the name of your Son
and in the power of your Spirit.

Open our eyes to see the evil we have done.
Touch our hearts and convert us to you so that
we might live free from sin and free for you.
We ask this in Jesus' name.

All: Amen.

CELEBRATION OF THE WORD OF GOD

Celebrant: *(In these or similar words)*
Let me set the scene for you. Jesus is on the mountain, the

crowds have gathered, and the disciples are there, too. All the people know who these disciples are, for until recently they had been completely identified with the crowds. These disciples blend well with the crowd. What makes them somewhat distinct is that they have entered into a special relationship with Jesus and are now trying to learn more about what that relationship means for them.

Up until a short time ago, these disciples carried on in their ordinary workaday world. There was nothing really special, dramatic, or sophisticated about them or their work. Then they met this man, Jesus. There was something about Jesus that attracted them to him. These disciples have been following him around now for days trying to get in touch with what it is that made Jesus so attractively human. The disciples watch him as he greets people, cares for the sick and the hungry, and has compassion on the lonely, the poor, the outcast, and the sinner.

The disciples are so eager to get in touch with this special something in Jesus that they not only watch with wonder the things that he does, but they also listen attentively to whatever he says. The disciples have experienced within themselves the very kinds of things they see happening in other people who meet Jesus. They experience a sense of worth in themselves. They feel something good being drawn out of themselves. And all of this often comes to their great amazement, since they did not think they were really as good as Jesus shows them to be. They also have experienced in Jesus new energies for life, new directions, fresh hope, a reason to live.

They know that this gathering on the mountain is going to be one of those special moments when Jesus reveals something more of what it is within him that makes him the sort of person that he is. This is going to be one of those moments when they will hear Jesus explain something about what it means to be human the way Jesus sees it and lives it. They know this is going to be a special moment to learn something more about what it will mean to live as one especially chosen to follow Jesus and imitate his way of life in the world where they spend most of their lives.

So, they are ready to listen; they are eager to learn. This is what they hear:

Speaker: Fortunate are those who know they are spiritually poor;
the kingdom of heaven belongs to them.

Celebrant:

To become a person as Jesus was means to be able to accept that all gifts come from the Father. This is real poverty—to know we can't go it alone. Poverty is to know we have needs. Above all, we need the Father's love. To know our poverty is to know we don't have it all together yet, and we never will. We will always be dependent on the Father, and on each other. Our poverty calls us to be open to something new, to be ready and willing to change, to know our needs.

All: Father, forgive us for taking your gifts for granted and hoarding the good things you have given us. Pardon us for our failure to accept our poverty. Forgive us for trying to go it alone without you. Lord, have mercy on us.

Speaker: Fortunate are the gentle;
they shall receive what God has promised.

Celebrant: Opportunities come, and opportunities go. Another chance to call our brothers and sisters to life, and we missed it again. The gentle and the meek have room in their lives for someone else. They have enough space in their lives to make room for another's needs. The meek and the gentle enable the other to be all that he or she can be. The meek and the gentle are free enough to be open, and quiet enough to listen.

All: Father, forgive us for filling up our lives with our own arrogance and self-centeredness. Forgive us for leaving no room for anyone else. Pardon us for seeing only what we want to see, or hearing only what we want to hear. Give us the grace to accept another's faults without bitterness, and to admit our own without regret. Christ, have mercy on us.

(Pause for quiet reflection)

Song: "We Are the Light of the World," verses 3–4.

Speaker: Fortunate are those who mourn;
God will comfort them.

Celebrant: Those who mourn are fortunate because they can accept their own emptiness before God. Those who know how to mourn know how to suffer with another, to feel the pain of another, to walk in another's shoes. Yes, such people know what it means—they have been there themselves.

All: Father, forgive us for failing to bring comfort to those who have come to us in their brokenness. Pardon us for not being able to recognize and welcome another in need. Lord, have mercy on us.

Speaker: Fortunate are those whose greatest desire
is to do what God requires;
God will satisfy them fully.

Celebrant: How fortunate are we to have high ideals, strong values, noble goals, and the motivation to build up what is best in ourselves and draw out the best in others. Yet, the temptation to conform, the temptation to be like everyone else, the temptation to be satisfied with being average is never far away. But those who desire to do what God requires feel the urge deep within themselves to forget self for the moment and to let another approach in their loneliness and distress, and even in their hope and enthusiasm.

All: Father, forgive us for continuing to make life miserable for others and for ourselves. Pardon us for hungering and thirsting after things without our thinking about whether they will help us serve others and you. Christ, have mercy on us.

(Pause for quiet reflection)

Song: "We Are the Light of the World," verses 5–6.

Speaker: Fortunate are those who show mercy to others;
God will show mercy to them.

Celebrant: Mercy hallmarks the Christian life. Mercy is the love with which God loves us. This merciful love is compassion without conditions. Mercy is being sensitive and responsive without defenses. If we fail to be merciful, if we fail to let others approach us in their weakness and in ours, we pay a high price— loneliness.

All: Father, forgive us for having compassion without passion. Forgive us for failing to forgive or to accept forgiveness. Pardon us for being indifferent, for holding grudges, and for enjoying the criticism we freely make of others. Lord, have mercy on us.

Speaker: Fortunate are the pure of heart;
they will see God.

Celebrant: Oh, how happy we would be if we could take off our masks, be free of false images, and simply be the persons we are. To be pure of heart is sincerely to be singlehearted. It is not to have double intentions, hidden agendas, secret desires to advance ourselves when dealing with another. The pure of heart can congratulate and support another without seeking to advance themselves.

All: Father, forgive us for being envious of another's successes. Pardon us for the ridicule we have made of those who act according to their heart's desire. Christ, have mercy on us.

(Pause for quiet reflection)

Song: "We Are the Light of the World," verses 7–8.

Speaker: Fortunate are those who work for peace;
God will call them his own.

Celebrant: "Peace! This is my gift to you," says Jesus. St. Paul tells us that by his death on the cross, Jesus united two—Gentile and Jew—into one with himself, thus making peace.

Oh, how fortunate we would be to build bridges instead of walls, to help others to live in harmony rather than with division.

All: Father, forgive us for being a source of strife or ill-feeling. Pardon us for making war on others in our hearts. Forgive us for brooding over hurts and grievances, and pardon us for being satisfied with the walls that rise up between us. Lord, have mercy on us.

Speaker: Fortunate are those who suffer persecution
    because they do what God requires;
    the Kingdom of heaven belongs to them.

Celebrant: The cross of Jesus is a sign of victory, not defeat. We can celebrate with the cross for it is our great sign of life. The persecution of another's displeasure or jealousy should not stop us from witnessing to the mission that is ours from God. When we live under the sign of the cross, we can accept hostility and anger without trying to hurt in return.

All: Father, forgive us for being so willing to compromise our witness to what is right and good. Pardon us for failing to accept suffering in our lives when it comes because of our commitment to you. Forgive us for persecuting in our hearts, or by our actions, those who do not see things our way. Pardon us for hesitating to hear your word, and forgive us for not acting upon your word when we hear it. Christ, have mercy on us.

(Pause for quiet reflection)

RITE OF RECONCILIATION

General Confession of Sins:
Celebrant: We are not only guilty before God, our Father, and the Lord Jesus for taking the gifts of the Spirit for granted, but

we are also guilty before each other. Through our sins, love has grown cold within the body of Christ, within our homes, our communities, our businesses, our neighborhood, ourselves. Therefore, we need to be reconciled not only with God but with each other.

Please stand, and bow your heads to pray together for ourselves and for one another:

I confess . . .

Litany of Response:
Celebrant: The Lord is indeed full of compassionate love, slow to anger, but quick with kindness. Let us ask the Lord to be near us as we confess our sins.
   C: Give us the grace of true conversion, we pray: Lord, hear us.
All: Lord, hear us.
   C: Renew the spirit of hope within us, we pray:
All: Lord, hear us.
   C: Strengthen us to bear witness to your love, we pray:
All: Lord, hear us.
   C: Keep us mindful always of your freeing presence, we pray:
All: Lord, hear us.

Lord's Prayer:
Celebrant: We now pray to God our Father in the words our Savior gave us asking for forgiveness and freedom from evil.
All: Our Father . . .
   C: Father, you know our weakness and our desire to be reconciled with you and with one another. In the power of the Spirit, and through the ministry of the Church, renew our spirit so that we can be free to express the gifts you have given us, and so give you thanks and praise. We ask this through Christ, our Lord.
All: Amen.

INDIVIDUAL CONFESSION AND ABSOLUTION

(At the beginning of this segment, the meditation song "Lay Your Hands" from Carey Landry's album *Abba Father* begins.

During the second verse, the priests take their confessional stations. During the individual confessions, quiet music continues
to play in the background.)

(The penitents go to the priests for individual confession, a penance, and absolution at this time. After each confesses, each
penitent then goes to the bowl of water to wash the hands of
another penitent, and then dries them with the towel. This is the
reconciling action in which all penitents participate as a sign of
commitment to being agents of reconciliation in the community.)

PROCLAMATION OF PRAISE AND THANKSGIVING

(After all have confessed, the priests gather in the front of the
sanctuary around the celebrant who invites everyone to stand
and join in the hymn of praise and thanksgiving, "Now Thank
We All Our God.")

CONCLUDING PRAYER OF THANKSGIVING

(After the hymn of thanksgiving, the celebrant concludes with this prayer:)
God the Father of us all,
you have forgiven our sins.
Help us now to be free enough to forgive one another,
and to work together to establish peace in the world.
We ask this through Christ, our Lord.
All: Amen.

CONCLUDING RITE

Blessing:
C: May the Lord guide your hearts in the way of his love,
and fill you with Christ-like patience.
All: Amen.
C: May he give you strength to walk together again
in the newness of life.
All: Amen

C: May Almighty God bless you, †
the Father, and the Son, and the Holy Spirit.
All: Amen.
Dismissal:
C: The lord has forgiven your sins. Go in peace.
All: Thanks be to God.
(All process out of the Church to the accompaniment of organ music.)

Rite for Reconciliation of Several Penitents
with General Confession and Absolution

Remote Preparations
This service uses the Gospel story of the Merciful Father (Lk 15:11–32) as its only reading. The reading, homily, and examination of conscience will all be of one piece. The Gospel will be read in parts by different readers. The reading will be interrupted with petitions which will serve both as homiletic reflections and as an examination of conscience. At the end of each series of petitions is a common prayer said by the assembly. To facilitate the celebration of this service, a program with the order of worship and the common prayers of the assembly needs to be prepared in advance.

Ministers needed for this service are the following:
Readers:

> Narrator (N)
> Merciful Father (MF)
> Prodigal Son (PS)
> Elder Son (ES)
> Servant (S)
> Petitioner (P)

also, music ministers (cantor and organist), technician to operate the tape recorder, and one priest as celebrant.

The readers ought to rehearse the reading beforehand to achieve proper timing and coordination. The technician ought to be sure that the tape recorder with adequate amplification for the size of the room is in working order. Also, the technician ought to see that a tape of "My Son Has Gone Away" from the album *Earthen Vessels* is available. The technician also needs to be clear on when recorded music is to begin and end, and have a copy of the full text of this service available to follow during the service. The cantor and organist ought to see that the song of praise and thanksgiving, "Now Thank We All Our God," from the hymnal, *We Celebrate With Song,* is available for the assembly.

Preliminary Preparations

Programs can be distributed as the people enter the church. Five minutes before the beginning of the service, all ministers involved in this service take their positions. The music ministers can then rehearse the community. Any further instructions or announcements that will clarify the movement of this service can be given at this time. When these preliminary preparations are completed, the celebrant invites the assembly to take a few moments of silence in preparation for the beginning of the service.

INTRODUCTORY RITE

Song: "My Son Has Gone Away" (recorded)
Greeting:
> **C:** Grace, mercy, and peace of God our Father, and the Lord, Jesus Christ, be with you.

All: And also with you.
Introduction:
> **C:** Tonight we come to pray for forgiveness.
> Let us come with confidence to the Lord,
> and allow him to set us free
> so that we can walk together again
> with our God and with one another.

Prayer:
> **C:** God calls us to be sorry for our sins;
> let us pray for the strength to be able to change our lives.

Father of mercy, hear our repentant prayer this day.
Forgive us our sins, and in your merciful love
grant us your pardon and peace.
We ask this through Christ, our Lord.

All: Amen.

CELEBRATION OF THE WORD OF GOD

N.   There was once a man who had two sons.
      The younger son said to his father,
PS.   Father, give me my share of the property now.
N.   So the man divided the property between his two sons.
      After a few days the younger son sold his part of the
      property and left home with the money. He went to a
      country far away, where he wasted his money in reckless
      living.

Petitions

P.   Father, we pray for those who are trying to find life
      apart from you. Lord, have mercy.
All: Lord, have mercy.
P.   Father, we pray for those who have taken the gifts
      you have given them for granted, and who have used
      them selfishly and carelessly. Christ, have mercy.
All: Christ, have mercy.
P.   Father, we pray for those who keep their distance from
      you by keeping themselves separated from their brothers
      and sisters. Lord, have mercy.
All: Lord, have mercy.
Common Prayer:
Father, we pray for ourselves now, too. A part of us is like the
prodigal son. We bring that prodigal part of us to you now for
healing.
(Brief pause for personal prayers for healing and forgiveness)
N.   He spent everything he had. Then a severe famine spread
      over that country, and he was left without a thing. So he

went to work for one of the citizens of that country, who sent him out to his farm to take care of the pigs. He wished he could fill himself with the bean pods the pigs ate, but no one gave him anything to eat.

Petitions

P. Father, we pray for those who feel forsaken, alone, or troubled. Lord, have mercy.
All: Lord, have mercy.
P. Father, we pray for those whose human dignity is violated by being treated in inhuman ways. Christ, have mercy.
All: Christ, have mercy.
P. Father, we pray for those who feel used rather than loved, and we pray for those who use others rather than show love to them. Lord, have mercy.
All: Lord, have mercy.

Common Prayer:
Father, now we want to pray for ourselves. We know how it feels to be forsaken, alone, troubled, and treated inhumanly. We have been there ourselves. We bring to you now that part of us that is hurting and in need of healing.
(Brief pause for personal prayers for healing and forgiveness)
N. At last he came to his senses and said,
PS. All my father's hired workers have more than they can eat, and here I am about to starve! I will get up and go to my father and say, "Father, I have sinned against God and against you. I am no longer fit to be called your son; treat me as one of your hired workers."

Petitions

P. Father, we pray for those in whom your light is dawning, who are coming to recognize how you have gifted them. Lord, have mercy.
All: Lord, have mercy.

P. Father, we pray for those who long to know their sin
and have the strength to change their lives.
Christ, have mercy.
All Christ, have mercy.
P. Father, we pray for those who are truly sorry for their
sins and long to be reconciled with you and with us.
Lord, have mercy.
All: Lord, have mercy.

Common Prayer:
Father, part of us is still broken and yet repentant. We pray for
ourselves now, and we bring to you that broken, yearning part
of ourselves for healing and forgiveness.
(Brief pause for personal prayers of healing and forgiveness)
N. So he got up and started back to his father. He was still a
long way from home when his father saw him; his heart
was filled with pity, and he ran, threw his arms around
his son, and kissed him.
PS. Father, I have sinned against God and against you.
I am no longer fit to be called your son.
N. But the father called his servants,
MF. Hurry! Bring the best robe and put it on him.
Put a ring on his finger and shoes on his feet. Then go
and get the prize calf and kill it, and let us celebrate with
a feast! For this son of mine was dead, but now he is
alive; he was lost but now he has been found.
N. And so the feasting began.

Petitions

P. Father, we pray for those who cannot be a father like
this, but who must be demanding and critical. Lord, have
mercy.
All: Lord, have mercy.
P. Father, we pray for all who have had to earn their
forgiveness, and so never really feel forgiven. Christ,
have mercy.
All: Christ, have mercy.
P. Father, we pray for those who are discovering the kind of

father you are and are beginning to experience your forgiveness and love. Lord, have mercy.

All: Lord, have mercy.

Common Prayer:

Father, a part of us longs for forgiveness, while a part of us already experiences forgiveness. We pray for ourselves now, and bring to you our divided selves and ask to be made whole.

(Brief pause for personal prayers of healing and forgiveness)

N.   In the meantime, the elder son was out in the field. On his way back, when he came close to the house, he heard the music and dancing. So he called to one of the servants,

ES.   What's going on?

S.   Your brother has come back home, and your father has killed the prize calf, because he got him back safe and sound.

N.   The elder brother was so angry that he would not go into the house; so his father went out and begged him to come in. But he spoke back to his father,

ES.   Look, all these years I have worked for you like a slave, and I have never disobeyed your orders. What have you given me? Not even a goat for me to have a feast with my friends! But this son of yours wasted all your property on prostitutes, and when he comes back home, you kill the prize calf for him!

MF.   My son, you are always here with me, and everything I have is yours. But we had to celebrate and be happy, because your brother was dead, but now he is alive; he was lost, but now he has been found.

Petitions

P.   Father, we pray for those who are unforgiving, condemning, and spiteful. Lord, have mercy.

All: Lord, have mercy.

P.   Father, we pray for those who are quick to see weakness in others, but slow to see and admit their own faults. Christ, have mercy.

All: Christ, have mercy.

P. Father, we pray for those who feel left out of the party, and who are angry because others are celebrating. Lord, have mercy.

All: Lord, have mercy.

Common Prayer:

Father, we pray for ourselves now, because a part of us is like the elder son. Father, we bring to you the elder son part of us, the resentful, the unforgiving, the ungrateful, and the righteous parts of ourselves. We bring all this to you for your forgiveness and healing.

(Brief pause for personal prayers of healing and forgiveness)

INSTRUCTION

Celebrant:

Those who wish to receive general absolution are called by the Gospel and reminded by the Church to repent of their sins, to resolve to turn away from these sins, and to make up for any scandal and harm one may have caused. A further expectation of the Church is that all grave sins which cannot be confessed individually now are to be confessed individually at some proper time before receiving general absolution again.

For a penance, each is to fast this coming Friday. You may add some other penance if you so desire, or if this penance of fasting is not possible for you.

GENERAL CONFESSION

Sign of Penance

Celebrant:

Will those who wish to receive sacramental absolution please kneel and acknowledge that you are sinners.

General Confession of Sins:

Celebrant:

Confess your sins and pray for each other, that you may be healed.

All: I confess . . .

Litany of Repentance
Celebrant:
God our Father waits for the return of those who are lost and welcomes them back as his children. Let us pray that we may turn back to him and be received with kindness into his house.
   C: That we may have the grace of true conversion,
      we pray, Lord hear us.

All: Lord hear us.
   C: For a renewed spirit of hope within us, we pray,
All: Lord hear us.
   C: For the strength to bear witness to your love, we pray,
All: Lord hear us.
   C: That we may live as a people reconciled with you
and with each other, we pray,
All: Lord hear us.
   C: That your love which forgives us our sins
      may teach us to love others
      and forgive their sins against us,
      we pray,
All: Lord hear us.

Lord's Prayer:
Celebrant: Let us now pray to God our Father
in the words our Savior gave us
asking for forgiveness and freedom from evil.
All: Our Father . . .
Celebrant: Father, you know our sins and our desire to be reconciled with you and with one another. In the power of the Spirit, and through the ministry of the Church, renew our spirit so that we can be free to express the gifts you give us and so give you thanks and praise. We ask this through Christ, our Lord.
All: Amen.

GENERAL ABSOLUTION

(Celebrant extends his hands over the penitents while saying:)

    God, the Father of mercies,
    through the death and resurrection of his Son

has reconciled the world to himself
and sent the Holy Spirit among us
for the forgiveness of sins;
through the ministry of the Church
may God give you pardon and peace,
and I absolve you from your sins
in the name of the Father, and of the Son,
and of the Holy Spirit.

All: Amen.

PROCLAMATION OF PRAISE AND CONCLUSION

Song: "Now Thank We All Our God"

Blessing:

C: May the Father bless us, for we are his children, born to eternal life.

All: Amen.

C: May the Son show us his saving power,
for he died and rose for us.

All: Amen.

C: May the Spirit give us his gift of holiness,
and lead us by the right path,
for he dwells in our hearts.

All: Amen.

Dismissal

C: The Lord has freed you from your sins.
Go in peace.

All: Thanks be to God.

(All process out with organ music accompaniment.)

Non-Sacramental Celebration of Repentance

The services thus far presented are all forms of the sacramental celebration of reconciliation. The Introduction to the Rite of Penance also speaks of penitential celebrations which are non-sacramental (see nos. 36–37). The Rite of Penance ritual also includes some of these non-sacramental celebrations in its

Appendix II. These non-sacramental services can be especially helpful in catechesis to develop a spirit of penance, and in forming the community so that it may celebrate sacramental reconciliation on other occasions. As the ritual advises, particular conditions of life, the manner of speaking, and the educational level of the congregation or special group need to be considered when preparing one of these celebrations. Appendix II of the ritual book provides sample non-sacramental services for Lent, for Advent, for general celebrations, for children, for young people, and for the sick.

The following dramatic expression of repentance shares in the spirit of these non-sacramental services. It was prepared by Mrs. Marguerite Fletcher for use with a teenage confirmation class in a small suburban parish. It is reproduced here with her permission.

This portrayal of repentance is designed to express several aspects of repentance. One is the recognition of our sins and their destructive effects. Another is the understanding of repentance as conversion, or turning around, in order to walk together again. A third aspect is the understanding of repentance as a gradual process, where our ability to recognize our sinfulness and respond in true repentance and reconciliation are a lifetime process of growing in grace.

The characters, situations, and dialogue were designed from the life experiences and imaginations of a teenage confirmation class. The basic movement of the play could be translated into a variety of situations with the ages and lives of the participants adding fresh ideas and alternative dialogue. The liturgical season for this performance was Advent. The imagery could be changed to accommodate the Lenten season, or some other occasion. (Some may even find this appropriate as a dramatic homily for the Gospel of the Second Sunday of Advent.)

The story is of two young teenagers rushing to their junior high school to decorate for a holiday dance. In their impatient self-involvement, they sin against family, stranger, and friend in three fateful encounters. Confronted by an "Angel of Repentance" they are invited to turn around and change their lives. Only after living through the same events two more times are they transformed by the call to repentance. The action of the play takes place in three movements, each replaying the original dialogue, until "paths are made straight" and the wholeness of the Kingdom is at hand.

The characters are an "Angel of Repentance" disguised as an evangelical streetwalker carrying a sign with the word "RE-PENT" printed in bold letters. WILL and ERIC are classmates, friends, full of self-confidence and high energy. AMY is Eric's little sister, grade school age. The SALVATION ARMY GIRL is collecting Christmas donations at a sidewalk stand. TASHA is a shy, not very popular girl from Will's and Eric's class.

Prologue

The *Angel of Repentance* walks slowly and silently from the sanctuary down the center aisle, holding high the *REPENT* sign. Then *Angel* waits in the rear of the Church behind all the people to watch the action of the first movement.

First Movement

Will enters from a side door of the sanctuary rushing noisily, laden with large bags and boxes. He crosses the sanctuary to another door and knocks loudly.

Will: *(shouting)* C'mon, Eric! We're going to be late!

Eric: *(Comes out of the door carrying more bags and boxes. He is irritated.)* What took you so long?

Amy: *(Rushing out the door after Eric. She is very anxious and upset.)* Eric, Eric! Help me! I don't know what to get Mom and Dad for Christmas.

Eric: *(Treating her with maximum sibling rudeness)* Oh, Amy. Get out of here! I don't have time for you!
(Amy slumps down, sits looking hurt and defeated. The boys pause to check their agenda.)

Eric: Have you got the decorations?

Will: Yeah, you've got the refreshments?

Eric: Yeah. Okay. Let's go!
(They run a few steps. Not looking where they are going. Will bumps into the Salvation Army Girl. She nearly falls spilling her collection box. Will nearly drops his load. As they are all recovering their balance, parcels, and money, the boys are grumbling. They are embarrassed, but see the incident as mostly due to her inappropriate presence.)

Will: Hey! What are you doing in the middle of the sidewalk?

Eric: Now we're really going to be late.
(They proceed a few steps and catch sight of Tasha who is standing quietly, shyly, halfway down the center aisle.)

Will: *(Nudging Eric, whispers)* Oh, no! It's Tasha!
(They exchange knowing glances and hurry past her, pretending not to notice her in their hurry. Tasha looks after them and walks slowly to the front of the aisle as they proceed toward the rear. The three girls now present a frozen tableaux of rejected, hurt, isolated humanity. The Angel of Repentance meets the boys partway up the aisle, greeting them with an authoritative, stern but understanding countenance. The Angel is not a punishing figure.)

Angel: Repent! The Kingdom is at hand!

Will and **Eric:** *(incredulous, confused)* What? What is this?

Angel: *(Putting hands on their shoulders, turns them around and walks them a few steps toward the girls.)* I think you guys ought to turn around and start all over again.
(The boys look at the human tableaux, look at each other, shrug their shoul-

299

ders. Then all move quietly and quickly back to their original positions. The Angel goes to rear of the church to watch the Second Movement.)

Second Movement

(Same action as before and practically the same dialogue. This time as each sinful action is done, the Angel will ring a bell. The bell stops the boys in mid-action, and signals the moment of coming to awareness. This recognition is clear enough to alter their behavior, but not to transform their hearts just yet. They try to change, but their apologies are half-hearted, and they are continually rationalizing their behavior.)

Will: *(After rushing in as before, knocking loudly)* C'mon, Eric. We're going to be late!

Eric: *(rushing out)* What took you so long?

Amy: Eric, Eric! Wait! Help me! I don't know what to get Mom and Dad for Christmas!

Eric: Amy, get out of here! I don't have time for you.
(Bell Rings. Eric pauses, turns around to Amy, then awkwardly and impatiently apologizes.)

Eric: Uh, Amy . . . I'm sorry, but I really don't have time to talk to you. We're late.
(They turn uncomfortably, and leave. Amy sits down sadly. The boys check their agendas as before. They are engrossed in plans for the dance as they hurry on. Will again bumps into the collection girl. Same results. Same impatience.)

Will: Hey, why are you doing this in the middle ot the street?
(Bell Rings. Will and Eric look at each other. They turn to watch her as she picks up her fallen items.)

Will: Sorry we ran into you. But, uh, you really shouldn't stand there. Somebody could get hurt, you know.

300

Eric: Boy, we're really going to be late now!
(They proceed. See Tasha as before. Exchange glances with the impulse to hurry past her. This time as they approach her, the Bell Rings. Their self-confidence disappears, and they look at Tasha with slightly embarrassed, forced friendliness. Mumbling some stiff hellos to her, they hurry by. Tasha looks after them, slightly confused. She goes on to the front where they are met again by the Angel.)

Angel: Repent! The Kingdom is at hand!

Will: Wait a minute!

Eric: We already did that!
(Angel puts hands on their shoulders, turns them around, points to the sad display of hurt humanity. The boys look and are very moved by the scene.)

Will: Look at the mess. Boy, are they sad!

Eric: WE did that.

Angel: I think you boys should start all over again. Don't give up now.
(They look at each other, now with excitement and resolve.)

Will and **Eric:** Yeah! Let's start all over again!
(They run back to their places.)

Third Movement

Will: *(Rushes in with the same hurry)* C'mon, Eric! We're going to be late!

Eric: What took you so long?

Amy: Eric, Eric! Wait! Help me! I don't know what to get Mom and Dad for Christmas!

Eric: *(Starting with same impatience)* Oh, Amy!
(He hears his own voice. He stops, puts down his bag. He takes her shoulders, and looks right at her.)

Eric: Amy, that was rude of me. I'm sorry. I *really* care about Mom and Dad, too. How about this afternoon when I get home, we'll sit down together and plan for them. Okay?

Amy: *(Smiles, very glad for his attention and care)* Sure, okay.

Eric: Good, All right! *(They grin at each other.)* Now *(turning to Will)*, you've got the decorations?

Will: Yeah. You've got the refreshments? Let's go!
(Involved again in their hurry, they bump into the collection girl again. After an exclamation of disgust and impatience, Will and Eric look at each other and at the girl. Eric immediately gets down to help her pick herself up.)

Will: We're really sorry. We were so busy, we didn't look where we were going. Are you okay? *(She nods, a bit dazed.)*

Eric: *(Helping her, notices how red and cold her hands are.)* Hey, you've been working really hard. It's cold out here. How about some hot chocolate? *(He takes a thermos from his bag and pours her a cup.)*

Will: You sure you're okay? *(She nods and smiles.)*

Eric: We're really going to be late now!

Will: Oh, no. There's Tasha! *(They start to exchange the old glance and look at each other with a new recognition.)* It's Tasha. Hi, Tasha!

Eric: *(With enthusiasm)* Hey, we're going to decorate for the party. Want to come with us and help? We need you. *(Tasha nods with pleasure. Satisfaction is voiced all around.)*

Eric: Here! Will you carry a bag?
(They share their load of boxes, and proceed laughing together. As they pass

by the Angel, who is smiling at their pleasure, they hear beautiful chimes. A choir organ, or bells, begins the first stanza of "Joy to the World.")

Will and **Eric:** Hey, what is that? Sounds like music.

Angel: Those are the sounds of the Kingdom! *(Angel ushers them out.)*

End

Notes

INTRODUCTION

1. Washington, D.C.: The Liturgical Conference, 1975.
2. New York: Harper and Row, 1981.
3. *Ibid.,* pp. 184–232. Those who wish to use this book by follow-ing Thomas Groome's method, but who are not yet familiar with this method, will find these pages in Groome's book very helpful.

CHAPTER 1

1. Edward J. Farrell, *The Father Is Very Fond of Me* (Denville, N.J.: Dimension Books, Inc., 1975), p. 5.
2. *The Challenge of Jesus* (Garden City: Doubleday & Co., Inc., 1977), pp. 93–113.
3. *Theological Dynamics* (Nashville: Abingdon Press, 1977), pp. 70–71.
4. *The Transformation of Man* (Springfield, Ill.: Templegate, 1967).
5. *Ibid.,* pp. 88–115.
6. *Ibid.,* p. 97.
7. *Ibid.,* pp. 242–280.
8. Boston: Little, Brown & Co., 1973, p. 3.
9. "From Cruelty to Goodness," *The Hastings Center Report,* Vol. 11 (June 1981): 23–28 at p. 26.
10. *Ibid.,* pp. 27–28.
11. *The Ministry of the Celebrating Community* (Glendale: Pastoral Arts Associates of North America, 1977), pp. 14ff.

12. *Ibid.*, p. 17.
13. *Reaching Out* (Garden City: Doubleday & Co., Inc., 1975), pp. 45–78.
14. *Ibid.*, p. 46.
15. *Ibid.*,

CHAPTER 2

1. *What Can You Say About God?* trans. Henry J. Koren (New York: Paulist Press, 1971), pp. 4–5.
2. *Do You Believe in God?* trans. Richard Strachen (New York: Newman Press, 1969), pp. 112–113.
3. *Faith and Doctrine: A Contemporary View* (New York: Paulist Press, 1969), pp. 74–81.
4. "The Unawareness of God," in *The God Experience,* ed. Joseph P. Whelan (New York: Newman Press, 1971), pp. 8–15.
5. *A Rumor of Angels* (Garden City: Doubleday and Co., Inc., 1969), pp. 65–94.
6. *Poems by Gerard Manley Hopkins,* 3rd ed. (London: Oxford University Press, 1948), p. 70.
7. *The New Life of Grace,* trans. Georges Dupont (New York: Desclee Company, 1969), pp. 7–9.
8. *The Shaking of the Foundations* (New York: Charles Scribner's Sons, 1948), pp. 161–162.
9. This summary of the effects of grace in modern language is taken from Roger Haight, *The Experience and Language of Grace* (Ramsey: Paulist Press, 1979), pp. 151–154.

CHAPTER 3

1. *The Story of My Life* (New York: Grosset & Dunlap, 1902), pp. 23–24.
2. New York: Sheed and Ward, 1963.
3. For a fine introduction to RCIA with pastoral implications, see James B. Dunning, *New Wine: New Wineskins* (New York: William H. Sadlier, Inc., 1981).
4. "Theologian's Challenge to Liturgy," *Theological Studies,* 35 (June 1974): 243.
5. *Music in Catholic Worship* (Washington, D.C.: USCC, 1972), p. 1.
6. For a forceful recent expression of this theme, see Regis Duffy, *Real Presence* (San Francisco: Harper and Row, 1982).

7. Old Hickory: Pastoral Arts Associates of North America, 1977.
8. *Ibid.,* p. 16.
9. *Ibid.* p. 17.
10. *Ibid.,* p. 18.
11. *Music in Catholic Worship,* p. 1.

CHAPTER 4

1. *The Moral Teaching of the New Testament* (New York: Herder and Herder, 1965), p. 95.
2. *The Responsible Self* (New York: Harper & Row, 1963), pp. 61–65.
3. *Ibid.,* p. 65.
4. Bernard Häring's writings are vast and wide-ranging. His early three-volume work, *The Law of Christ,* was one of the first major works by a Catholic moral theologian to rethink morality in light of the biblical renewal. His most recent three-volume work, *Free and Faithful in Christ* (New York: Seabury Press, 1978, 1979, 1981), is an expression of Häring's more mature thought. This work is not a revision of *The Law of Christ,* but a completely new work. Charles E. Curran, a student of Häring's, has followed his teacher's lead in making efforts at renewing moral theology in light of the biblical renewal. Some of Curran's pertinent articles are "The Relevancy of the Ethical Teaching of Jesus" and "Conversion: The Moral Message of Jesus" in *A New Look at Christian Morality* (Notre Dame: Fides Publishers, Inc., 1968), pp. 1–23 and 25–71.
5. *The Responsible Self,* p. 126.
6. *To Live in Christ Jesus* (Washington: USCC, 1976), p. 5; cf. *Sharing the Light of Faith* (Washington: USCC, 1979), #98.
7. *Biography as Theology* (Nashville: Abingdon Press, 1974), p. 19.
8. See especially Timothy E. O'Connell, *Principles for a Catholic Morality* (New York: Seabury Press, 1978), pp. 51–55.
9. Ken Kelsey, *One Flew Over the Cuckoo's Nest* (New York: New American Library, 1962), p. 126.
10. See especially Chapter Five, pp. 164–222.
11. Similarly, a more recent ecclesiastical document, *Lineamenta,* designed by the Synod Secretariat to promote discussion and input in preparation for the 1983 international Synod of Bishops, holds a similar position when it says:

Certainly the life of a man must be evaluated on the basis of the fundamental option which he makes with regard to God:

accepting him as the supreme good or rejecting him. But this fundamental option is not at all reducible to an "intention" empty of any well-defined binding content, to an intention to which an efficacious effort in the various areas of the moral life does not correspond. In reality, the existence of man works itself out within history and within personal events. For this reason, the fundamental and global orientation of human liberty demands that it be concretized in concrete determinate choices; and also in one of these choices it is possible to effect a revision of the very global orientation, either in the sense of rejecting God or in the sense of returning to him.

Here we find another positive expression of the essence of the fundamental option theory which captures the proper relationship between fundamental option and the person's fundamental orientation, or stance. In "Reconciliation and Penance in the Mission of the Church," *Origins* 11 (February 18, 1982), p. 575.

12. See especially pp. 64–66, 70–74.

13. *Free and Faithful in Christ,* Vol. 1: *General Moral Theology,* pp. 168–177, esp. pp. 172–175.

14. *Ibid.,* p. 189.

15. Pope John Paul II, *Catechesi Tradendae, Apostolic Exhortation on Catechetics* issued October 25, 1979 as found in *Official Catholic Teachings, Update 1979* (Wilmington, N.C.: McGrath Publishing Co., 1980), pp. 368–426, quotation at p. 397.

16. *Free and Faithful in Christ,* Vol,. 1, p. 403.

17. *Ibid.,* p. 407.

18. *Ibid.,* p. 215.

19. *Ibid.,* p. 5.

20. *Free and Faithful in Christ,* Vol. 1, pp. 213–214.

CHAPTER 5

1. *Principles for a Catholic Morality* (New York: Seabury Press, 1978), pp. 88–93.

2. New York: Random House, Inc., Vintage Books, 1962.

3. *Ibid.,* pp. 52–53.

4. *Ibid.,* p. 71.

5. *Ibid.,* pp. 76–77.

6. *The Moral Choice* (Garden City: Doubleday and Co., 1978), p. 379.

7. *Becoming* (New Haven: Yale University Press, 1955), pp. 70–71.

8. In C. Ellis Nelson, ed., *Conscience: Theological and Psychological Perspectives* (New York: Newman Press, 1973), pp. 167–188.

9. *Ibid.,* p. 181.

10. *Ibid.*

11. *Ibid.,* p. 182.

12. Frank J. McNulty and Edward Watkin, *Should You Ever Feel Guilty?* (Ramsey: Paulist Press, 1978), pp. 53–54.

13. *Vision and Character* (Ramsey: Paulist Press, 1981), p. 1. This book offers a careful critique of Kohlberg as well as a proposal for an alternative to moral education based on a "visional ethics" rather than the standard "juridical ethics" promoted by Kohlberg.

14. See, for example, Donald Evans, "Does Religious Faith Conflict with Moral Freedom," *Faith, Authenticity, and Morality* (Toronto: University of Toronto Press, 1980), pp. 197–246.

15. New York: Random House, Inc., Vintage Books, 1962, p. 81.

16. Recent years have shown an increasing interest in *character* in moral theology. This interest in ethics has developed along with the increasing interest in *story,* or narrative, in other areas of theology. Stanley Hauerwas of the University of Notre Dame has been a consistent advocate of an "ethics of character." See, for example, his major work, *Character and the Christian Life: A Study of Theological Ethics* (San Antonio: Trinity University Press, 1975); also, his collections of essays: *Vision and Virtue* (Notre Dame: Fides Publishers, Inc., 1974); with Richard Bondi and David Burrell, *Truthfulness and Tragedy* (Notre Dame: University of Notre Dame Press, 1977); and *A Community of Character* (Nortre Dame: University of Notre Dame Press, 1981).

17. "Vision and Choice in Morality" in Ian T. Ramsey, ed., *Christian Ethics and Contemporary Philosophy* (New York: The Macmillan Co., 1966), p. 200.

18. As quoted by David Burrell and Stanley Hauerwas in "From System to Story: An Alternative Pattern for Rationality in Ethics," in *Truthfulness and Tragedy,* pp. 206–207.

19. *Can Ethics Be Christian?* (Chicago: University of Chicago Press, 1975), p. 69.

20. Berkeley: University of California Press, 1976, p. 196.

21. Gustafson, *Can Ethics Be Christian?* p. 65.

22. *Bible and Ethics in the Christian Life* (Minneapolis: Augusburg Publishing Co., 1976), p. 106.

23. *The Moral Choice,* pp. 128–188.

CHAPTER 6

1. *The Gospel According to John XIII–XXI*, 29A: *The Anchor Bible* (Garden City: Doubleday and Company, Inc, 1970), pp. 1044–1045.

2. Some useful references on the shape of the canonical penance are Bernard Poschmann, *Penance and the Anointing of the Sick*, trans. Francis Courtney (New York: Herder and Herder, 1964), see especially 19–121; C. Vogel,"Sin and Penance," in *Pastoral Treatment of Sin*, P. Delhaye, J. Leclerc, B. Häring, C.Vogel, and C.H. Nodet (New York: Desclee Company, 1968), especially pp. 177–259; for excerpts of pertinent documents from this era, see Paul F. Palmer, *Sacraments and Forgiveness*, Vol. II: *Sources of Christian Theology* (Westminster, Md.: The Newman Press, 1959).

3. For a list of penances and lengths of times used in the canonical penance rite, see C. Vogel, "Sin and Penance," in *Pastoral Treatment of Sin*, pp. 234–235.

4. John T. McNeill and Helena M. Gamer, *Medieval Handbooks of Penance* (New York: Octagon Books, Inc., 1965), p. 99.

5. *Ibid.*, p. 101.

6. *Ibid.*, pp. 92–93.

7. *Ibid.*,p. 251.

8. *Ibid.*, p. 46.

9. *Ibid.*, p. 88.

10. *Ibid.*, p. 108.

11. *Ibid.*, p. 255.

12. *Ibid.*, pp. 143–144.

13. James Dallen, "The Absence of a Ritual of Reconciliation in Celtic Penance," *The Journey of Western Spirituality*, ed. A.W. Sadler. *The Annual Publication of the College Theology Society*, 1980 (Chico, Cal.: Scholars Press, 1981): 79–106.

14. John T. McNeill, *The Celtic Churches: A History A.D. 200 to 1200* (Chicago: The University of Chicago Press, 1974).

15. *Ibid.*, p. 84.

16. Poschmann, *Penance*, pp. 144–145.

17. Dallen, "The Absence of a Ritual," in *The Journey*, p. 87.

18. Appendix B #2, p. 162.

19. For historical sketches of the debates in the Scholastic period, and for different interpretations of these debates, see Poschmann, *Penance*, pp. 155–193, and Joseph Martos, *Doors to the Sacred* (Garden City: Doubleday and Company, Inc., 1981), pp. 335–345. For pertinent documents of this time, see Palmer, *Sacraments and Forgiveness*, pp. 185–223.

20. The principal texts of Trent which pertain to Penance can be found in Palmer, *Sacraments and Forgiveness,* pp. 237–253.

21. Charles E. Curran, "The Sacrament of Penance Today," *Contemporary Problems in Moral Theology* (Notre Dame: Fides Publishers, 1970), p. 160.

22. Carl J. Peter, "Auricular Confession and the Council of Trent," *Proceedings of the Catholic Theological Society of America* 22 (1967): 185–200. For an updated version of this study, see his "Integral Confession and the Council of Trent," in *Sacramental Reconciliation,* ed. E. Schillebeeckx, *New Concilium,* Vol. 61 (1971): 99–109

23. Peter, "Auricular Confession," *CTSA Proceedings,* pp. 198–199.

24. *Ibid.,* p. 200.

25. *AAS* Vol. 35 (1943), p. 235.

26. John Dedek, "The Theology of Devotional Confession," *Proceedings of the Catholic Theological Society of America* 22 (1967): 218. The article which Dedek summarizes of Rahner is "Vom Sinn der haufigen Andachtcbeicht," *Zeitschrift fur Aszese und Mystik* 9 (1934): 323–336.

CHAPTER 7

1. *Reaching Out* (Garden City: Doubleday and Co., Inc., 1975), p. 70.

2. *Sin, Liberty and Law* (New York: Sheed and Ward, 1965), pp. 52–53.

3. *Make Your Tomorrow Better* (Ramsey: Paulist Press, 1980), p. 255.

4. Nouwen, *Reaching Out,* pp. 69–70.

5. *The Rite of Penance: Commentaries,* Vol. 1: *Understanding the Document* (Washington: The Liturgical Conference, 1975), pp. 116–117.

6. *Ibid.,* p. 117.

7. *Ibid.,* pp. 121–122.